1

MUKHIYA: Tumhaar khopdi ghoom gayi hai,
Bhuvan!...khud to doobogey, hum sab ka bhi
laikey doobogey!
(Have you gone crazy Bhuvan?...not only you, we will all
be ruined!)
— LAGAAN

"There was a certain degree of madness in me."
ASHUTOSH GOWARIKER
Writer- Director

1 An idea that nearly died

30th July 1996

The bonnet of a car is probably not the best location to narrate a script idea, but in a way, that's where our story begins. The place: the compound of Marina Apartments in Mumbai, where Aamir Khan lives. The time: the wee hours of dawn, with the earth still wet from the downpour of the night gone past.

Ashutosh Gowariker is so obsessed with his story idea, he has to share it then and there, even if it means narrating while Aamir Khan leans back on the windscreen of his car. After all, Aamir has always lent his ideas a willing ear. Ashutosh, however, has entered the compound of Marina Apartments at exactly the same time at which Aamir has returned home exhausted after a night of shooting. Ordinarily, Ashutosh would have waited for a better time and place for something as important as a narration. Today, however, Aamir's state of mind and body does not deter Ashutosh. He believes his story idea is so powerful, even a sleeping man will spring to life on hearing it. He has only to mention his idea to Aamir for the onward journey to celluloid to begin…at any rate, this is what Ashutosh thinks.

The day has yet to begin for the denizens of Marina Apartments. Barring the odd milkman and paper delivery boy, the Marina compound is asleep. Ashutosh's mind however is in overdrive. This day could change his life. In five swift minutes he sketches the contours of his story. What Aamir learns is this: The tale is set in the British Raj in a small village in central India. It hasn't rained for a couple of years and the villagers are unable to pay the tax known as *lagaan*. Near the village is a British cantonment headed by a capricious officer. The villagers get into a situation where the officer agrees to cancel the tax if the villagers are able to beat the British at a game of cricket. If they lose the wager, the villagers will have to pay thrice the *lagaan* that is due. Ultimately, the villagers beat the British at cricket and hence are freed of the burden of *lagaan*.

Ashutosh concludes his narration with a flourish and waits eagerly for

Aamir's response.

Aamir splutters, "It's outlandish Ash, completely implausible."

Ashutosh's mind starts reeling. This was not the reaction he expected.

"British Raj…villagers playing cricket to cancel the tax…I don't know what to make of it Ash and I doubt whether the audience will either."

Desperately, Ashutosh tries to provide a defence. "But Aamir this is only the skeleton, when I flesh it out…"

"Forget it Ash!" Aamir interjects. "I am definitely not interested in this idea and as a friend, I suggest that you do not waste your time on it either."

"But…Aamir…"

Ashutosh is bluntly cut short.

"Look Ash, you've already made two films that haven't worked. This time round you must make something safe, something nice, not some weird story about villagers in the British Raj."

Ashutosh falls silent as Aamir drives home the nails. He is shattered.

Quietly, he leaves the Marina compound, with the look of a man who has been cast into the abyss. A defining moment in the life of *Lagaan*.

Ashutosh's career as a film director hangs on the edge of a steep precipice. One more fall and it's all over. One of the handicaps of showbiz is that everyone knows exactly how your career is doing. Most other professions provide a modicum of opacity to one's career graph. One is not entirely sure of the fortunes of a banker, a lawyer or a clerk. The fate of an actor, a singer or a film director is however, naked to the sky.

No one needed to ask to know that Ashutosh Gowariker's career was going nowhere. F-L-O-P! The word hurts. It is as painful as the branding of a horse, burnt with fire across the body. An awful four-letter word. The ultimate sin in the film industry. And Ashutosh had committed the sin twice. Both his directorial ventures, *Pehla Nasha* and *Baazi* had flopped. And now, Aamir's harsh judgement on his precious story idea…almost like a death sentence.

It is difficult to describe all that Ashutosh feels that morning. Disappointment, dejection, hurt, pain, shock, horror…nothing can quite capture it. What Aamir has trashed is not just another story idea he had tossed up for consideration. This is *his* baby, born in *his* heart, conceived through suffering and pain. Ashutosh decides not to panic and not to take any decision in a hurry. He must endure this moment by thinking and reflecting on the journey that has brought him so far.

Ashutosh was the perpetual 'ne'er do well' of the Gowariker family. Despite his obvious intelligence and distinguished background (his father, Ashok Gowariker, a senior police officer, one of his uncles, the famous scientist, Vasant Gowariker, who served as the scientific adviser to the prime minister of India), Ashutosh couldn't quite make it in academics. His failure to reach the middle class meccas of medicine or engineering pushed him to a bachelor's degree in science at Mithibai College in suburban Mumbai. By the Maharashtrian middle class standards that he was brought up on, Ashutosh did not have much of a future.

In college, Ashutosh compounded his academic ineptitude by relegating his studies to a marginal activity and focussing instead on the intoxicating world of inter-collegiate theatre festivals. Yet, the academic delinquent appeared to have a spark after all and despite the growing anxiety of his parents, he seemed to have found his feet in theatre. Ketan Mehta spotted Ashutosh on the theatre circuit and cast him in a major role in his *Holi*, an offbeat film about ragging in college. On the *Holi* sets, Ashutosh met a fresher actor playing a rather insignificant role. His name was Aamir Khan.

The actor Ashutosh (centre), in Saeed Mirza's *Salim Langde Pe Mat Ro*

Holi never made it beyond the art film circuit, but it launched the careers of both Ashutosh Gowariker and Aamir Khan. Aamir's performance sufficiently impressed cousin Mansoor Khan and uncle Nasir Husain for them to cast him in the film *Qayamat Se Qayamat Tak* which launched Aamir as a top rung star, a position he consolidated over the years. Ashutosh, despite his lanky six foot one inch build, curly hair, sensuous lips and abundant enthusiasm, hovered around the charmed periphery of fame and success, but never quite made it as an actor. He bagged major roles in Kundan Shah's *Kabhi Haan Kabhi Naa* and in Saeed Mirza's *Salim Langde Pe Mat Ro*, but the better roles and the big banners eluded him and with each passing year they seemed ever further.

His dwindling prospects as an actor did not deter Ashutosh from a career in films. His exposure to the myriad processes through which a story is told with pictures and sound had convinced him that his world was cinema.

Even in his actor *avatar*, Ashutosh loved working as the director's assistant. His shot canned, Ashutosh would don his assistant's cap — giving other actors their cues, giving the clap, doing just about anything that would enable him to observe and absorb the intricate craft of movie-making. Amol Palekar, Saeed Mirza, Mahesh Bhat, Kundan Shah… these were illustrious directors who he acted under, but none of them was his guru. In that sense, Ashutosh was self taught and had the confidence, even cockiness of a person who has learnt on his own. So even as his acting career fizzled out, Ashutosh revised his targets upwards – he decided to become a director.

I n India's caste-ridden society, most professions are relatively closed circles where sons succeed fathers. The lawyer's son inherits his father's clients, the businessman's son the business and the politician's son his father's constituency. Films could scarcely be different. While it was easy for the failed actor Ashutosh to dream of making films, actually breaking in would be a miracle.

Yet, the miracle occurred. In 1992, Ashutosh then only twenty-eight, without even a period of formal directorial assistance to his credit, directed his first film, *Pehla Nasha,* starring Deepak Tijori, Pooja Bhatt and Raveena Tandon. The film, a murder mystery geared to the box office, flopped. Critically too, it was clobbered.

Ashutosh's directorial debut, *Pehla Nasha:* with Deepak Tijori (centre) and Neeraj Vora

Despite the debacle of *Pehla Nasha,* the dreamer was on to bigger things. Ashutosh's next directorial venture was *Baazi* – a *Die Hard* remake, starring a now well established Aamir Khan. For *Baazi*, Ashutosh pulled out all stops as far as box office *masala* was concerned. He had a bare-legged Aamir do a 'sexy' dance number masquerading as a woman, the hero and heroine drooling over each other and large quantities of mind-numbing violence. The *masala* created massive indigestion both critically and commercially. The dreamer came down to earth with a thud. With two resounding flops, Ashutosh's directorial career was finished…or at least that is how it then seemed.

Through the making of *Baazi*, Aamir had been unhappy with the way the film was turning out. Even Ashutosh was creatively dissatisfied – *Baazi* was a film aimed at the box office; it was not a film that appealed to his sensibility. Despite his flops, Aamir was convinced that Ashutosh had a touch of genius. Aamir was also convinced that genius would die, unless his friend was roused to take a stand and believe in himself. "You'll never make a good director Ash, unless you display guts. If you don't have conviction in what you do, if you make films you don't believe in, you'll never succeed."

Aamir and Ashutosh on the sets of *Baazi*

Perhaps, Ashutosh did not need Aamir to tell him this. His own experiences were telling him that he needed to beat another path.

A shutosh went into an exile from direction enforced by a lack of backers. More than the 'flop' label, he was frustrated with the lack of success in his own eyes. Neither *Pehla Nasha* nor *Baazi* were films that he was proud of. Yet, they had served an important purpose. If *Pehla Nasha* and *Baazi* had not been made, or if either of them had succeeded, Ashutosh would probably never have made *Lagaan*. It was important for *Lagaan* that these two films should have been made and that they should have bombed, because it was their debacle that forced him into creative hibernation and to ask the all important 'why' a person asks himself when he is at the crossroads.

Ashutosh decided that he was through with making films for the box office. He had tried the known route. He had tried the *masala* ingredients and drawn a blank. He now knew that nothing about the box office was certain. Rather than trying to guess what the audience wanted, it was far better to make something that he, Ashutosh Gowariker, believed in and then hope that the audience too would like it. That way, he joked, "At least one person in the world will love the film!" So, Ashutosh decided to write a film that he would be proud of.

One of the advantages of failure is that it provides a lot of time for study. Ashutosh used his years in exile to see and study films — an exploration that took him back to Guru Dutt, Bimal Roy, K. Asif and Mehboob Khan. Ashutosh was awe-struck by the audacity with which these masters picked just about any subject that moved them and proceeded to make a movie, completely ignoring the prevailing trend at the box office. Like, who would believe that a film about a dreamer poet, *Pyaasa*, or a film about a pauperised farmer who pulled hand-rickshaws in Calcutta to repay his debt, *Do Bigha Zameen,* could be a mainstream superhit?

Inspired by these masters, Ashutosh resolved never again to write a script he did not believe in. In the muggy heat of October 1996, Ashutosh decided to write a script with angst.

In the India of the mid-nineties, angst had all but disappeared from the mindscape of the urban media. The articulate urban middle class that dominates public discourse was revelling in the consumerist dream. It was only rural India or Bharat that was simmering. Protests erupted periodically as in the struggle of tribals against the Narmada Dam or of the Konkan villagers fighting Enron. To Ashutosh, the unequal battle of humble villagers pitted against giant corporations seemed intrinsically heroic, a David versus Goliath scenario.

Ashutosh on the drums in Kundan Shah's *Kabhi Haan Kabhi Naa*

He worked out various plots and stories in this setting, but ran into a problem — hackneyed characters. The politician, the police, the landlord …all these had been done to death in Hindi films, albeit with a different purpose and vulgar sensibility. Even the 'truth' had become stale! Ashutosh found himself gridlocked.

Once again, the masters showed the way forward. "Imagine," says Ashutosh, "a film about two lovers whose parents are opposed to their marriage. What could be more hackneyed. Now set this same film in the reign of Emperor Akbar and you have *Mughal-e-Azam!*"

This insight led the writer Ashutosh back in time to British rule and to the drought-stricken decades of the 1890s, when the struggle against *lagaan* or land tax was a burning question. The changed period gave birth to a completely different array of characters – the Maharaja with his pomp and pageantry, the tyrannical, capricious British officer and most important, the protagonists, humble farmers in rural India. Suddenly, Ashutosh found his plot had a 'never before' feel. The dreamer was excited.

The big question Ashutosh now faced was this: in what form should the conflict between the villagers and the British be played out? How could he make plausible a story where all-powerful rulers lose and humble peasants win? His solution was as simple as it was audacious. While it would have been impossible to conceive of farmers defeating the British in armed struggle in 1893, it was definitely possible to accept the 'sporting' British being defeated on the cricket field of Champaner. Ashutosh had found a way of quietly inserting a fictitious tale within the pages of history.

All the pain and frustration of his past and a deeply felt artistic hunger gave birth to the *Lagaan* idea. From the moment he conceived the idea of a group of humble villagers taking on the mighty British Raj on a cricket field, Ashutosh was a man possessed. Finally, he had an idea that came from the heart. Finally he had the outlines of a story *he* was proud of. And now Aamir was advising him to junk the 'weird story about villagers in the British Raj'!

In the life of the still embryonic *Lagaan*, this is a crucial moment. It is simplicity itself for Ashutosh to give up on this idea and try yet another and still yet another, until he has Aamir or some major star showing serious interest. That is the only *practical* plan of action. But Ashutosh is past being practical. He has reached that point where he can validate his life only by being *impractical*, by following his conviction and dream even if it means being labelled crazy and possessed.

Ashutosh's long years as an actor, the two flop films and above all his own desperate artistic thirst, all combine to save the *Lagaan* seed. In a superb act of irony, Ashutosh

Ashutosh with parents Ashok Gowariker and Kishori Gowariker, sister Ashlesha (left) and wife Sunita (right)

decides to show conviction by ignoring the advice of the man who had exhorted him to show conviction. He decides to swallow Aamir's biting reaction to the *Lagaan* idea. "Maybe Aamir just cannot see the film as I see it because it still needs to be developed," is how he consoles himself.

With his career in doldrums and with no backer in sight, Ashutosh decides to develop his story idea into a full-fledged script. Ashutosh leaves Mumbai and goes into seclusion to write the dialogue version of *Lagaan*.

It's all about guts

Like his counterpart, Bhuvan, Aamir would accept the challenge

CAPTAIN RUSSELL: Tum...bolo... doogana lagaan doge, ki sharat manjoor hai?
(You...tell me...will you pay double tax? Or do you accept the bet?)
BHUVAN: Sarat manjoor hai!
(I accept the challenge!)
— LAGAAN

"Produce! No way! That's the last thing I want to do. I have seen the hell my father has been through as a producer."

AAMIR KHAN
Actor-Producer, in various interviews since 1988

It's all about guts

August 1996

The decision to persist with *Lagaan* in the face of dire opposition from Aamir gives Ashutosh a strange strength. Perhaps, if *Lagaan* had been written with the mandate of Aamir Khan or another big star, it would not have turned out as it did. It would have been too comfortable and easy. An audacious script like *Lagaan* could only emerge as an act of defiance from a writer who has decided to please himself, the world be damned.

Ashutosh has virtually downed his acting shutters to develop the *Lagaan* idea. This has meant giving up regular paid work to chase what essentially is a dream that brings home no bread. Day after day Ashutosh is at his writing table while his parents and wife wonder what exactly he is up to. His children, Konark and Vishwang, even ask their mother, Sunita, why their daddy sits at home all day, when all other daddies go out and work in offices. These are lonely days and it is only the inner conviction that keeps the flame alive.

1st December 1996-7th January 1997

Ashutosh has taken on board Kumar Dave and Sanjay Dayma as his collaborators. He borrows a friend's farmhouse at Kollote, two hours away from Mumbai and the three work through December 1996, building the *Lagaan* story into a full-fledged script.

Kollote is the perfect place to write *Lagaan*. Electric supply is intermittent and telephones are non-existent. The writers, physically isolated from the rest of the world, are placed in a setting at sharp variance with modern life – the ideal work environment for a period film.

On the third day of January 1997, the trio returns home triumphantly with a start to finish script of *Lagaan*. Whether or not the world agrees, the writers believe they have penned a script that will shake the world.

9th January 1997

Once again, Ashutosh asks for a meeting with Aamir. The two have not met for five months. Aamir who has been wondering where Ashutosh disappeared, is delighted to hear that his friend has used that period to write a script and immediately agrees to hear it. Then, on an afterthought, Aamir asks, "Has this script been developed from that same cricket story you narrated earlier?"

Ashutosh lowers his head, runs his hand through his hair and tries to sidestep the question, "Aamir, in seed it is the same — but after hearing it in its developed form, you'll feel it's completely transformed."

Aamir cannot trust his ears. He cannot believe that Ashutosh has wasted his time on what he feels is an outlandish and implausible idea.

"Ash I'm shocked that you've wasted five full months on that weird story about villagers in the British Raj. Anyway, you want to waste your time, that's your problem, but I don't want to waste my time."

The conversation comes to an end with Aamir's outright refusal to even listen to the script. In Ashutosh's mind, the bells are now tolling for *Lagaan*. He meets Aamir again two days later. This time he digs his heels in.

"Aamir, reject it if you must, but at least hear the full script before you do that."

Aamir is irritated, but never in his life has he seen Ashutosh almost plead with him.

"Look Ash, there's no chance that I'll change my mind. But since you've spent five months working on this, I'll respect the work you've done and hear it."

With his mind deeply biased against the *Lagaan* script, Aamir braces himself for a narration.

9th March 1997

Three months pass before Aamir can bring himself to hear the narration. Ashutosh has spent a sleepless night focussing and bringing to bear all his years in theatre, all his roles in films, all the work he has ever done, just for this one narration. Now, he performs brilliantly. With all the resources at his command he tries to communicate the film he has seen in his mind's eye. When Ashutosh finishes, Aamir is shell-shocked. He has laughed. He has sighed. His eyes are moist. He is deeply moved by the script of *Lagaan*.

"How did you even conceive of such an idea Ash? It's simply superb…" Aamir cannot stop praising the script.

Ashutosh is enjoying every moment of it and is sharing his creative journey with Aamir, when he suddenly notices that Aamir has fallen silent.

"What's the matter Aamir?" asks Ashutosh.

"It's a wonderful script Ash, but…" Aamir trails off.

"But what?"

"But it's an extremely scary film to be part of and I don't know whether I have the guts to do it."

Ashutosh is pleased and dismayed. Has he come so far only to be a victim of the success of his script? He tries desperately to persuade Aamir, but to no avail.

"Look Ash, I loved the script and I would love to see it made, but I don't know whether this film *can* be made. Whether any producer will allow it to be made the way it should."

"Let's try and work it out Aamir," Ashutosh persists.

"Ash, the sensibility of your film makes it an experiment and a very expensive experiment, for which it needs to be a mainstream film and I don't know whether the mainstream audience will accept this sensibility. It's just too different. I mean I would have to be crazy to do this film…"

Aamir goes on and on about why he is terrified to touch *Lagaan* and Ashutosh persists in trying to bring him on board, until finally, Aamir hits upon a via media.

"Ash let's do it this way. *You* get a producer to do this film on the strength of this script and I'm with you. What I mean is that the producer must back your script *without knowing that I would like to act in it*. He must back it on his reading of whether the audience will accept this script. If he does that, then you can surprise the producer and tell him that Aamir would like to act in it."

"But why shouldn't I just tell the producers that you'll star in the film?" Ashutosh questions, reluctant to accept that he will not be able to use his trump card.

"That won't work for me and that will be dangerous for the film," says Aamir. "In that manner you may get ten producers who would be doing the film - not because they believe in your script, but because I have agreed to do the film. Such a producer may later force creative compromises that make it impossible for the potential of the script to be realised. Ash, you must get a producer who believes in the script as much as you do."

Ashutosh leaves Aamir's house disturbed by the encounter. If Aamir is afraid to do *Lagaan*, who will have the courage to do it? Ashutosh has written without an eye on the box office. Now he must face the market eyeball to eyeball and pass its test.

10th March 1997 – December 1997

Script in hand and head held high, Ashutosh the dreamer hits the road, narrating to producer after producer. Sadly, no producer buys the dream. Three factors work against him.

The first is his own unsuccessful track record as the director of *Pehla Nasha* and *Baazi*.

The second is that his script has violated the market's sacred commandments. Thou shalt not make period films! Thou shalt not make rural films! Thou shalt not make films with a sports climax! Thou shalt not dress a hero in a *dhoti* and *bundi*! ... the list continues. The sensibility and setting of *Lagaan* are alien to mainstream Hindi cinema and producers who claim to understand the pulse of the market make outrageous demands on Ashutosh. One such producer demands that Ashutosh make the climax more action packed by getting Bhuvan to gore Captain Russell with a stump on the cricket field after the winning shot!

The third factor that damages the prospects of *Lagaan* is that a sizable section of the film market is not interested in scripts. The Mumbai film industry revolves around stars. In most cases, the stars are primary; the script is incidental. The stars are not there to do justice to the script. The script is meant to serve and promote the stars. Barring the projects of a few A-list producers or directors, a big budget film needs one or more major stars, without whom it is very difficult to raise the funds required. In this star-driven system, Ashutosh is trying to make a film on the strength of his script alone!

Even producers who like the script invariably ask the critical question - "Do you have a star who has agreed to act in it?"

Despite having Aamir, one of the biggest stars in the industry, Ashutosh is honour bound to grit his teeth and say, "No sir," thereby bringing further discussion to an end.

A few months into the process, and Aamir, who is more than a little unhappy about the tragedy of Ashutosh's superb script finding no takers, meets with him.

"Ash, I don't want you to lose time in filming your script only because I don't have the guts to do it. Why don't you narrate your script to some other star who might be comfortable with the idea of using his name to find a producer. If any of them agrees, that's just fine and I'll have no hard feelings."

Ashutosh spreads his net wider to include some stars and continues with his narrations. Ashok Amritraj, Shahrukh Khan and many others are impressed by the *Lagaan* script, but for one reason or the other, the project falls through. Every time it looks like *Lagaan* will finally find a substantial backer, something goes wrong. It appears as if the stars are configured against Ashutosh's simple tale making it to celluloid.

Through the year 1997, Ashutosh searches for a producer or a star who will share his dream and have the guts to see it through. Emotionally his life is on a roller coaster. Everytime a Shahrukh or an Ashok Amritraj expresses interest, he is on a high, then there is a pause, a period of waiting and uncertainty before the proposal is called off and down goes the roller coaster into depression...and then...up once again.

Through all this, Ashutosh keeps Aamir informed.

"Today I went to ABCL and..."

"Shahrukh and Ashok Amritraj liked the script but..."

"Tomorrow I am meeting Goodnight Mohan..."

Aamir listens attentively, but the rejection by producer after producer confirms his strong suspicion that Ashutosh's fantastic script is commercially utterly unviable. This is no longer just his opinion or hunch. This is what the market is saying and confirming every day. The *Lagaan* script may be marvellous, but India is not ready for it. The market for a film of this sensibility is just not large enough.

30th January 1998

The market rules the market place but passion is possessive. None of what the market has said allows Aamir to forget just what he experienced when he heard the script. He had experienced a work of great artistic beauty and power and no market ratings could take away from that. Once more, Aamir asks Ashutosh to narrate the script of *Lagaan* to see whether it could stir the same magic.

Once again, Ashutosh makes his way to the study in Aamir's flat at Marina Apartments, reads one hundred and thirty-five pages of screenplay and performs the sixty-eight speaking parts to bring the village of Champaner and its British cantonment to life.

Once again, Aamir falls in love with the script of *Lagaan*.

Once again he hesitates to embrace it.

"It's superb Ash, but I still don't know whether I have the guts to do it."

Ashutosh would perhaps have liked to remind Aamir about the need to have conviction and guts, but he says nothing. He knows that Aamir takes time to make up his mind, but once he does so, he spares no effort to accomplish the task he undertakes. Ashutosh will simply have to be patient and calm.

Calm is what Aamir is most certainly not. His mind is in turmoil. He badly wants to do *Lagaan*, but as an actor. Ashutosh's prolonged efforts in trying to find a producer on the strength of the script have convinced Aamir that if *Lagaan* is to be filmed with the integrity with which it has been written, then *he*, Aamir Khan will have to produce it. Yet, if there is one thing Aamir has always known right through his film career, it is that he did not want to ever produce a film. The power of the *Lagaan* script is now compelling him to reconsider this decision. Aamir's mind is in a state of war struggling with contradictory emotions and impulses, reflecting on the myriad experiences that have shaped him.

A amir, unlike Ashutosh, grew up in a film family. His father, producer Tahir Husain and uncle, producer-director Nasir Husain, have been phenomenally successful at the box office. The happy part of being born to a film family was that even as a child, Aamir was exposed to the process of film making – to script narrations, to music sittings with giants like R. D. Burman and to screenings of

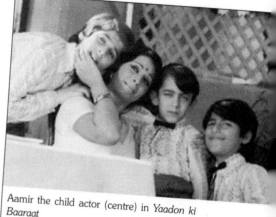

Aamir the child actor (centre) in *Yaadon ki Baaraat*

films at various stages of post-production.

A film background gave him more than just knowledge of the creative and technical processes of cinema. It exposed him to the caprice, cruelty and ruthlessness of the money market that powers films. Aamir's father, Tahir Husain had produced superhits like *Caravan*, *Zakhmee* and *Anamika*, despite which the child Aamir Khan had lived through the trauma of seeing the family fortunes go to the very brink of disaster more than once. As a child he had felt helpless as the vultures moved in for the kill and Aamir had vowed never to be in that position again.

From his catapult to stardom on his debut, *Qayamat Se Qayamat Tak*,

Aamir the assistant director with his uncle, producer-director Nasir Husain (extreme left)

Aamir treated the market with respect and selected films carefully, striking a balance between films made aggressively for the market and those that appealed to his own sensibility. His choice in this matter was somewhat restricted, because Aamir made his debut in 1988, when Hindi cinema was at its nadir. The eighties were the dark ages when Hindi cinema was consigned to the dung heap of the worst of mass culture.

Qayamat Se Qayamat Tak was a turning point. It was a lotus in the muck, heralding the emergence of a new generation of film makers like Sooraj Barjatya, Aditya Chopra, Karan Johar and of course Aamir's cousin Mansoor Khan. Hindi cinema began emerging out of the swamp, but with a lot of dirt still clinging to it.

Aamir trod a delicate path in which he did the loud and vulgar *Ishq* and the sexist *Raja Hindustani*, yet was the one big star who stuck his neck out to back bold and unusual scripts. Unlike some of his contemporaries, Aamir refused to get typecast and have a standard screen persona and redefined himself from role to role. From Mansoor Khan's offbeat *Jo Jeeta Wohi Sikander* to the delightful comedies *Dil Hai Ki Maanta Nahi* and *Andaz Apna Apna* and films like *Sarfarosh* and *Earth* that discuss serious contemporary issues, Aamir stood out as the thinking star.

For Aamir, his journey through the potboilers was his period of preparation and waiting – waiting for the day when *he* could dictate terms and do the kind of films he really believed in. But better films require better scripts and the culture of the first three decades after independence that had nurtured genuine writers is now in an advanced state of *rigor mortis*.

The nineties saw a new generation of film makers break the hold of the hackneyed and tacky action films of the eighties. With *Hum Aapke Hain Kaun, Dilwale Dulhania Le Jayenge, Dil To Pagal Hai* and *Kuch Kuch Hota Hai,* they created a new dominant paradigm of romance and *rishtas* (matrimonial proposals). For the first time since Salim-Javed institutionalised the wronged-by-circumstances avenging hero in the early seventies, violence moved away from centre stage.

The new formula treated wealth and affluence as a given and in that sense marginalised the expression of class anger, which albeit in *filmi* form, had been a part and parcel of films for several decades. Now, suddenly and strangely, everyone on screen was rich. Poverty and oppression disappeared from the screen, a reflection of the mindscape of the post-liberalisation upper middle class.

For all its novelty in form, the new paradigm in content, did not move beyond the boundaries of the romance-*rishta* formula and rapidly grew predictable. The newness was increasingly defined by exotic locales, glamorous wardrobes, chic sets and sophisticated shot taking. It soon became apparent that it had no new story to tell.

Qayamat Se Qayamat Tak propels Aamir to stardom

Strangely enough for the actor who had begun his career as a romantic hero, Aamir allowed the romance-*rishta* bandwagon to pass him by. Unlike the other two Khans, Shahrukh and Salman, Aamir did not have a single romance-*rishta* film after the mid-nineties and beat his own path as it were, selecting his characters from script to script. Each of his successive roles in *Rangeela, Ghulam, Sarfarosh* and *Earth,* were completely unlike each other.

Despite his success in picking the right scripts, Aamir has never quite lost his distrust and fear of the market. He knows that the journey downward is swift and brutal. So, when Ashutosh's *Lagaan* stares him in the face saying, "Here I am, do you have the guts to accept the challenge?" Aamir is torn apart. On the one hand, he knows that *Lagaan* could mean box office disaster and a huge setback for his career. On the other hand, *this* is his big chance to do something he has always believed in.

Aamir faces a dilemma. He knows that *Lagaan* will be enormously expensive to make and financially could well destroy him. He has no stomach for a re-run of the traumas his producer father went through. He knows that even if *Lagaan* were to do well, he would earn several times more money by utilising the same time as an actor — a fact that his chartered accountant, Bimal Parekh, never lets him forget. He knows that *Lagaan* is pitted against the swell and tide of mainstream Hindi cinema. Yet, given his creative ambition and love for challenge, it is these very factors that make *Lagaan* irresistible. If this means that he must turn producer, then so be it!

There is one last hurdle that Ashutosh must cross before Aamir is willing to finally embrace *Lagaan*. Aamir asks Ashutosh to narrate *Lagaan* to his parents, his wife Reena and the financier Jhamu Sughand. This, for Aamir, is the litmus test. If Ashutosh's script can carry this audience, then Aamir Husain Khan is willing to forget his lifetime vow against producing a film.

25th April 1998

Once again, Ashutosh wends his way to the study in Marina Apartments to narrate *Lagaan*. Aamir has picked the audience for the narration with great care.

Facing Aamir is Jhamu Sughand, a film financier with an unorthodox, yet shrewd sense of what the audience wants. Jhamu had financed the Aamir starrer *Rangeela* and had developed a deep respect for Aamir's financial integrity and creative skill. Jhamu had repeatedly suggested to Aamir that they team up as producer-financier, but scarred by the traumas his father had experienced, Aamir had always declined. Aamir wants Jhamu to hear the *Lagaan* script, both to see how the shrewd financier reacts and also so that Jhamu may decide whether or not he would like to finance *Lagaan*.

On Aamir's left are his parents. His father, Tahir Husain, is a veteran producer and no ordinary one at that. Tahir Husain has always given primacy to the script rather than to stars and has made bold and unorthodox movies, generally with first-time directors. Aamir's mother, Zeenat, also comes from a film family – her uncles the well known Fazli brothers — and the influence had rubbed off on her. Aamir has grown up listening to his parents discussing film scripts at the dinner table. Now he must see whether his parents like the story he has fallen in love with.

On Aamir's right is wife Reena – hearing a narration for the first time in her life. She is the only 'outsider' to films among those present, yet someone whose instincts as an audience, Aamir deeply respects.

Ashutosh pours himself into the narration. By now, every inflection and deflection, every movement of the hand, every pause, has become part of his persona. Aamir fights against the pull of the script to keep a close eye on the reactions of the others. As the narration proceeds, Aamir witnesses the magic of *Lagaan*. Tahir Husain, Zeenat Husain, Jhamu Sughand and Reena Datta are all overcome with emotion. Aamir's parents urge him to do the film. Jhamu too is overwhelmed by the story. Reena in characteristic undertone says, "I loved the script. Whether you should do it is something that *you* should decide."

Aamir *is* finally ready to decide. Nearly two years after he urged Ashutosh to junk the 'weird story about villagers in the British Raj' and over a year after he first fell in love with the script, Aamir is willing to embrace it with both hands. He is now ready to both act in and produce the film. In the life of the infant *Lagaan*, this is the turning point. Ashutosh is no longer carrying the baby alone. With Aamir on board, it is certain that he will use his considerable abilities and talents to ensure that the tiny seed Ashutosh conceived as a flight of fantasy, will reach maturity.

The baby gets a father

Reena and Aamir in the early days after marriage

GAURI: Main tohre saath hoon. Bharosa hai mohe, tujhpe, tohri himmat pe.
(I am with you. I have faith in you, in your courage.)
— LAGAAN

"I could not have made this film without Reena. And I am not saying this as a husband. I mean I just *could not* have made this film without her."
AAMIR KHAN
Actor - Producer

3
The baby gets a father

"If the director is the mother of a film, then the producer is the father." This is Aamir's favourite film analogy. In the *Lagaan* journey, the mother has finished her most lonely phase, whereas for the father, his journey is just beginning. Even before Aamir can settle into his new role, the 'baby' has a hiccup. Two days after commiting himself to financing *Lagaan*, Jhamu Sughand has second thoughts.

"Ashu's script is very good, but Aamir, now that you are open to producing a film, I have scripts by some other directors. Why don't you hear them before deciding which film you want as your first production?"

The alarm bells in Aamir's mind start clanging. "Why is Jhamu saying this? Didn't he like the script? Has he changed his mind?"

Aamir decides to be direct and force Jhamu to foreclose his options. If Jhamu wants to bet on him, he will have to go the whole hog. He will have to believe in Aamir's instincts about the *Lagaan* script and its director.

"Jhamu, I would love to hear whatever scripts your directors have to narrate to me, but I want you to know one thing. The first film I'll produce will be *Lagaan*. If you have any doubts about the script of *Lagaan* or about the fact that Ashutosh is the director, then please feel free to back off. I want you to *believe* in this film – if you don't believe in it, don't get into it. And it's not that I'll feel upset. I'll respect it and we'll work on some other film later."

"No, no, I didn't mean it that way. I am interested in financing *Lagaan*. There are no second thoughts…" interjects Jhamu.

"Are you sure? Otherwise, please take your time," insists Aamir.

"I *am* sure," says Jhamu, but by now Aamir is adamant.

"Jhamu, for the sake of the film, I *insist* that you take your time and let me know your answer only after a week."

4th May 1998

Jhamu calls Aamir to confirm that he is indeed financing *Lagaan*. Aamir's method is transparent. If you want to be involved with *Lagaan*, you must believe in it. You must believe in the script and you must believe in the director. Jhamu would probably have financed *Lagaan* just on Aamir's word, without even hearing the script. That is the way most financiers in the Hindi film industry have always worked. Aamir has instead placed Jhamu in the situation of making a decision on the basis of the script, precisely because he knows that making this film will be like climbing a mountain that can only be conquered with loads of conviction and guts. Forcing Jhamu to see the scale of the task and its inherent risks will steel him for the climb ahead.

The discussion turns out to be critical. From this point on, Jhamu Sughand never looks back. No matter how much the film overshoots its budget, no matter how great the delay in its release, no matter how many times aesthetic and creative decisions override practical considerations, he will back *Lagaan* without ever questioning Aamir.

May 1998 – January 1999

Although Aamir has decided to produce *Lagaan*, it is as an actor that his life and priorities are organised. *Sarfarosh* is due for release and requires publicity support from him. *Mann* and *Mela* are approaching completion and he is required for shooting and in the dubbing theatre. He simply does not have the time right now to be a hands-on producer. This is weighing on his mind.

Jhamu Sughand - *Lagaan*'s gutsy financier

Aamir is deeply aware of the extent and nature of his duties. Producing a film requires a lot more than putting money on the table. Sometimes, that can be the easiest part of the process. Producing a film is like setting up a mammoth factory – it is building a team, getting department heads, the cameraman, the production designer, the sound recordist, the head of wardrobe, make-up, hair, negotiating contracts with actors and blocking their dates, hiring locations, building sets, hiring lightmen, production boys, set workers, assistants in every department, sourcing a thousand different kinds of equipment, buying raw stock, catering food, making arrangements for transport, booking hotels and countless other jobs. It is only when all this and more is done that the camera will expose its valuable contents to light at the rate of twenty-four frames per second and the images frozen in a script will be recorded for posterity.

Despite the obvious importance of the production department, there is no film institute which trains for production tasks. The only training is on the job and is an extremely feudal process, where the producer keeps a tight control over decision-making and the money. Production staff are not viewed as skilled professionals, but are hired basically for running errands, which is why they are referred to as 'runners'! Yes, there is generally a production controller who runs the show on behalf of the producer, but rarely does he enjoy the producer's trust or the respect of the creative team.

Aamir has repeatedly seen how production goof-ups impact the creative team in various ways. He has seen how moneybag producers treat these goof-ups as matters of course, to be resolved by a volley of abuse hurled at the production staff. He is determined not to let this happen in Lagaan. He is determined that the creative team should have the fullest production support, for which a properly organised and professional production department imbued with a modern work culture needs to be set up. But who on earth is going to do that?

In the meantime, Ashutosh has started work in right earnest. Nitin Desai has joined the team as the production designer and they have started their search for locations. Ashutosh has started making a budget and is also looking around for actors. The pre-production of a mammoth film has started without any production systems in place. There is no office, no staff and other than making money available, there is no producer. Reena can see the utter lack of organisation and this irritates her.

"Aamir, if you want to produce a film, do it properly, not in this half-hearted manner."

"Aamir, your papers are all over the house. You can't find a thing when you need it. How will you make a film like this."

"Aamir, you call yourself a producer, but you have no production systems …"

Reena's wifely admonitions fall on Aamir's somewhat blocked ears. His mind, however, is whirring, working out a plan – that of getting Reena involved with the production of Lagaan. Aamir knows that his basic focus will be on the creative side. He desperately needs someone to oversee if not directly handle the mammoth production work in the film. Yet, he knows that nothing in Reena's past has equipped her for the task he is proposing.

The upbringing and background of young Reena Datta couldn't have been more different from that of the child Aamir Khan. Aamir grew up in a film - business environment, where he, his two sisters Nikhat and Farhat and brother Faisal breathed the intoxicating air of films, while academically, were pretty much left to do their own thing. Reena's father was a senior officer in Air India, and as in the households of most employed professionals, in the Datta family too, films were looked down upon, while academics was given prime importance. Unlike Aamir, Reena was academically bright and had scored high marks right through her schooling upto her graduation in statistics from St. Xavier's College. What Aamir and Reena really shared through their youth was an accident of architecture, namely the view from their balconies, which faced each other. This view was to prove decisive to their lives.

Aamir then and even today lives in a building called Marina Apartments. This building faces the Air India building where Reena lived. So full of pretty girls was the Air India building that Aamir and his younger brother Faisal fondly referred to their balcony as the place to sight 'jannat ki pariyan' (heavenly fairies). Ultimately, Aamir fixed his sight on one *pari* called Reena Datta and after a dramatic romance in the face of parental opposition, they had a registered marriage at the minimum permissible legal age. Thus was the *pari* called Reena Datta safely ensconced in the Khan flat adjoining the opposite balcony.

"Will you marry me?" Aamir in QSQT with Reena Datta in her only screen appearance

Even after marrying Aamir, Reena stayed miles away from filmdom. She rarely went for Aamir's shoots, she did not attend film parties, she had no film friends, she did not read film books or magazines and she did not even see many films. She had always wanted to start a career in computer software, but Aamir's crazy schedules meant she was bringing up their children and managing the household single-handed. Had she launched her own career, probably Aamir and she would not have seen each other at all. So, through twelve years of married life, Reena has been a homemaker. On the face of it, Reena cannot be more unprepared to handle the production of a giant film.

Yet, Aamir is in a spot and Reena just might fit the bill. And then, hasn't

Reena repeatedly asked him what career she should pursue? So, after the kids have fallen asleep, lying in bed at night, Aamir pops the question.

The newly-weds with Aamir's parents, Tahir Husain and Zeenat Husain

"Reena, I need someone in production whom I can trust completely. Would you like to give it a shot?"

Reena is perhaps half expecting the question. She can see that Aamir needs her help, yet her inexperience bothers her.

"I'd like to Aamir, but I don't know anything about film making."

Aamir promptly assures Reena that he will teach her and help her. Reena joins the Lagaan team.

February 1999 – May 1999

A mir is unsure of whether Reena will take to her new vocation and to what extent she will cope with the work. He hopes she can oversee at least the financial aspects, so that the budget does not go haywire.

Reena herself is unsure about her role and at first, sets herself modest targets. As a student of statistics, she feels that numbers are her strength, so she decides to make the budget for *Lagaan*. She is shocked to discover that in the film industry, what generally passes as a budget are a few pages allocating approximate sums of money under broad heads, like actors' fees, equipment hire, location hire. This really is a wish list divorced from reality.

Reena starts the other way around. She gets hold of the final accounts of a film after it has been released and discovers that there are over 5,000 separate heads of expenditure running into nearly eighty pages of an Excel worksheet, for each of which she needs specific quotations. For three months, Reena pours herself into the task, meeting hundreds of suppliers, vendors, transporters…the works.

Reena realises that the eight crore budget first prepared by Ashutosh is inadequate and that *Lagaan* will cost not less than fourteen crores of rupees. Aamir feels that this is the outer limit and given the market potential for *Lagaan*, any further expenditure will drive the project into the red. He repeatedly warns Reena that she must ensure that financially the film does not become a runaway horse, with the producer dragged in its wake. Aamir's brief to his executive producer is clear: "Reena, you must ensure that *Lagaan* does not exceed its budget and we are not forced to put in endless amounts of money to complete the film. If that means you have to clamp down on me, please do so."

Reena listens calmly and stores it all for future recall. Her husband is inviting her to read him the riot act if necessary. He cannot complain about this later.

Preparing the budget does much more for Reena than telling her what *Lagaan* would cost. The process of preparing the budget compels her to study the equipment, the skills, the manpower and the time required to shoot a particular scene. In short, it compels her to acquire a working knowledge of all the technical processes of cinema. Reena plunges into her film education. In the first couple of weeks she refers her technical queries to Aamir. Later, she begins speaking to the experts in each field directly. At this stage, she is a sponge, absorbing all she can about film making and its processes.

By the time Reena is through with the budget, she has tasted film making and savoured it. Different people come to cinema in different ways. The path of Reena, married to Aamir Khan for twelve years, is through the budget of *Lagaan*!

Aamir now sees that the reins in the production office are in capable hands. Whether or not Reena needs *Lagaan*, no one can doubt that *Lagaan* needs Reena.

June 1999

A amir asks Reena to formally take over as the executive producer of the film. From that point on, Aamir's role as producer is focussed only on the big policy decisions. At the operational level, Reena is the boss.

Reena's involvement has a strong romantic angle for Aamir. Not just personally, but professionally too, they are building something together. It is a new and hitherto unexplored dimension to their relationship. They are both experiencing facets of the other's personality not fully known despite twelve years of married life. There is growing mutual respect for new and different reasons. Yet, anything that has the power to build also has the power to destroy and neither Aamir nor Reena at this stage know that their professional relationship in *Lagaan* will test their personal lives as never before.

A team that shares the dream

Aamir and Ashutosh borrow a leaf in team building from Bhuvan's book

Jo hai tumre man mein, wohi humre man mein,
Jo sapna hai tumra, sapna wohi humra hai jeevan
mein
(What's in your heart is in my heart too
The dream you have is also my dream in life)
— Song from LAGAAN

"For any film, the core team you choose is a make or break decision. Only those who were passionate about the *Lagaan* script were in the film."
AAMIR KHAN
Actor - Producer

A team that shares the dream

In the history of mankind, perhaps no artistic activity has been as much a collaborative effort as film making. A poet pens his verse alone, a painter's companions are his easel and brush and a composer may write his music in solitude. However, a film director, no matter how inspired and brilliant, must work with his cinematographer, music director, sound designer, editor, production designer, costume designer, actors and so many others. The vision of the director's creative team determines in large measure the kind of film that will be made.

Aamir is deeply aware of the importance of bringing together the right team and also the challenges he faces in this regard. Given Ashutosh's track record, anybody who joins the team will do so, because it is Aamir's film and yet it is Ashutosh's creative leadership that every team member must unquestioningly accept. By his words and deeds, Aamir must get the entire team to feel the same. At this stage itself, he must ensure that only those who believe in Ashutosh and in *Lagaan,* may join the team.

The producer Aamir Khan has another important concern. *Lagaan* is an extremely expensive film to make and an extremely difficult script to film. The only way to realise the potential of the script without making *Lagaan* financially unviable, is to create a different work culture and put in place systems at sharp variance with those prevailing in the Hindi film industry.

Most Hindi films are shot over several schedules of a few weeks each, that stretch over a couple of years. A large part of the reason for this is that the system of financing Hindi films is driven by stars who work in upto a dozen films at the same time and so cannot spare more than a few weeks at a stretch for any single film. As a result, the creative energies of the entire unit, from the lightmen to the cameraman, are divided in more than one 'project'. Busy actors shoot for a few hours on one set, then dub for a few hours in a recording studio and shoot for a third film at night. Juggling dates to get the entire team together is the ultimate nightmare of a producer.

This anarchic work culture has calamitous consequences on the creative process. For *Lagaan*, Aamir knows that this work culture will be fatal. With its jumbo cast of actors, dates simply cannot be juggled. Creatively too, it will be disastrous for the unit to divide its attention across more than one film. The entire film must be shot from start to finish in a single schedule, in which every unit member will only live the world of *Lagaan*.

A hundred decisions must be taken to create a different work culture. Can this be done? Can the existing system be tamed? Can a new work culture be created among those used to working the old way?

Aamir knows this will not be easy. The only way to create a different work culture will be to put all his cards on the table, to inform every prospective unit member that *this* is how *Lagaan* is going to be made. Whether it is the cameraman, the music director or any of the actors, they can be part of *Lagaan* only if they accept its work culture.

October 1998 – March 1999

Aamir must test his resolve in the casting of the music director. Both Ashutosh and Aamir are convinced that A. R. Rahman is indispensable for *Lagaan*. By hook or by crook they must get him.

Aamir is anxious whether Rahman will agree to do *Lagaan*. His own previous interaction with Rahman has not been entirely smooth. Not that Rahman and Aamir have ever clashed, it is just that they have entirely different temperaments and ways of working.

As the son of a producer, Aamir Khan the actor has always been highly sensitive to the problems of the producer. As a child he had seen how the crisis of dates on the film *Locket* all but destroyed his father. So, as a star, he has made it his mission to stick to the clock, raising punctuality almost to the level of a fetish. Then again, being an actor has forced Aamir to remain constantly in the public gaze and though shy as a child, over the years he has learnt to genuinely enjoy his interaction with colleagues of different backgrounds and temperaments.

A. R. Rahman, music director

Rahman, on the other hand, is a recluse, introvert to the point of being afraid of any public interface. His work as a composer takes place through the dead of the night, in his studio lit by the candles of a holy *dargah*. Silence and loneliness are his constant companions at work. Perhaps, it is only the inspiration that comes from such a spiritual journey that could have produced the music he has. Were Rahman sensitive to the tensions of producers, could he ever have been creatively as fertile!

With such a sharp difference in temperament and approach, it would be a wonder if Aamir and Rahman had spontaneously hit it off. Back in 1996, Rahman had made Aamir wait for three hours in a theatre in Chennai for a pre-release screening of *Rangeela* to commence, without either an explanation or apology. Aamir had then decided that while Rahman was indubitably a genius, their paths must necessarily be different.

The turning point for Aamir was Deepa Mehta's *1947 Earth*, which also had a marvellous score by Rahman. It was Deepa who convinced Aamir that the genius from Chennai may be guilty of giving his music late, but not of a supercilious attitude. What appeared from a distance to be arrogance was in fact extreme shyness.

This history has made Aamir doubly nervous about Rahman — about the possibility of Rahman agreeing to do the film as also about the quality of the working relationship between Ashutosh and Rahman. Yet, Rahman is a must and when Jhamu Sughand assures Aamir that he will get Rahman, there is a palpable sense of relief. As in other matters, Jhamu is as good as his word and sure enough, Rahman agrees to do *Lagaan*.

Ashutosh is thrilled, but Aamir is curiously unmoved by the news that Rahman is on board. Aamir is determined that Rahman must not say yes to a Jhamu Sughand or an Aamir Khan. He must believe in the script of *Lagaan* and its director Ashutosh Gowariker. So Aamir calls Chennai and asks Rahman to hear Ashutosh narrate the script before making up his mind about whether he wants to do the film. Rahman is probably a little surprised. He turns down half a dozen producers daily and now Aamir is insisting that he hear a script before committing himself!

A shutosh's vehicle winds its way through the narrow lanes leading to Rahman's house in Chennai. Mercifully, no car approaches from the opposite direction to stop his progress. A good omen, thinks Ashutosh. The tiny lanes are flanked by simple, single-storeyed structures. The entire area has a middle class ambience. Then, on the third turn in the labyrinth, Ashutosh sees a plot of modest size with a gigantic structure on it. Rahman has built his bungalow in the middle class area he grew up in and has added storeys as he went along.

Inside Rahman's gates are two state of the art studios with work in progress on a third. Violinists, guitarists, *tabla* and *ghattam* players are packing their instruments after a night's work. Half a dozen producers loiter around. "Waiting in queue for Rahman," Ashutosh learns. Eyes bleary from lack of sleep, they look as if they have merged into their surroundings, a little like devotees who wait in long lines at temples for a *darshan*, an audience with the deity. The thought flashes through Ashutosh's mind – "Someday, will I too…"

Rahman sees a nervous Ashutosh soon enough. Ashutosh narrates the script, dialogues and all. The normally impassive Rahman is responsive. Narration done, there is no vacillation or hesitation. Rahman immediately agrees to do the film. So enthusiastic is Rahman, that he instantly calls Aamir who is then shooting for *Mela* and tells him that he loved the *Lagaan* script.

Aamir receives the call at the tiny motel where he is staying, located on the highway to Bangalore. He is delighted at the news. Rahman is now doing *Lagaan* on the strength of its script and director. Yet, Aamir is not quite through with his apprehensions.

"Rahman, there's one more thing I'd like to discuss before you commit to doing the film."

"What?" asks an intrigued Rahman.

"I'll come to Chennai and discuss it with you."

Rahman is baffled. What on earth could Aamir want to talk about?

Aamir makes the pilgrimage to Chennai. He is swift and direct. "Rahman, I am thrilled that you have agreed to do the film. But I want you to know that the film is being shot in a single schedule and so we will need all the songs at least two months before shooting starts. Only you know whether your pending commitments will permit you to meet our deadline."

Rahman is relieved. So this is all Aamir wanted to speak to him about. He is perhaps a little irritated by Aamir's nervousness. There is roughly a year for the shoot to start. Aamir's anxiety makes no sense to him. True to form, there is no hearty assurance to relieve Aamir. There is only a quiet, "Yes, I will finish on time."

Aamir must simply accept this at face value. Before he leaves, Aamir tells Rahman that henceforth Ashutosh alone would be interacting with him and that he will not be involved in the creative process at all. Rahman is characteristically expressionless. Aamir heads back to Mumbai satisfied that perhaps *the* critical member of the team has joined, but all his instincts are telling him: monitor the pace at which the music is made with a hawk's eye. Delay could destroy *Lagaan*!

Production designer Nitin Chandrakant Desai is for Ashutosh akin to home team. Nitin instinctively gears himself to Ashutosh's thinking. He has done both of Ashutosh's previous films and they are superbly tuned to each other's aesthetics. In a career spanning barely a decade, Nitin has handled a huge variety of work — highly successful commercial films like *Hum Dil De Chuke Sanam* and *Josh*, critically acclaimed films like *Ambedkar* and foreign films like *Jungle Book* on which he collaborated.

Nitin Desai, production designer

Ashutosh's brief to Nitin is simple: Forget the gloss, forget the sets that send the audience into a make-believe world. I want the audience to smell the cow dung of Champaner.

Despite his extensive experience, the decision to play out the *Lagaan* fantasy in a highly realistic manner means a unique challenge for Nitin Desai. Creating beauty out of gloss is simplicity itself; he must now make the viewer fall in love with structures made out of the mud, cow dung and stones of India. What is more, for single schedule *Lagaan*, Nitin must complete all the sets well before the shooting starts. It is a challenge he relishes.

Ashutosh and Aamir have zeroed on Anil Mehta as *Lagaan*'s cinematographer. Anil is an old friend. He was assistant director on Ketan Mehta's *Holi*, which had launched the careers of both Ashutosh and Aamir. Anil had dabbled in acting and modelling and ultimately consolidated a career in cinematography. The problem for Anil has always been an embarrassment of choices. His first Hindi feature film, *Khamoshi* and his second, *Hum Dil De Chuke Sanam*, won so much admiration for his work, that he was inundated with film offers. Anil has to think hard and long about whether he really wants to do *Lagaan*.

Director of photography, Anil Mehta

What excites Anil about *Lagaan* is that it will be a single schedule film where the entire unit of actors and technicians will be camping together for four months at a remote location — something unheard of in mainstream Hindi cinema. For Anil, a film is much more than the final product on celluloid. It is the *process* of film making that engages him – the process by which hundreds of people of different backgrounds and outlooks come together for a common purpose.

Lagaan with its single location, single schedule shoot promises a rich and engaging life experience. How is he to know that the single schedule on a single location will later create an intense professional and personal crisis!

Reena asks Aamir's beautiful elder sister, Nikhat, to help her out. Nikhat has dabbled in films on and off, but has never handled production responsibilities. Nikhat and Reena are well matched in their lack of experience, a deficit they make up with their enthusiasm and commitment. Nikhat sets up shop using part of the space at her father Tahir Hussain's production office.

Reena's biggest advantage in handling the work is her lack of experience. This has relieved her of the burden of 'industry practices' or settled ways of doing things, which essentially are a compendium of how *not* to do things. Reena has only a robust common sense to guide her and a desire to do things right. Sometimes, that counts more than a degree in business management or a diploma in film making!

A shutosh meets Bhanu Athaiya, aka Bhanutai, for the costumes of *Lagaan*. Bhanutai has the reputation of being reclusive, almost mysterious. Also, other than Satyajit Ray, she has for the costumes of Sir Richard Attenborough's *Gandhi,* won the only Oscar awarded to an Indian. In her long career, she has designed costumes for over seven hundred films including the films of Ashutosh's idol, Guru Dutt. Working with Bhanutai is in a sense connecting with the best cinematic traditions of India. Ashutosh knows all this and is more than a little in awe of her.

Bhanu Athaiya, costume designer

The meeting with Bhanutai is more than cordial. She is from Kolhapur as is Ashutosh and the ties of small towns are ties that still matter and bind. Ashutosh narrates the story of *Lagaan* and gives her a bound script as well. Bhanutai loves the narration and is impressed by his level of preparation.

The costumes for *Lagaan* are important to recreate the period feel. The wardrobe of Elizabeth and the others in the British cantonment will play a large part in bringing the Raj alive. Bhanutai requires no prompting. Meticulous research is her forte and the Raj an area of special interest. After a long time she is doing a mainstream period film – an exciting prospect.

April 1999

R eena and Nikhat are groaning under the pressure of work. Aamir's personal manager, the flamboyant Ashish Tharthare has joined the team, but the work keeps spiralling out of control. Obtaining a thousand and one quotations, making travel arrangements for Ashutosh and Nitin, coordinating with Bhanutai for the costumes…the list never ends. Then again, both Reena and Nikhat are new to films. They desperately need a production controller, someone with experience, to join the team.

One name comes to Aamir spontaneously – B. Shrinivas Rao. Aamir had seen Rao work as production controller on *Jo Jeeta Wohi Sikander.* Now when he needs him most, he is unable to track down Rao. Reena meets a number of production controllers from the industry, but their rough and ready methods put her off.

Finally, Rao is tracked down in Neerja Guleri Productions where he has a plum job handling the television superhit, *Chandrakanta*. Rao is very different from the other production controllers she has met. He is soft-spoken, articulate and even in the brief meeting, displays a superb sense of organisation. For a moment, Reena wonders how such a soft-spoken man will move the army of workers on a film like *Lagaan,* but she likes this approach. A different work culture will need a different personality to make things happen.

May 1999

B. Shrinivas Rao, chief executive – production

A amir is busy shooting for *Mela*, yet, one part of his mind is constantly tuned to *Lagaan*. Perhaps Aamir's biggest anxiety is adhering to the shooting schedule. The budget, the actors' dates, finishing the shoot before the monsoon …there are just too many eggs in that one basket and major delays in shooting could sink the whole project.

The only way to stick to the schedule is to have a First Assistant Director aka the First AD as in the west. In Hollywood and Europe, the First AD is the chief administrator on the set. In consultation with the producer and the director, he prepares the schedule for the entire film and then ensures that the shots assigned for each day are canned.

If one were to compare his powers within a factory set-up, the First AD combines the roles of a shop floor foreman and a general manager, operations. The First AD is even entitled to push the director to ensure that the film meets its schedule. The director thus cedes part of his powers to the First AD, but in return, a huge administrative burden is taken off the director's back, enabling him to concentrate exclusively on the creative process.

Hindi films generally do not require First ADs in the Hollywood sense. Where films are made without a bound script, where stories change as the shooting progresses, where there is no tradition of paperwork and planning, a First AD makes no sense. For single schedule *Lagaan*, Aamir knows a First AD is indispensable. The problem is: a First AD will have to be imported.

They are not 'made in India'.

Aamir's idea of 'importing' a First AD runs into opposition from Ashutosh. "I already have my assistants!" he protests.

Aamir is convinced that the skills and methods of a western First AD are not yet available in the Hindi film industry. He feels that sooner rather than later Ashutosh will come round to his point of view. Aamir begins correspondence with some assistant directors in the west. At around this time, Farhan Akhtar who has been talking to Aamir about his directorial debut film, *Dil Chahta Hai,* suggests Apoorva Lakhia who regularly works as an assistant director in Hollywood.

Apoorva believes he is a star in his own right. A build like Van Damme, the swagger of Indiana Jones and a portfolio that includes work with top Hollywood stars like Robert De Niro and Harrison Ford, reinforce that belief.

Apoorva and Aamir meet first in Mumbai and after Apoorva returns to the United States they continue negotiations electronically. Ultimately, Apoorva and Aamir meet at 3 a.m. in New York after Aamir has finished a stage show at midnight. Apoorva is impressed by a man who sets up a meeting at 3 a.m. and then continues till dawn! The deal is sealed and Apoorva joins the *Lagaan* team as First AD.

The present draft of the *Lagaan* script has dialogues that sound too contemporary and urban for the nineteenth century. Even today, people in the villages of central India, speak dialects like Braj Bhasha and Bhojpuri. Credibility demands that the people of Champaner must also speak in a dialect. Yet, the idea of making a film for the multi-lingual all-India market in a local dialect is preposterous, as a huge portion of the market for Hindi films lies outside north and central India, where north Indian dialects are not understood. Using a dialect could easily mean losing these audiences. A balance must be struck between the conflicting pulls of authenticity and comprehensibility, by using a watered down version of a north Indian dialect, which can communicate to an all-India audience even while preserving a rustic and period flavour.

Ashutosh now needs a dialogue writer who can perform this delicate balancing act. Ashutosh is convinced that the dialogue writer for *Lagaan* must be from the world of literature. Specifically, Ashutosh recalls the poet K. P. Saxena, whose poetry he had heard at a poetry conference several years ago. Ashutosh tracks him down in semi-retirement in Lucknow.

After the initial pleasantries and introduction, Saxena asks him, "What is the name of your film?"

"*Lagaan,*" replies Ashu.

Without further ado, Saxena tells him, "I'm doing the film. Your title tells me everything."

In western and southern India nobody even knows the word '*lagaan*'. Like the Raj, the word belongs to a forgotten era. But for Saxena, who has a strong sense of history, the word '*lagaan*' resonates with meaning. He realises that a film with that title must perforce be different.

Saxena suggests that the dialogues of *Lagaan* be written in Awadhi, as it would be the most widely understood dialect in India. However, it is a language which neither the writer-director nor the producer-star have a substantial grasp over! As with a hundred other things in *Lagaan*, they will learn along the way.

June 1999

"**A**shu, I'm really keen on shooting *Lagaan* with sync sound. What do you feel?" Aamir sets the cat among the pigeons in a manner only he can.

Shyam Benegal and a few others making smaller, less expensive films have consistently used sync sound, but in mainstream cinema, sync sound has disappeared for several decades now. The rule in commercial cinema is to shoot films using rudimentary sound equipment that will record pilot sound and then dub all the dialogues and background sounds in a studio after the entire shoot is over. As a result, actors have got used to being casual about their dialogue delivery on set, directors to pumping up the emotional levels while dubbing and the unit members to functioning in a noisy fashion during the shoot. The system of dubbing is much more than the technique of recording sound. It is part of a work culture.

Aamir had always been frustrated with this work culture and had tried persuading his directors to use sync sound, but without success. Everyone felt that the system simply was not conducive. Then, Aamir shot with sync sound for Deepa Mehta's *Earth* and tasted the power of a performance recorded entirely on location. Now, he is determined to use it for *Lagaan*.

Ashutosh is technically proficient with sync sound, but is apprehensive of its practical implications. It means that every take must be technically okay not only for camera, but also for the sound recordist. This means a massive addition to the creative burden during the shoot, an increase in the total number of takes and hence, rise in the number of shooting days. For a film whose financial viability is critically dependent on adhering to the shooting schedule, sync sound could well mean disaster.

Ashutosh points out all these factors to Aamir, who is unmoved.

Nakul Kamte, sound recordist

"Ashu, factor in the extra takes when you're making the schedule. If it means an increase in the number of shooting days, we'll spend that much more, but let's get it right."

Ashutosh is unconvinced. "Aamir, what if an actor's performance needs to be improved in dubbing?"

"Ash, don't worry. If it comes to that we'll spend some more money and dub those portions."

Practical issues addressed, the search for a sound recordist who can handle sync sound begins. Initially, some sound recordists in England are contacted, but using a recordist who does not understand Hindi seems hazardous. Ultimately, Ashutosh and Aamir meet Nakul Kamte who has done a film, *Bhopal Express,* using sync sound. Ashutosh and Aamir see two reels of *Bhopal Express* and are impressed by the capacities of a recordist who can record clean sound at a crowded railway station. Then they meet with Nakul and discover that the tall, flamboyant, former musician has a quiet aesthetic, in tune with the sensibility of *Lagaan,* and a strong streak of irritability so important for a recordist who insists on getting his takes just right.

"Sound is one half of the film and no one should forget that," Nakul says repeatedly.

October 1999

Ashutosh and Aamir are in Javed Akhtar's beautiful living room in his flat at Juhu. Ashutosh must narrate his script to the Javed of Salim-Javed, perhaps the only star writers in the history of Hindi cinema. Narrating to the legendary writer is not easy, but Ashutosh must do his best, for both he and Aamir have decided that Javed Akhtar will pen the lyrics for *Lagaan*.

Ashutosh finishes the narration and waits hopefully for the *wah, wah*.

Javed Akhtar looks at Ashutosh and Aamir and feels terrible about what he is going to say. Being a writer himself, he knows how appreciation is the best reward a writer can receive. And yet, he feels it is his duty to be frank.

Javed Akhtar is brutally direct.

Javed Akhtar, lyricist

"I have many problems with this script. If one were to compile a list of the 'don'ts' of mainstream Hindi cinema, this script contains all of them."

For a moment, Ashutosh and Aamir are shaken. The shoot is less than three months away and one of the most successful script writers in the history of Hindi cinema is telling them that their film may not work! But they recover swiftly. It is not easy to tell the Don Bradman of script writing that they disagree with his script analysis, but that is what they do – politely – and after thanking him for his effort and candour.

The confidence of the duo impresses Javed Akhtar. It appears to him almost an act of madness, of commercial suicide in pursuing an artistic dream. Ironically, this is the kind of film he longs to work for. So, despite his reservations about the script, Javed Akhtar will write the lyrics for *Lagaan*.

The heads of department fall into place. A. R. Rahman, Javed Akhtar, Bhanu Athaiya, Nitin Desai, Anil Mehta…each is a star, arguably at the top in his or her field – a 'dream team' of cinema. Perhaps as important as their stature and talent is that each has joined with a shared excitement about the *Lagaan* script. None of them has joined the team without accepting the work culture of *Lagaan*.

In the days to come, the talents and the endurance of each team member will be tested to the limits. This is when Ashutosh and Aamir will be glad that they have much more than just a 'dream team' — they have a team that shares the *Lagaan* dream.

Think big, think cinemascope

Ashutosh surveys the vast expanses

BHUVAN: Haan Arjan, hum sapna dekhat hain. Aur sapna wohi saakaar kar pavey hain, jo unhe dekhat hain.

(Yes Arjan, I dream, because only those who dream can make dreams come true.)
— LAGAAN

"I gave Ash only one guideline: Don't compromise. Don't tell me later, 'I wish I had got this'. Whatever you want, you are going to get."

AAMIR KHAN
Actor - Producer

5 Think big, think cinemascope

"I've found the perfect location for Champaner," Ashutosh triumphantly tells Aamir. "Both Nitin and I think that Kutch is ideal."

Aamir listens quietly, but he is unconvinced – not with the decision but with the process by which it is being taken. He is afraid that Ashutosh is being satisfied too easily.

"Ashu, I have nothing against Kutch and it may well turn out to be the perfect location, but why don't you look at other places as well, they may just turn out to be more exciting. I would recommend that Nitin and you actually go to various parts of the country and then choose. Don't make up your mind so fast."

Ashutosh is pleasantly surprised. Any other producer would have been relieved that his director had finalised the location without further loss of time and money. Aamir is suggesting just the opposite. In fact, this has become a regular pattern – of Aamir telling him, "Ash, think big, think David Lean, think cinemascope."

" If you need a hundred people for a scene, ask for three hundred."

"If you think of a palace it should be as grand as they come…"

Ashutosh, however, needs no prompting. The scale of his vision is embedded in his script, which mandates a big film. Aamir's solid backing makes available the resources necessary to realise his creative vision.

The ambitious thinking has however been worrying the production department. Production head Rao is opposed to leaving Mumbai and has instead urged the use of Film City in Mumbai as the principal shooting location. Shooting outside Mumbai will mean huge additional expenditure on hotels, food and transport for the entire unit, fifty percent extra payment per shift for the unionised workers and higher expenditure across the board. Rao has even prepared a table comparing the costs. On considerations of economy alone, Film City in Mumbai is unbeatable.

But, Ashutosh is clear that Champaner and the cricket ground must be dramatically different from anything seen on screen before. This rules out Film City in Mumbai as it is overexposed, both on the big screen and on television. Moreover, Aamir is convinced that creative justice can be done to the *Lagaan* script only by escaping from Mumbai and its sorry method of work in which everyone's attention is divided between various projects. He is determined that during the shoot, the entire unit must have no working life other than *Lagaan*. If that means spending fifty percent more money, so be it.

December 1998 – May 1999

Ashutosh and Nitin continue the search for Champaner. Maharashtra, Uttar Pradesh, Madhya Pradesh, Karnataka, Gujarat…and their jeep still rolls on through the Indian subcontinent. Somehow, they just cannot find the dry, parched look of agricultural terrain where it hasn't rained. The Chambal ravines are too rocky, the Rajasthan desert too sandy, Maharashtra and Karnataka too green.

Ashutosh is seeking a piece of land on which he can build Champaner from scratch. His dream location must not betray modernity in any way – no overhead electricity and telegraph wires, transmission towers, structures made of brick and cement, advertisements…

Champaner is elusive – Ashutosh checking out locations

Although Champaner is proving elusive, Ashutosh and Nitin put their journeys through rural India to good use. Even as their wheels roll, Bharat (rural India) speaks to them, prompting their sensibility in a hundred ways. Nitin is continuously recording every interesting object or person he sees. A conical straw rooftop in Gujarat, an unusual outhouse to a temple in Karnataka, impressive tiles for the village headman's house from Maharashtra…all images that will ultimately find their way into Champaner. Thinking big has its advantages.

As the days go by, Reena wonders whether Ashutosh has given up the idea of making *Lagaan* until he finishes seeing all of rural India. Ashutosh's wife Sunni wonders if he has settled down in some village.

W hile Ashutosh and Nitin continue their search for the perfect look on screen, the production team follows up on the availability of shooting permissions, hotel and transport infrastructure and other production arrangements.

In Kutch, a crucial consideration is the use of the palaces of the former king of Kutch, its Maharao. The financier Jhamu Sughand, who knows the Maharao, has already requested him for the use of his palaces, but without success. Ashutosh, however, is in love with the palaces and asks Aamir to try his charms.

Aamir drives into the home of the Maharao in Bhuj — itself a massive palace, inhabited by the royal couple, the Maharao and his wife, the Maharani. The palace has huge outhouses and annexes, sprawling gardens dotted with marble statues and even a massive bath in the porch! No one can mistake the wealth and prosperity its rulers once enjoyed. The walls of the winding corridor leading around the palace are lined with the stuffed heads of wild buffaloes, leopards and deer, animals shot by forefathers of the present Maharao. Next to the stuffed heads are photographs of royalty posing with their kill. One look at the palace and it is obvious that within these walls lie all the properties necessary to recreate the British Raj and the maharaja's *durbar* (court). Aamir's mind is rustling with possibilities, but will the Maharao accept his *firyad* (request)?

The Vijay Vilas Palace – summer resort of the rulers of Kutch

The Maharao is a tall man, with a prominent nose, piercing eyes, bushy moustache, dressed in British tweeds. From his gait and manner, to his habit of referring to himself by the royal 'we', it is obvious that here is a man who believes that he *is* 'royal', a status that Aamir accepts then and thereafter. Perhaps this is what makes the Maharao trust Aamir instinctively.

"You have come to us with a request. You can ask for anything. We cannot say no to you."

Thus does royalty extend its hand in friendship to 'royalty'!

Back in Chennai, there is no sign of Rahman starting work on *Lagaan*. He is simply too busy. The industry is rife with stories of producers and directors sleeping outside Rahman's house to get their songs and complete their films. A nervous Aamir meets Rahman.

"Rahman, please don't forget *Lagaan* is going to be a single schedule film. Once the schedule starts, there will be no opportunity for Ashutosh to come away. We simply must have every song in advance," Aamir stumblingly tells Rahman.

"When are you planning to begin the shoot?" Rahman asks.

"The first week of January 2000," replies Aamir.

Rahman makes a mental calculation. He has eight months. No big deal!

"Don't worry, Aamir, you'll have your songs in time." Rahman tries to allay Aamir's fears.

But Aamir is not satisfied. True to form, he must rub in his sense of urgency.

"Look Rahman, we are very excited that you're doing *Lagaan*, but if you have even a shadow of doubt that you can't deliver the songs on time, please do not hesitate to back out of the film even now."

Aamir is petrified even as he speaks. Half the world is persuading Rahman to do their films and Rahman is ruthlessly declining even the biggest guns in the industry. Here he has Rahman signed on and yet is offering the musical genius a way out of his commitment. If Rahman accepts Aamir's offer and actually backs out of the film, Aamir will probably never forgive himself.

Rahman stares at Aamir perplexed. What exactly does this man want him to do? Does he want him to back out of the film? Apparently not. Then, how can he get this man to stop offering him an exit route out of *Lagaan*? It is only after a lot of explanation that Rahman finally reads Aamir's desperate insecurity about not getting the songs ready on time. Yet again he assures Aamir that he will deliver, but this time, Rahman puts some conviction into the assurance.

Aamir comes away relieved that Rahman is still on.

Ashutosh requires ten cricketing teammates for Bhuvan and nearly ten other speaking parts. He is convinced that only an actor who looks the part, who simply *is* the character, must get the role. The best way to put this theory into practice is to audition the actors. This is highly unusual in the Hindi film industry where screen tests are conducted basically for aspiring novices and many of the seniors are unhappy about being auditioned. *Lagaan* is now the buzz of the industry and there is no route to being cast other than through an audition.

Conducting so many auditions is no cakewalk. There are more than half a dozen actors shortlisted for each role. This means screen testing nearly two hundred actors in all, a time consuming and expensive exercise. In order to check the suitability of the look, the actors don costumes and make-up for the auditions. Even props are procured so that Ashutosh may see how compatible the character looks with his properties. An axe is procured for casting the woodcutter Lakha, pots for casting the potter Ismail and medicinal herbs for the village doctor Ishwarkaka.

As the audition marathon continues, Ashutosh is increasingly convinced that if for nothing else, he must get a citation for having conducted the maximum number of auditions for a film in India!

Raghuveer Yadav as Bhura, Rajesh Vivek as Guran, Suhasini Mulay as Mai, Amin Hajee as Bagha…gradually the actors for the village cast fall into place.

Amin Hajee is the first actor to start working on his role. As the mute Bagha, he expresses himself through an oversized drum or *dhol*. Amin finds an orchestra that accompanies religious processions and starts learning various beats. In the festival season Amin and his drum will hit the road with the orchestra.

A critical creative decision must be taken. This one has huge commercial implications. Where will the British cast in the film be found? Indian producers have always used locally available Indian 'whites' for British roles, rather than fly British actors to India and pay them 'fancy' salaries in pounds. The time-honoured solution would have been to cast Anglo-Indians and white actors settled in India.

However, both Ashutosh and Aamir know that only British actors could create the authenticity required for the *Lagaan* fantasy to be believable. But casting actors from Britain is no easy decision to make. There is a huge financial implication to consider. Other than the major characters of Captain Russell and Elizabeth, the script requires ten British cricketers, three British seniors and at least thirty British junior artists. Paying the London-Mumbai airfare and salaries denominated in pound sterling will cost an arm and a leg. Thinking big will come with a big price tag!

Fortunately for *Lagaan*, casting in England was never in question for Aamir. The real issue is whether British actors want to be cast in an Indian production.

Barring the expatriate Indians, nobody in the British film industry may have heard of Aamir Khan, so there will be no queuing up for roles. Then again, by British standards, *Lagaan* is a low budget film being shot in a third world country. What's more, the system of casting in England is driven by agents and casting directors and presents a fresh set of challenges to Indians used to directly negotiating with actors.

All in all, a superstar actor-producer leaves Indian shores with his director and executive producer, armed with the discomfiting knowledge that when he lands in England, Aamir Khan is a nobody, an unknown third world producer trying to sign up professional British actors.

4ᵗʰ June 1999 – 13ᵗʰ June 1999

Aamir, Ashutosh and Reena land in London, buy a copy of the listings directory of the British film industry and scan the pages. They start by setting up meetings with prospective casting directors. The first meetings are invariably a little comic.

"Has your production house made any film before?" the casting directors quiz Aamir.

"No, this is my first film as producer," Aamir modestly replies.

"In which language are you making your film?"

"Hindi," says Aamir, even as the casting director gets more nervous.

"In which language are the British actors you want to cast, supposed to perform?" they continue.

"Also Hindi," says Aamir.

"So, you are making your first film in Hindi for an Indian audience for which you want British actors who will speak in Hindi…!" Many of them just cannot fathom whether the trio from India is serious!

The tide turns when they read the script. All of them realise that they are dealing with an artistically ambitious film. Some of the more hard-working casting directors do their homework and since the producer mentioned that he is also an actor, they do an Internet search on *"Aamir + Khan"*. At the next meeting, the *Lagaan* team is treated with a new respect.

Ultimately, the trio meets Danielle Roffe at her apartment, which also serves as her office. Vivacious and enthusiastic, Danielle loves the script and importantly, she is affordable. She also has a British assistant of Indian descent by the name of Urvashi Chugani, who, though she speaks no Hindi, somehow connects the firm of Danielle Roffe Associates with India. Also, since this is the only film that Danielle will be doing for the moment, she can devote all her energies to *Lagaan*. So, Danielle joins the *Lagaan* team. Aamir, Ashutosh and Reena return to Mumbai, secure in the knowledge that *Lagaan* now has an outpost in the land of the Raj.

The paramount consideration for casting is always the suitability of an actor for a particular role. For *Lagaan*, Danielle has a daunting list of additional requirements:

WANTED

For the role of Elizabeth, a British girl

- who can dance and lip sync to songs, AND
- is willing to learn Hindi, AND
- is willing to learn how to ride a horse side saddle.

For the role of Captain Russell, an actor

- with a menacing look AND
- who is an excellent horse rider AND
- plays excellent cricket AND
- who is willing to learn Hindi.

For the role of ten other members of the cricket team

- cricketers who act or actors who play cricket.

And all actors must be –

- willing to shoot in a dry and hot spot in India
- in third world living conditions
- although the film will probably do nothing for their careers in British cinema.

Even the generally optimistic Danielle wonders if she has bitten off more than she can chew.

15th June 1999 – August 1999

The heroine, Gauri, is proving to be elusive. Namrata Shirodkar, Amisha Patel, Nandita Das and several others have auditioned. Each has her strengths, but Ashutosh has a particular look in mind and he is yet to find his Gauri.

No one would have blamed Ashutosh for casting a star heroine in Gauri's role, someone who could lend glamour to a film in great danger of being labelled arty. But Ashutosh is clear that the heroine's star value is irrelevant. She simply must look the part.

It is afternoon on 20th July and Ashutosh is in the production office. Joshi, a veteran industry secretary drops in to meet Ashutosh. With him is a new actress called Gracy Singh. It is her birthday, but nobody knows that as yet. Gracy is not conventionally glamorous, but Ashutosh immediately notices that she has a quiet beauty with a very *bharatiya* (Indian) quality about it.

Ashutosh calls Gracy for a screen test.

Amir is present for the test to perform the romantic scene between Bhuvan and Gauri. Gracy belongs to a younger generation of actors than Aamir. In her teens, Aamir's poster adorned her walls. She is now romancing her pin-up boy on camera. The entire exercise is unreal.

Aamir notices that Gauri is very silent before the audition. Her face displays neither nervousness nor excitement. The quiet girl from Delhi is painfully shy and says little – a sharp contrast to the confident and bubbly girls that abound in the Hindi film industry. Yet, the flip side of this apparent lack of 'attitude' and 'personality' is that Gracy is able to transform herself into a character of her choice.

Gracy Singh, has the Gauri look

When Ashutosh rolls the camera, Gracy performs brilliantly.

Ashutosh and Aamir watch all the Gauri screen tests at one go into the late hours of the night. Both unhesitatingly choose Gracy over the others. The quiet girl from Delhi will join her adolescent crush on the *Lagaan* poster.

The search for Champaner has been on and with less than six months for the shoot to commence, a decision cannot be deferred. Ashutosh and Nitin have travelled extensively, checking out various possibilities and the choice has narrowed down to two. Ashutosh's first choice is still Kutch. The dry parched look of Kutch is ideal for the village and the cricket ground. Moreover, the permission to use the Maharao's palaces means that the entire film can be shot from a single base in Bhuj without shifting the unit elsewhere.

The other strong contender is Nasik in western India for the village and the cricket ground and the Pataudi palace in north India for the British cantonment. Aamir finds the undulating terrain of Nasik more picturesque than austere Kutch and tells Ashutosh as much. Ashutosh, however, sticks to his first love, Kutch.

Aamir is in turmoil. He loves the look of Nasik and is tempted to use his powers of persuasion with Ashutosh, but then he pauses. The location is crucial for the creative vision of the director. He must not tamper with the integrity of Ashutosh's creative vision. Champaner shall be built in Kutch, a decision that is to prove vital to *Lagaan*.

In the tiny production office, the atmosphere is tense. Production head Rao is holding his head in his hands.

"You mean we are going to have a single schedule shoot with a multinational cast and crew in Bhuj!" Rao has been dreading the decision.

"How will we make arrangements for such a large unit in Bhuj? Where will the foreigners stay? How will people travel there? Where does one get the materials continuously required in a shoot? What if people fall ill?"

The entire production team is sitting around and the questions are aimed at no one in particular.

Aamir calmly tells Rao, "That's what you're there for Mr. Rao. I know you'll find an answer to all these questions."

Rao knows perfectly well that a decision taken on creative grounds is not going to be changed for the convenience of production. He is merely venting his frustration at the hand he has been dealt. Rao could scarcely be blamed. Kutch is an intimidating place to deal with. Nature and geography have made it both remote and austere.

Kutch is a peninsula with its only road link to the rest of India being through the Surajbari Bridge built over a hundred years ago by the British.

Most of Kutch is a salt desert, dominated by the Rann of Kutch. In summer, temperatures rise to above forty degrees centigrade and the desert winds that sweep unchallenged, scorch all life that stands in their path. In winter, the temperatures fall to a single digit and the winds cut to the very bone. Rainfall is becoming increasingly scarce, turning vast areas of Kutch, including the erstwhile pasture lands of Banni, into saline deserts like the Rann.

In the seventies, the government, in order to halt the relentless march of the Rann, introduced the seeds of a 'miracle plant' known by the botanical name *prosopis juliflora*, locally known as the *ganda babool*, and even arially sprayed the seeds. The miracle multiplied like wildfire and took deep root in the desert soil. But the cure was worse than the disease. The *babool* was poisonous to cattle, a catastrophe in an economy heavily dependent on cattle rearing! Worse, the miracle plant sucked precious water from the soil, leading to the death of all other trees and vegetation.

With Kutch turning increasingly hostile to human habitation, the twentieth century has seen a continuing exodus out of the district. Those who survive in the desert, thrive in better-endowed lands. The hardy Kutchis turned out to be enterprising businessmen and over the past century fanned out all over the world, prospering wherever they went.

The Kutchi diaspora spends a lot of money in Kutch, building mansions in their ancestral village homes and on charity. The Kutch economy thrives on these remmitances. The modest needs of the less ambitious Kutchis who resist the temptation of greener pastures outside Kutch are relatively easily satisfied. This diaspora-driven economy has contributed to the creation of a laid-back work culture and nurtured the dignity of a people for whom honour and respect count far more than lucre. Ironically, for a region that exports so many aggressive capitalists, Kutch is astonishingly gentle, almost a forgotten land only barely exposed to the winds of change.

The contrast of Kutch with Mumbai in terms of climate, geography, culture and people, cannot be greater. Yet, Champaner is in Kutch and it is in Kutch that Aamir Khan's production team now has to strike roots. The creative team had been told to think big, now it is the turn of the production team to match the size of that vision.

A million things to do

NUMBER EACH ITEM

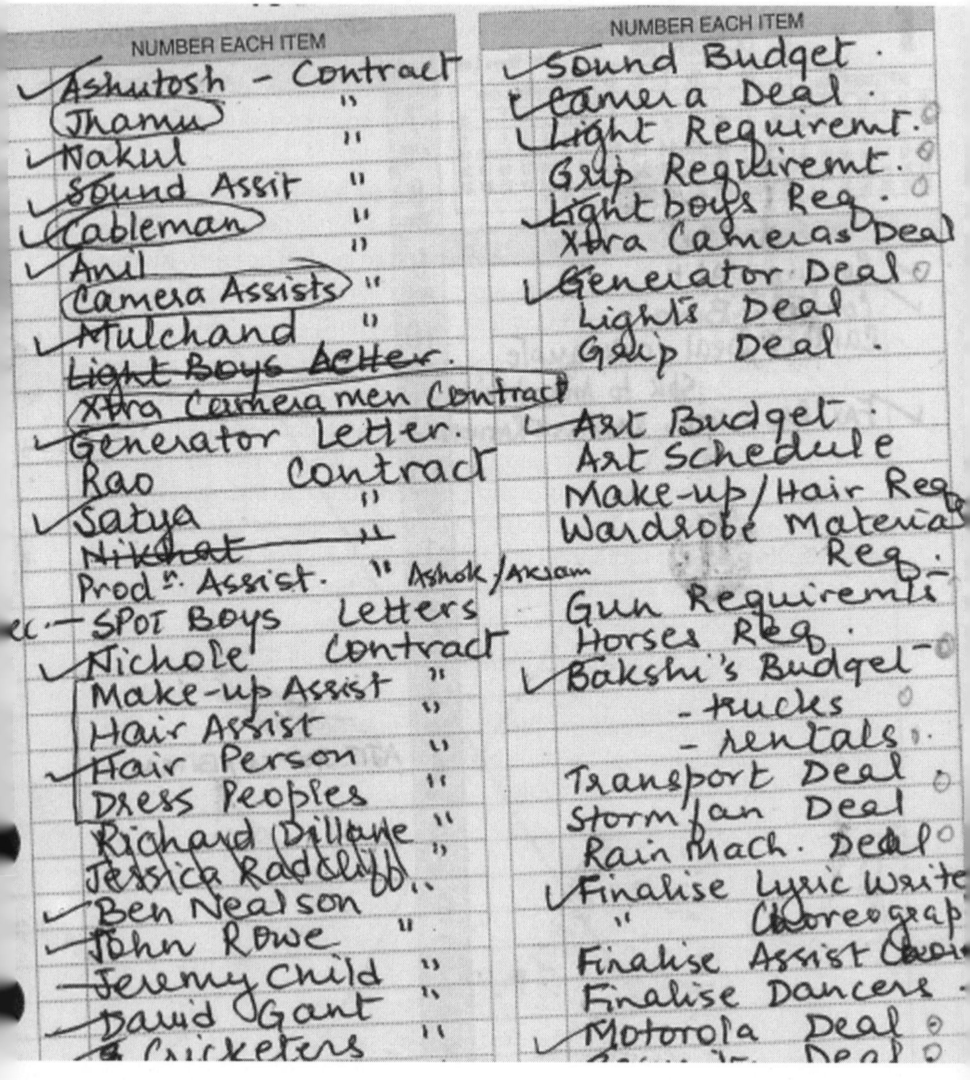

Ashutosh - Contract
Jhamu "
Nakul "
Sound Assit "
Cableman "
Anil "
Camera Assists "
Mulchand "
Light Boys Letter.
Xtra Cameramen Contract
Generator Letter.
Rao Contract
Satya "
Nikhat "
Prodn. Assist. " Ashok/Aksam
SPOT BOYS Letters
Nichole Contract
Make-up Assist "
Hair Assist "
Hair Person "
Dress Peoples "
Richard Dillane "
Jessica Radcliff "
Ben Nealson "
John Rowe "
Jeremy Child "
David Gant "
Cricketers "

NUMBER EACH ITEM

Sound Budget.
Camera Deal.
Light Requiremt.
Grip Requiremt.
Light boys Req.
Xtra Cameras Deal
Generator Deal
Lights Deal
Grip Deal.
Art Budget.
Art Schedule
Make-up/Hair Req
Wardrobe Material Req.
Gun Requiremts
Horses Req.
Bakshi's Budget
- trucks
- rentals
Transport Deal
Storm fan Deal
Rain Mach. Deal
Finalise Lyric Write
" Choreograp
Finalise Assist Chore
Finalise Dancers.
Motorola Deal

A day in the life of Reena Datta

Aaja re aaja re, aaja re aaja re
Bhale kitne lambey ho raste ho
Thake na tera yeh tan ho
(Come, yes come on
However long the path may be
This body of yours shall not grow weary)
— Song from LAGAAN

"There were so many things happening at the same time, that I could not believe that it would all ever come together. That a shot would ultimately be taken."
REENA DATTA
Executive Producer

6 A million things to do

Reena, Nikhat, Rao and Ashish arrive by second class train at Gandhidham station and travel further by road to Bhuj in a battered jeep-taxi. They must try out every mode of transport and every form of stay in Bhuj. This is no excursion. Production needs to set up shop in Bhuj. In six months time, the *muhurat* (first) shot of *Lagaan* will be taken and the production team has to create the extensive infrastructure mandated by a single schedule shoot. The production team has come to Bhuj to stay and will leave this town only well after the last shot has been canned.

As the cab rattles its way to the hotel, Rao is absorbing the town, his forehead wrinkled with worry. Already, there is a steely determination in his eyes. *Lagaan* will be the challenge of his life. It will require all his organisational skills to make it happen. One thing the production team is unanimous about: given the sheer length of the prospective stay in Kutch, they cannot remain outsiders or guests. They must get to know Kutch as well as the Kutchis. They will have to strike deep roots here.

The first task is to figure out the lodging facilities for a jumbo cast and unit. They try out the half dozen hotels and tiny lodges in Bhuj, eat at all its restaurants and discover where the food leads to a tummy upset. They check the cleanliness in the hotel rooms and discover which ones have dry taps or defective boilers. At first, the hotel owners are surprised to see the name of Aamir Khan's wife and sister on their guest list and the service is passable. Then, as the novelty wears off, habit takes over. The celebrity guests lose laundry, miss room keys, endure empty flush tanks and do without room service. They discover that although the people of Bhuj are very hospitable, as an industry, hospitality is yet to arrive.

And yet, if Amir Khan Productions does not bring the hospitality industry to Bhuj, it will have a mutiny on its hands. Imagine a unit of 400 people, many of them used to a high standard of living, several of them from England, forced to live together for more than four months, with unclean linen, geysers that don't work, doors that do not close properly and food that is inedible. Then imagine this disgruntled lot giving an enthusiastic performance!

28th June 1999

While the living arrangements are being checked and worked out, the primary focus is on building Champaner. The team makes the pilgrimage to the holy spot chosen by Ashutosh for building his dream village. The last part of the journey is on a mud track. Daily, hundreds of people will have to be transported to and from this location before any ACTION can begin. When they finally arrive at the spot where Champaner will have to be built, Reena and Nikhat cannot believe their eyes. It is the most godforsaken place they have ever seen.

Their first hurdle is the discovery that the plot of land selected by Ashutosh is owned by twenty-odd farmers of a village called Kunnaria. It is difficult to get even one individual to part with his land in India, imagine persuading two dozen! If even one of these farmers refuses, Ashutosh will have to begin his search for Champaner all over again. The vision of seeing Ashutosh and Nitin roaming around in a jeep for a few more months terrifies everyone.

Nikhat and Rao contact the sarpanch (village chief) of Kunnaria and set up a meeting with the landowners. It is a curious congregation. On one side are two dozen villagers – their faces impassive, giving little away. On the other side are Nikhat and Rao trying to explain in Hindi to the villagers, why they should consider leasing their lands for a year for the shooting of a film. Most of the villagers understand very little Hindi and speak none. As for films, let alone grasping the concept of a shoot, many have never been to a theatre in their lives! Rao drones on in his South Indian Hindi accent and the villagers make a show of listening. "Our land must have something precious," is what their faces say.

Nikhat is confident of one thing. The name of Aamir Khan. She has seen how her brother's name has unlocked not just hearts, but also all kinds of doors. She's convinced that this time too it will work the miracle for them.

The villagers continue listening. Now, they seem more than slightly bored. Finally one of the villagers looks at the Mumbaiwallas with an air of curiosity and simply asks, "Who is Aamir Khan?"

Needless to mention, the meeting ends with the villagers ambling home, without making any commitment.

30ᵗʰ June 1999

Ashutosh is on to the next task: working out the design of the village and other sets with Nitin Desai. Both are sticklers for detail and both have strong opinions on the set design. Each spends endless hours trying to convert the other to his point of view. That Bhuvan's house shall face Gauri's, that the mukhiya's house should have a commanding location in the village, that Bhura's house and Goli's field shall be adjacent…there are a thousand and one details to work out and fight over.

The process is exhausting, but leads to a great deal of clarity. For Ashutosh, it is a trial run in his head of every scene in the film. Through this creative war in designing the village, he now knows exactly from where every character will enter and exit in each scene. He knows who will be in the background and who will not. No decision on set design is taken by default, every aspect is thought through.

2ⁿᵈ July 1999

The village has been designed on paper. The next task is that of actually building it. Most shooting sets consist of exterior walls without interiors. What the camera sees is built, building anything else is a waste.

Ashutosh, Aamir and Nitin decide to break with established practice. They decide to build a real village with real houses one can live in. Yes, there will be massive 'wastage' of money in that process, but building a real village will have incalculable advantages. It could allow the actors to forget they are acting on a set and create the atmosphere of a village to which they belong. Also, this will allow Ashutosh and the cameraman Anil Mehta infinite flexibility in shot taking — at no stage will they have to worry about the camera seeing an incomplete structure.

Who will build this real village? Nitin is keen on using his regular crew from Mumbai. This is the tried and tested solution. Aamir and his production team are, however, hell-bent on using local labour. For Aamir, this is a policy, part of his overall approach to Kutch. Aamir Khan Productions must strike deep roots in the Kutch soil. It must provide employment to as many people as possible. Whatever is available locally must be bought locally. The people of Kutch must feel this is *their* film. They must have a stake in it. Using local labour to build Champaner will be an important step in this direction.

Even creatively, Aamir feels that local labour will be more suitable. The Mumbai crew will end up building a set, while the villagers will build a real village with real houses. Perhaps, Champaner will be a little crude and the villagers may face some difficulty in following Nitin's drawings, but the lack of finish is precisely what could give it the authenticity Ashutosh is so desperately seeking.

But, how does one source the villagers to build the set? There are barely four months left for the shoot to start and *Lagaan* is running out of time.

4th July 1999

The production team has been scouring Kutch for a contractor who can build Champaner. There are plenty of contractors willing to build roads, buildings and other cement concrete structures, but none who can build a traditional Kutchi village.

Rao hears of a contractor, Danabhai Ahir, who does a lot of work for the government and lives in a village called Kotai, not far from the site for Champaner. Rao is told that if anyone can build Champaner on time, it is Danabhai.

Rao meets Danabhai, who seems to have the wherewithal to pull it off and offers him the contract, expecting him to feel thrilled and honoured. He is in for a surprise. Danabhai is curiously non-committal and is suspicious of a person from the film world. Time is running out and no alternatives are at hand. A worried Rao sets up a meeting between Danabhai and Aamir in Mumbai.

7th July 1999

Danabhai, a millionaire of sorts, yet a Kutchi villager at heart, boards a second class compartment on the Kutch Express and 14 hours later telephones Aamir from the railway station at Mumbai. Aamir sends his car for Danabhai and instead of meeting him at his office, invites him home for lunch. Over the meal, Aamir explains to Danabhai the importance which the village Champaner has for the film and what Danabhai is required to do.

Although Danabhai Ahir, standard IV pass, resident of village Kotai, and Aamir Khan, belong to vastly different worlds, the lunch initiates the process of melting their differences and flags off a shared journey into the world of *Lagaan* which will dominate their lives over the next 12 months.

Danabhai would later confess to Rao, "I came prepared to meet a film star and I met a human being instead."

With Danabhai joining the team, Production has much more than procured a contractor to build the village. It has bonded Bharat with India. With Danabhai comes a massive network of contacts throughout Kutch, in particular among the Ahirs who are the dominant *jati* or sub-caste in the villages in and around where Champaner is located. The power of the network is soon evident.

Danabhai Ramji Ahir – the man who built Champaner

The farmers of Kunnaria who had earlier been suspicious and afraid of letting out their land, now give their consent immediately. The villagers themselves suggest the rent, an amount equivalent to the price of their entire crop had it rained and had they cultivated the land. Reena agrees instantly and the deal is struck.

Then, something important happens. To ensure that there is no ambiguity or misunderstanding, both Danabhai and Reena insist that written agreements are prepared in Gujarati and read out to the villagers before they sign them. Since I had practised as an advocate for ten years in Mumbai, I land up with the task of getting the agreements drawn up by a local lawyer.

The entire exercise is a bit unusual. In India, nobody draws up agreements with humble, unlettered villagers and that too in their mother tongue. All you do is strike deals with power brokers who get the villagers to fall in line. The task of reading out the agreements takes days and only when each of the villagers is satisfied are their signatures or thumb impressions affixed. It is obviously a new experience for them.

The elaborate effort sets the relationship between Aamir Khan Productions and the villagers on a sound foundation of mutual respect. It is a relationship that will play a role far more important than anyone could have ever imagined.

15th August 1999

Back in Mumbai at Aamir's house, Ashutosh narrates the script of *Lagaan* for the entire cast and crew finalised so far. My wife, Svati and I are the only non-unit members at the narration. For one of us that will change soon enough.

5th September 1999 - 11th September 1999

Ashutosh and Reena are in England to cast the British actors. Aamir is unavailable as he is away in North America doing stage shows. When they left England in April, they had been a little uncertain about how many actors would be willing to work in hostile climatic conditions in a third world country. These fears are now completely belied. Adversity has worked to their advantage. The prospect of shooting in India has lured actors like bees to honey. Dozens and dozens of actors have auditioned for the parts and the casting director, Danielle, has been sending tapes of the auditions to India. Ashutosh has been through these and has sent Danielle a shortlist of those whom he wants to recall, namely those who will now audition in his presence. Danielle is superbly organised and the auditions proceed like clockwork.

Auditions done, Ashutosh selects Jane Silverstone and Robert Croft for the role of Elizabeth and Captain Russell. Reena also concurs with Ashutosh's choice. Reena faxes Aamir the photographs of Silverstone and Croft, asking whether he has any suggestions before they are finalised. The fax is in black and white and Aamir cannot really judge the photographs too well. But, Aamir has full faith in Ashutosh and Reena and replies saying, "This is your call. Go ahead and do what you have to, I trust your judgment."

Ashutosh is delighted that he has the casting for the two major British characters wrapped up. Little does he suspect the twists and turns that lie ahead.

Meanwhile, Danielle and her assistant Urvashi spread the casting net for the cricketers who can act or actors who play cricket. It's an unusual combination, but the nursery of cricket nurtures an almost unbelievable number of professional actors who play cricket regularly for various clubs and who want to travel to Kutch and shoot there. There are far more candidates than roles and Ashutosh has an embarrassment of riches. The question is: how is he to choose?

Ashutosh finds a simple solution. He asks the cricketer-actors to play a regular cricket match. A county ground is hired, teams are formed and a game is played. Ashutosh squats at square leg, camera in hand, shooting the proceedings. While the cricketers enjoy their match, Ashutosh shortlists the players on the basis of their cricketing skills and of different kinds of looks, so that the team will appear interesting.

While Ashutosh selects his actors, Reena handles the back office – speaking to the actors' agents, negotiating fees and other conditions of work. At a level, this is a routine task. What is unusual in England is that in addition to actors' fees, numerous other things must be negotiated. The food to be served, the 'turnaround time', which is the number of hours between pack-up on a shooting day and the time at which the actors depart for set the next day...these and a hundred other issues must be haggled over. Reena rapidly makes decisions that she must live with till the end of the shoot.

Apart from the negotiations, Reena is busy 'warning' the actors about what they can expect in India. Both Reena and Ashutosh sit with every shortlisted actor and provide a graphic description of the desert heat and the absence of amenities in Kutch. "If anyone has reservations about shooting in these conditions, then please don't sign on," is their candid warning. Curiously, the adversity heightens the lure of shooting in India. It becomes a challenge that the actors are keen to face.

Reena's candour will pay rich dividends in the difficult days to come. Nothing can fully prepare the actors for the intensity of the trial they shall undergo, but the honest warnings create the foundation of a relationship based on truth, which the actors will reciprocate and respect.

20th September 1999

R ahman was to have started his work by mid-April, yet by mid-August, Ashutosh is still to have a single sitting with him. There are just four months left for the shoot to begin and there are no tunes in sight. Reena's emotions are a mixture of fury and desperation. She dials Rahman in Chennai. Despite repeated attempts, she cannot get him on the line. His Man Friday, Noell, who handles everything from studio bookings to dates with directors, answers for him. Reena unleashes her fury on Noell. Five minutes later, Rahman calls.

27th September – 5th October 1999

A shutosh makes his way through the winding lanes leading to Rahman's house in Chennai, with a spring in his stride. Finally, work is to start on the music of *Lagaan*...well almost. Rahman spends quality time with Ashutosh. Lots of quality time. Reena relaxes in Mumbai. Finally, the work has begun.

For one full week, Ashutosh and Rahman discuss everything under the sun, but the music of *Lagaan*. They talk about politics, about the state of affairs in India, about cinema, about different kinds of music — Hindustani classical, folk, the music of the great Hridaynath Mangeshkar... everything except the music of *Lagaan*.

Another director would have had his heart sinking with every ticking minute. Not so Ashutosh Gowariker. This is his method of work enabling Rahman to tune in to his sensibility before he can compose his tunes.

Ashutosh leaves Chennai after a week of chatting with no tunes in his pocket. He has waited the better part of a year for Rahman's dates and now after a week of 'work', there are no songs forthcoming. But Ashutosh knows there is a method in this madness.

2nd October 1999

I make my first journey to Bhuj by the Kutch Express. Svati and our children, Nayantara and Nishant turn up to bid me goodbye. None of us have an inkling that it will be nearly a year before my Kutch saga will end.

I am travelling with my colleague in the production department, Ashish, who smiles at a tall, lean gentleman in the corridor of the train. Ashish turns round and says with a flourish:

This antique of the Maharao will be restored

"Satya, I'd like to introduce you to His Highness Maharao Pragmulji III, Sawai Bahadur of Kutch".

I can almost hear the trumpets heralding his presence as Ashish announces the name.

I hold my breath as I say, "How do you do, sir."

I know that the Maharao controls two massive palaces, which we require for the shoot. Somehow, the image of a king with fabulous palaces does not jell with the place of introduction. Just then the ticket collector approaches with the reservation chart and the Maharao must retreat to his berth to find his ticket.

The train enters Gandhidham and like us, the Maharao jumps on to the filth-caked tracks and clambers up the next platform to cross over on to the road outside the station. My sense of wonder about the king of Kutch increases, when outside the station I see a handsome, bearded gentleman, later introduced to me as Dilipbhai, bend low and salute the Maharao as a noble would his king. Such majestic irony!

This quick introduction to Kutch teaches me a valuable lesson: here, the old world and the new co-exist in a strange fashion and whatever my opinion about each might be, the purpose for which I have come can only be served by both the old and the new.

4th October 1999

Work on building Champaner is in full swing. Rao soon realises that everything he has heard about Danabhai's organisational abilities is more than true. Ensuring the smooth movement of labour and materials in the middle of nowhere is not an easy task, yet miraculously, just as one lot of stone is exhausted a truck carrying another lot appears. As the water tank is getting empty, a trailer-tractor with fresh supplies approaches.

For the houses of Champaner, Nitin and Ashutosh have settled on the conical mud and straw huts of Kutch known as *boongas*. Although the *boonga* is native to Kutch, the advent of electricity and the march of brick and cement have made it history. The first problem Danabai faces is that he just cannot find skilled workers who can build *boongas*.

It is only in the far flung cattle-rearing hamlets of Banni that people still live in *boongas*, and even these structures built a few generations earlier are being rapidly replaced by brick and cement homes. Only a handful of village elders still know how a genuine and sturdy *boonga* is built. Danabhai sends his men into the heart of the Banni grasslands and half a dozen wizened old men are found. Danabhai starts a kind of local training programme. The old teach the young the art of *boonga* building. In the process of creating the set for *Lagaan*, an ancient craft is being preserved.

To me, the work seems poetic in its rhythm. At six-thirty sharp the trailer-tractors arrive and the women wearing their red *bandhani* printed *ghagara cholis* and the men dressed in their *cheni kediyas* pour out. For half an hour, they have tea and engage in friendly banter and chat. Then, without any outward sign of being directed, they head for work and continue without a break till midday and lunch. After lunch, they sleep in the shade for an hour and all activity is at a standstill. Then, they all rise together and work till sundown. Strangely, everyone seems to know exactly what is expected of them and the work proceeds almost soundlessly.

The forgotten art of *boonga* building

In the evening, before sunset, the villagers climb into their tractors and leave for their village, Kotai. I climb up the hillock leading to the temple hilltop and gaze around me. For miles together I see undulating plains dotted by the cancerous green of the *babool*. There is not a soul in sight, there is no bustle of activity, no roar of vehicles; the only sound is that of the birds and of the breeze blowing through the barren plains. Vastness and silence overwhelm me.

5th October 1999

In Kutch, the construction work proceeds full steam ahead. So smoothly does the work progress, it seems that Champaner will be ready ahead of schedule…and then disaster strikes! Danabhai runs out of *gobar*! One of the key materials required for building Champaner is fresh *gobar* or cow dung, collected while it is still sticky, before it has hardened. It is used to plaster the walls, the floors of the houses and the platform outside each structure in Champaner. In India, even today, millions of women use *gobar* to plaster their homes. But the very nature of *gobar* does not lend itself to centralised collection and management.

The problem is that Danabhai requires an astronomical ten lakh kilograms or one thousand tonnes of *gobar* for Champaner. How is so much fresh cow dung to be procured? Unlike a factory-made product, production cannot be stepped up overnight for love or money.

The only way out is to spread the collection net wider. How this problem is confronted is a tale in itself. Danabhai sends men and tractors in the wee hours of the night into the far corners of the Banni grasslands, where cattle graze. The precious dung is scooped and collected before it can harden. Nobody knows how Danabhai deals with the owners of the cattle whose precious droppings are being carted away. All we know is that for days on end, a line of tractors empty their invaluable contents on location. In the history of the film industry, never has bullshit played such an important constructive role!

Plastering the Champaner houses with cow dung and mud

The mammoth Operation Gobar pays off and the set looks like it will be completed well within time.

7th October 1999

The construction of Champaner is in full swing. Seated on the temple steps, Ashutosh can see the villagers at work. Ashutosh needs nearly a hundred villagers as part of the background action for the scenes shot in Champaner. He has been dreading the prospect of casting suitable faces from the professional junior artists available in Mumbai. Suddenly it strikes him, why not use these villagers who are building the village. They would be absolutely authentic. It is a gamble considering that some of the villagers have never been to a cinema theatre in their lives. Will they understand shooting instructions? Will they resist staring at the camera? Will they be able to dance in the songs? Ashutosh knows that just because people are villagers does not mean they can play the part of villagers. Yet, he decides to take the risk. The builders of Champaner shall be the villagers of *Lagaan*.

In the midst of frenetic production activity, Rao lands a casting coup. Ashutosh needs at least sixty junior artists to play the family members of the main cast – roles like that of Goli's wife and Arjan's sister. Rao has discovered that Kutch has a large and active amateur theatre group that could provide actors for these roles. Ashutosh promptly begins auditions and is pleasantly surprised at the talent available. Sixty actors are cast from Kutch. They are excited at the opportunity to appear on the silver screen and be involved in the film making process.

The amateur actors bring to the table much more than acting skills – suddenly dozens of families, their next of kin and their neighbours, collectively running into a few thousand families, start getting bonded with the *Lagaan* unit. Just as Danabhai acts as our gateway to rural Kutch, the amateur actors integrate the towns of Bhuj and its outskirts with the *Lagaan* unit. The city of Bhuj is astir with news of the impending shoot. Articles start appearing in the local newspapers – some are not entirely complimentary. There is more than a touch of apprehension and anxiety about the arrival of the Mumbaiwallas. How will they behave? Will our girls be safe? Will they respect the local culture?

These are legitimate questions and anxieties, all of which Rao is extremely sensitive to. Production shall closely monitor the behaviour of the Mumbaiwallas on this count. The mores and norms of metropolitan Mumbai will not be permitted in Kutch. In Kutch, do as Kutchis do, shall be the motto!

19th October 1999

The task of purchasing period properties for the village begins. Nitin's chief assistant, Eknath Kadam, Rao, Ashish and I roam through the villages of Kutch looking for old pots and pans, *khaats* (cots), doors, door and window handles, boxes, cupboards, cradles…just about anything that is a hundred years old. The geographic isolation of Kutch has made it an old world place and the villages are treasure troves of antique properties. Yet, old world properties bring with them old world values and the villagers are unwilling to sell some of the properties for reasons that sound quaint to our Mumbai ears.

We come across a genuine nineteenth century potter's wheel, where the point of contact between the stone wheel and the base rests on a natural resin as opposed to the ball bearing joint of a modern wheel. The potter, Ahmed, is unwilling to sell the wheel for any price whatsoever. He tells us that the wheel has been handed down to him by his father who received it from his father who in turn received it from his father. Ahmed feels that selling the wheel would be like selling his legacy and no amount of money can persuade him otherwise. Ahmed changes his mind only when we explain to him that millions will see his family legacy in a film set in his great-grandfather's era. True to old world logic, he insists that we use the wheel for the film and then return it — the remuneration is totally irrelevant.

The same sentiment is attached to the *khaats* – beds made of bamboo and coir rope – the Kutchis simply refuse to sell them, insisting that we use them for the shoot and then return them – because of the old Kutchi saying, which is to the effect that when a person sells even his bed, it is a sign that he is completely destitute!

The search for period properties is giving us much more than old world objects, it is giving us an insight into old world values, where tradition and self-respect count for much more than money.

Ahmed working on his family legacy – a nineteenth century potter's wheel

21ˢᵗ October 1999

The situation on the hotel front continues to be grim. There are just not enough hotel rooms in Bhuj and to the extent they exist, there is a shortage of skills in running the hotels. It is not that the hotel owners or their staff do not try – it is simply that the prevailing work culture in laid back Bhuj does not make it possible for them to do things any differently than they are used to. Putting up with all this for more than four months is impossible. There is only one way out. Think big! With the audacity that is to characterise everything about *Lagaan*, Rao and Reena decide to create a 'hotel'.

Bhuj has been experiencing a construction boom. Modern multi-storied buildings are sprouting all over. Rao surveys many of these before zeroing in on a building known as Sahajanand Towers owned by one Bharat Chouthani. Rao approaches Bharatbhai with a proposal to hire out the top four floors. Hiring out flats instead of selling them would not ordinarily make commercial sense, but Bharatbhai shrewdly perceives that renting flats to Aamir Khan Productions will add a premium to his ultimate sale price. Despite objections by some local hoteliers, Bharatbhai hires out the top four floors of Sahajanand Towers for *Lagaan*.

As our needs grow, more and more vendors supply all kinds of goods to the unit. From refrigerators to pins, the house of Aamir Khan Productions daily laps up the thousands of diverse goods required to shoot a film. The economy of Bhuj receives a shot in the arm with all this spending. However, Production's method of payment by cheque after deducting tax at source is creating a small crisis. Despite their apparent affluence, most of the vendors are not registered with the income tax authorities and decline cheques. Reena refuses to buckle under.

She tells them firmly, "So far as we are concerned, in law we can only pay by cheque and after deducting tax at source. How you handle your tax problems is your headache."

The vendors grudgingly fall in line. I am delighted by this ardour for the law. By the time the shoot is over, the tax authorities will add a few hundred tax payers to their list.

Sahajanand Towers will become home to the *Lagaanites*

15th October 1999– 26th October 1999

Aamir stops over in UK on the way back from his shows and takes time off to meet Jane Silverstone and Robert Croft, who have been cast as Elizabeth and Captain Russell. This is the first time he is personally seeing either of them. The meeting is warm and friendly and Aamir can see that they are fine actors, but…to him they do not appear suitable for the roles they have been cast for! His radar is on high alert.

On getting home, the first thing Aamir does is to see their auditions on tape and when he does so, his heart sinks. A hundred alarm bells clang in Aamir's mind. Aamir is convinced that Elizabeth *must* possess ethereal beauty, if the Gauri jealousy angle has to work. The moment Elizabeth steps out of her carriage, Gauri must feel that faced by such a beautiful woman, Bhuvan is lost to her. In Aamir's opinion, Jane just does not have that kind of look. Aamir also strongly feels that Robert Croft does not have the persona of Captain Russell.

For three nights Aamir cannot sleep. He is convinced that the casting is a disaster that will sink the film. Yet, what can he say to either the actors or to Ashutosh and Reena. Aamir had repeatedly urged Ashutosh and Reena to finalise the casting in his absence, saying, "I trust your judgment". Also, Aamir is basically an actor. He can well imagine the trauma Robert and Jane will suffer if they are replaced now. No amount of, "We have no problems with your performance, it is just a question of looking the part," would assuage the hurt. He knows that Production is committed to the actors and it is perhaps too late in the day to change his mind.

Yet, another part of him tells him that this casting can make or break the film. If he does not speak, *Lagaan* could suffer a mortal blow.

Afterthree days and three nights of sleepless brooding, Aamir decides that propriety must yield to the interests of *Lagaan*. A meeting is called with Ashutosh and Reena and Aamir throws his bombshell.

"Ash, I have to tell you and Reena that the selection you've made for the characters of Captain Russell and Elizabeth doesn't seem right to me. They don't work for me at all."

Ashutosh and Reena hear Aamir out patiently and then the storm bursts. Reena is outraged.

"If you didn't trust us, you shouldn't have asked us to go ahead."

"You should have taken the trouble to be there."

"We've already committed ourselves orally Aamir, we cannot back out now."

Aamir takes the wise route on this. He simply admits that he was wrong and says he is sorry. Yes, he should have been present for the casting. Yes, he should not be changing the casting after assuring them that he trusts them, but still, his mistakes should not compromise the interests of *Lagaan*.

On the creative front, Ashutosh sticks to his guns. He is convinced that he is right on the casting. He feels that Jane's beauty will simply grow on the audience. Aamir and Ashutosh fight on and on and on, until for the first time, Aamir is tempted to use his clout as the producer. But Aamir knows that this will demoralise Ashutosh and destroy his confidence. Yet, Aamir is convinced that if he does not act decisively, *Lagaan* will suffer a deadly blow. What Aamir does is typical of the manner in which he shall make his presence felt as a producer in the months to come.

"Ashutosh, maybe as a producer, I made a mistake in giving you a finite budget for the casting of these two characters. Now, what I'm telling you is that there is no limit on the budget. So, go back to England and audition again. See if you can get someone better."

Ashutosh is still not convinced, but he knows Aamir intimately. He knows that Aamir just cannot do something that he is not convinced about. With a long shoot before him, it is critical that Aamir must be in the correct frame of mind for work. So, Danielle Roffe, the British casting director is asked to cast her net yet again and a fresh bunch of tapes makes its way from one end of the globe to another.

Aamir calls up the agents for Robert Croft and Jane Silverstone (names changed) and personally conveys the bad news, softened by an apology. The agents are beside themselves with rage – but Aamir weathers the storm. He assures them that notwithstanding the fact that the contracts for Robert and Jane are yet to be signed, they will be paid every pound of their entire remuneration had they shot. His production house has given its word and that word will be honoured – contract or no contract.

Aamir's commitment starts a curious *Lagaan* chapter at the Reserve Bank of India. The RBI officials believe they smell a rat, as they find it difficult to imagine that anyone will pay actors without a written contract such a huge sum of money for services that will never be rendered! After a great deal of questioning, the foreign currency is reluctantly released and Aamir's word can finally be honoured.

A shutosh and Aamir repeatedly watch the fresh round of auditions conducted in England by Danielle Roffe. None of the girls are impressive. Then, Aamir remembers that he had liked the first actress on the earlier lot of tapes sent by Danielle. Ashutosh and Aamir watch the earlier tape and are impressed by the actress, Rachel Shelley.

"I'll pitch for Rachel," concludes Aamir.

"You forget she's taller than you," reminds Ashutosh.

"We're doing so many new things in *Lagaan*, Ash. Let's also give the audience a heroine taller than the hero," replies Aamir wryly.

Settling the casting for Elizabeth clears the way for the casting of Captain Russell. Paul Blackthorne had always been Aamir's first choice. His quirky manner seemed just right for the capricious Captain Russell. But Paul, at six foot and three inches, towers over Aamir, a fact that weighs on Ashutosh's mind. Once again Aamir prevails, "Ash the taller he is the better. It will be David versus Goliath in every sense."

27th October 1999– 4th November 1999

A shutosh returns to England and the casting of Paul and Rachel is finally locked. Paul and Rachel had featured among the recalls, the actors shortlisted by Ashutosh to audition for him when he visited England. With some months having elapsed, both of them had assumed that they had lost out on *Lagaan*. Now, they are delighted at landing the roles unexpectedly.

The casting crisis has been a tense moment in the life of *Lagaan*. Fortunately, the father and mother of the baby *Lagaan* are back on the same track once again, but it is only the greatest sensitivity on the part of both towards each other, that has averted a crisis.

5th November 1999 - 30th November 1999

W ork starts on constructing the cricket ground. It is a mammoth task. First, earthmovers uproot the *babool* weed, following which over two hundred trucks of soil are deposited to level the ground. The soil has been carefully selected by Nitin to create a parched, drought-stricken look. The cricket pitch is laid and rolled daily. Alongside, the pavilion is erected. It is a mammoth organisational task, yet it is accomplished in less than a month.

Nitin surveys his work with relish. Bang in the middle of a desert he has managed to recreate a cricket field that could pass off as one belonging to a nineteenth century British county club. His joy is short-lived. Without any warning whatsoever, a mammoth twister unleashes its full power,

Building a 19th century cricket pavilion in the middle of the desert

knocking down one wall of the pavilion. One of the workers is injured, though not seriously. The wind has given due notice of its power and the havoc it can wreak in the days to come.

J ust over a month now remains for the shoot to start. Production rides a roller coaster of emotions. There is so much happening in Bhuj, so much in Mumbai, so much in England, so much in Chennai, that one wonders how it will all come together. A single setback could send all the carefully made plans into a tailspin, but there is no sign of it at least as yet. Aamir's sister Nikhat has dropped out of *Lagaan*. She is now four months into her pregnancy and her doctor has advised her to avoid the stress and strain of film making. Clearly, it is a wise decision.

Ashutosh has the look of a man convinced that nothing can now stop him. Aamir is cautiously confident. Reena and Rao are white with anxiety and exhaustion. Reena maintains her calm, but the strain is showing. She speaks very slowly, each word coming out of her mouth gradually, like a computer suffering from data overload. But even her radar shows no signs of unmanageable trouble. The juggernaut rolls on inexorably towards the first shooting day.

The die is cast

Finally, Champaner is ready to come to life

Bhaley ghor andhera chaavey
Chale chalo chale chalo
Koi raah mein na tham jaavey
Chale chalo
(Even if it is pitch dark, Let's walk ahead, let's walk ahead
Let no one stop halfway, Let's walk ahead)
— Song from LAGAAN

"After fifteen minutes of reading my first line in Hindi,
I could remember barely three syllables. I put my
head in my hands and thought, I've made a terrible
mistake. I must call the whole thing off."

PAUL BLACKTHORNE (Captain Russell)

7 The die is cast

shutosh is in Chennai with Rahman once again. There are less than five weeks left to compose and record six songs. Now, even Rahman is anxious. Rahman composes in his ground floor studio lit by candles from a famous *dargah*. Incense permeates the atmosphere. Working in a state of the art studio, Rahman appears to be a mystic in a cave performing such penance, as only he knows.

Rahman sleeps through the day and works at night. Ashutosh's body rhythms adjust to those of Rahman. Gradually, the tunes emerge. Most of them are characteristically difficult and the music must grow on the listener before he may enjoy its beauty. Ashutosh curbs his natural tendency to speak freely and trains himself to listen and absorb the notes.

Rahman records the raw tunes in his own voice with some instrumentation and gives Ashutosh the tapes. Ashutosh has been waiting for this moment. In his mind's ear, if there is such a thing, he has already heard the songs even as he was writing his script. Now, his thoughts are being translated into sound.

Ashutosh hears the tunes and panics. The tunes echo the *Lagaan* ambience superbly, but he believes that they do not quite fit the song situations they are meant for. What is he to do now?

Ashutosh immerses himself into Rahman's tunes, hearing them repeatedly, until in a flash it strikes him that he *does* have every song. All he needs to do is to gently nudge each tune to the correct song situation. So, the tune suggested for *ghanan* is used in the *mitwa* song situation. The tune suggested for the title and opening credits is used in the *ghanan* song situation. Rahman is a little shocked at Ashutosh's suggestions, but is extremely open and receptive. He begins respecting Ashutosh's music sense.

From Chennai, Ashutosh plays the selected tunes for Aamir, who is in Mumbai, via a Walkman held to the mouthpiece of a telephone. The technology is rather old fashioned, but what the hell, so are the songs.

Aamir is impressed by the music, but is still anxious about deadlines and pleads with Ashutosh to remember them.

Production had obtained possession of the four floors at the top of Sahajanand Towers in late October. The enormous number of goods required to furnish Sahajanand Towers, including air conditioners, geysers, beds and mattresses, have been obtained on hire. Getting these installed is easier said than done. There are problems every step of the way. The main power cables cannot take the load of so many air conditioners, so the cabling both inside and outside the building needs to be changed. Western style commodes need to be put into each room. Many of the goods need to be ordered from Ahmedabad and deliveries are delayed. A portion of the ground floor parking area is enclosed to serve as a mess and another portion fitted with a table tennis table. Setting up a 'hotel' overnight is not an easy task.

I have been stationed in Bhuj preparing 'Hotel Sahajanand Towers' and now it is virtually ready. I cannot believe that we have set up a sixty room fully air-conditioned facility in a little over a month. I know that nothing I have done in my life has equipped me for this task. And yet, in film making, at any rate in making *Lagaan*, the most incredible things are being treated as a matter of course. Perhaps for the first time in Indian film history, a 'hotel' has been set up to make a film!

Apoorva Lakhia aka Apu has landed in Mumbai. In the tiny office of Aamir Khan Productions, it seems as if Hollywood has arrived. Apoorva has swagger, attitude and Movie Magic. The last named is an incredible piece of software that allows the user to do everything from writing film scripts to preparing budgets and schedules. Apoorva tells me, "In Hollywood, if you don't write your script in Movie Magic, no producer will bother to look at your face."

Apoorva brings the magic of the software to *Lagaan*. To begin with he reads the script dozens of times, marking it with a huge set of highlighters, with different colours for properties, actors, animals... He then feeds this information into the software on the computer. Then he, Aamir and Ashutosh work on scheduling the film – deciding the date and time at which each scene will be shot.

This done, the software works its magic. It generates all kinds of lists –

the properties required on a particular day, the dates on which each actor is required … just about any piece of information about the film is a mouse click away. Modern technology is serving the ends of a period script in a marvellous fashion and everyone is seduced.

Nicole Demers, the make-up designer has arrived from Canada. She had worked with Aamir on Deepa Mehta's *1947 Earth* and they had established a good rapport. Aamir was keen on having Nicole for *Lagaan*, because with a racially mixed cast, there is a wide range of skin tones, which must be handled correctly in make-up. Also, in sharp contrast to the more obvious style of make-up in Hindi films, Ashutosh wants to use make-up sparingly, so that the characters look as natural as possible.

Bhuvan, keen on sporting a moustache, is overruled by Ashutosh

Nicole has begun working on the look of various characters even while in Canada. Now, she marks her script in various colours for different characters and starts working out their continuity. Even the make-up is generating a mountain of paperwork. She sits with several photographs of each actor and at sittings with Ashutosh works out the look of each character. The looks of the minor characters are being worked out in great detail too.

Aamir is keen on sporting a moustache. Even today, men in Indian villages generally sport a moustache. In nineteenth century India, it would be inconceivable that Bhuvan could have been clean-shaven. Aamir drives home his point with Ashutosh by provoking him.

"Ash, just imagine, Champaner is supposed to be drought-stricken. There is no water. And Bhuvan is wasting water each morning for a shave!"

Ashutosh is not amused. Aamir puts on all kinds of false moustaches to prove his point, but Ashutosh is unmoved. Ashutosh's instinct tells him that Aamir Khan should not sport a moustache and in this instance, he is willing to sacrifice logic at the altar of instinct.

5th December 1999

Aamir, Ashutosh and all the department heads land in Bhuj for the dry run of *Lagaan*. Since *Lagaan* is a single schedule film, there is really no scope for major changes during the shoot. It is critical that department heads check out all the locations and acquaint themselves with all the problems well in advance.

The director of photography, Anil Mehta is alarmed by the extent to which the sandy soil in the village reflects light. A decision is taken to cake the entire surface of the village with a mixture of cow dung and specially selected soil, to cut the glare and also to give Champaner more of the dry, cracked earth look of a drought-stricken village.

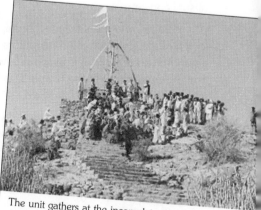

The unit gathers at the incomplete temple on the hilltop to view the village

The sound recordist, Nakul Kamte, is alarmed by the extent of the wind sound as also that of the jets. He makes a mental note that he must arm himself with the best windshields that are available.

Bhanu Athaiya is busy checking out the clothes the villagers wear. She is pleased. They are naturally period and the villagers require no special costumes to act in *Lagaan*. Bhanutai tells Rao that the costumes for the British women will be so long, that they will partially trail on the floor. The only way to keep them clean will be to carpet the wardrobe area. Also, all the toilets must have wide doors to allow the large billowing costumes to pass through smoothly. All these are small matters of detail, but attention paid to a hundred such details will aid efficiency.

Moolchand, the gaffer, who executes the lighting instructions of the cameraman, moves around with his compass mapping the arc of the sun through the winter sky. At every location he makes lists of the lights and rigs that Anil requires.

Nicole Demers realises that Kutch is far drier than humid Mumbai and that she will need to order large quantities of moisturiser to protect the actors' skins.

Danabhai's villagers finally meet the Aamir Khan for whom they have built a village, but whom they have never seen! The Bhuj actors are more than aware of who Aamir is and are thrilled to meet him.

Ashutosh tells the male actors from Bhuj to stop cutting their hair and shaving their beards. This will give him the greatest flexibility in shaping their look just before the shoot. Over the next month, Bhuj town shall develop a hirsute appearance!

Ashutosh estimates the number of villagers required to make Champaner look realistic. Between the Bhuj juniors and Danabhai's villagers, there are a hundred and fifty people available. Ashutosh, Anil, Aamir and the others from Mumbai climb to the temple hilltop and watch as the First AD, Apu and his assistants, direct the crowd.

The villagers wait inside the houses. As the team from Mumbai watches from the temple hilltop, the village square is empty. Then, Apu lets out an almighty yell, "Action!" and the villagers emerge from the houses and walk around the village as directed by Apu and his assistants. Ashutosh whispers to Nitin, "Champaner is coming to life for the first time." Nitin is overcome with emotion.

After this performance, Aamir and Ashutosh squat in the centre of a circle on the cricket field surrounded by the Kutchis and tell them just how

Aamir and Ashutosh share their dream with the Kutchis

important a role they are going to play in the film. It is a big moment. On one side are villagers living in remote, drought-stricken villages utterly removed from modern life. On the other side are a superstar and his director. They are worlds apart from each other. This quaint meeting on a cricket pitch in the middle of a semi-desert is bringing their worlds a little closer.

The villagers do not fully understand what Ashutosh and Aamir have to say about the film. What they definitely understand are subtle intangibles. The very fact that they are all sitting together on the ground is an important statement. Today, they are not hired labour. They have become partners. Aamir Khan is requesting their help and support to make the film successful. They listen in silence. On both sides, 'they' becomes 'we'. It is a special moment. Intuitively, everyone senses a mission is beginning.

A nasty twister envelopes the cricket ground blowing clouds of dust into everyone's eyes. For a moment, it seems as if the meeting will have to break up. Then everyone huddles closer together and the meeting continues. A war cry breaks out. *"Re bhaiyya chhoote lagaan!"* ("o brother, may we be free of the accursed tax!") The cricket ground resonates with the sound. The first links of a special bond have been forged.

6th December 1999

Aamir meets all the residents of Sahajanand Towers at a function organised in the basement of the building. This enables his fans in the building to meet him; more important, it enables Production to prepare the residents for what they will face a month later when the shoot starts.

"I'm really sorry for the inconvenience we might have caused," Aamir starts and then goes on to discuss the problems the residents may encounter because of the *Lagaan* unit's presence. Rao and I take over and through an open dialogue work out various systems necessary to keep the inconvenience caused by our presence to a minimum. The Sahajanand residents are touched by Production's efforts. Their cooperation as neighbours shall never flag through the shoot.

7th December 1999

It is the last day of the dry run. The heads of department sit together and add final touches to the schedule. Each department tries to get a little more time allocated for its work and some skirmishes break out before the schedule is 'locked', a term that will later cause great amusement.

Department heads meet on set during the dry run

Aamir takes time off to survey the living arrangements at Sahajanand

Towers. His eye for detail causes Production some headaches. "The basins are too small. Over six months they will irritate everyone," he insists and wants them all replaced. A small change, but replacing over a hundred basins requires a fair amount of plumbing work.

Reena finds the walls too bare. She goes to the Bhuj market and buys beautiful wall hangings for each apartment. The colours and native designs of Kutch enter our rooms.

With each passing day of the dry run I can see the suggestions for changes burgeoning and am more than a little relieved when the team finally leaves.

8th December 1999 - 19th December 1999

Aamir and Reena rush from Bhuj via Mumbai to London. Aamir meets the British cast. Two months later, forty actors are to leave for Mumbai. It is important that the producer meets them and gives them a sense of confidence about the shoot. If even a single actor does not turn up at the last minute, the film will be stranded.

The actors most relieved to see Aamir are Paul Blackthorne, who is now playing Captain Russell and Rachel Shelley, now cast as Elizabeth. Both have been struggling with their Hindi. Paul, in particular, has been reading and re-reading the script sent to him by Ashutosh. The script has the Hindi lines written phonetically in the Roman alphabet, along with the English translation. Yet, the whole business has been a nightmare. No matter what he does, nothing makes sense. A solution has to be found and fast.

Aamir goes to the Centre for Oriental and African Studies (SOAS) at the London University and meets a class, studying Indian cinema, conducted by a friend, Rachel Dwyer. One of Rachel's students, a Pakistani girl, Samin, is drafted to handle the challenge of teaching the two British actors Hindi in a month.

Samin gives Paul and Elizabeth a method to understand the gibberish that the Hindi appears to be. She reads the lines in Hindi and the actors write them down phonetically in English. Then, as the actors read the lines out in Hindi, she tells them the meaning of each word, which they then note.

Rachel swiftly gets into the groove, but two weeks into his lessons, Paul wants to give up both Hindi and the film. Samin encourages him to persist. Urged on by the burning desire to do *Lagaan*, Paul ultimately turns the tide. When it is time for Rachel and Paul to leave for India, they know their lines better than any other actor in *Lagaan*.

There is another nut that Aamir must crack, before he returns to India. He must find nineteenth century cricket gear. London, more than Mumbai, has dealers who sell or hire out properties for the stage and screen. Aamir and Reena go around London visiting them and are amazed at how well they are organised. These are not small shops. They are mammoth buildings with warehouses, each floor stocking properties belonging to a particular century. Fifteenth century swords jostle with tenth century helmets; practically whatever one could want is available, except period cricket gear.

Aamir and Reena spend days scouring shop after shop, until they are ready to give up. The last dealer they visit suggests they try the shop of one Shawn Arnold, who just might have what they need. The tired couple jumps into a cab for one last attempt and enters the shop in the evening, just before shutters are downed.

On entering the shop, Aamir sees a wicker basket full of cricket balls, with the old style stitching and without the stamp of the manufacturer invariably visible on modern balls. Aamir heaves a sigh of relief. At least the problem of the old balls has been solved. He then approaches the man at the counter asking, "Would you by any chance have old cricket…" Aamir stops in mid-sentence, for in front of him is an array of old cricket bats, including a genuine nineteenth century piece. He knows he has hit pay dirt.

The owner of the shop, Shawn Arnold, is an encyclopaedia of information on old cricketing gear. He explains the difference between the equipment of various decades and moreover has a book full of nineteenth century photographs of cricket. Aamir persuades a reluctant Shawn to sell the book and buys up everything from bats to stumps, pads, gloves…the works. Aamir's persistence has paid off. The cricket equipment in *Lagaan* will now be realistic to the last detail.

Javed Akhtar is in Chennai to work on the lyrics. Akhtar is a great proponent of the importance of phonetics in song writing. Working with Rahman has underlined this belief. "Rahman understands very little Hindi and reacts more to the sound and resonance of words than their meaning," he tells Ashutosh.

Javed Akhtar's effective use of phonetics is showcased in the onomatopoeic cloud song.

Ghanan, ghanan ghir ghir aaye badra,

ghane ghan ghor, kaale chaaye badra…

(Dark and dense come the swirling clouds

Darkly dense roar the spreading clouds)

As Javed Akhtar recites the lyrics, Ashutosh's eyes sparkle with tears and excitement. Sitting in Rahman's studio in Chennai, he can through misty eyes, see distant Champaner coming alive.

The singers, Udit Narayan and Alka Yagnik are also in Chennai to record the songs. Rahman likes each singer and each musician to bring his own creativity to the song. After explaining the basic structure of the tune, he encourages the singers to sing each stanza with as many variations as they want, until they are satisfied. He does not interrupt the singer's rhythm by getting her to imitate him.

His method with the instrumentalists is even more intriguing. Sultan Khan arrives with his *sarangi* (string and bow musical instrument). He is given only the beat and the tune of the opening verse and asked to play whatever he likes. Sultan Khan is recorded for two hours and leaves.

Through all this, Rahman sits at the digital console as his own recordist. Later he will be his own sound editor and cut and paste the best 'takes' of the singers and best pieces of the instrumentalists. Outwardly the path of creation appears to be a happy accident, yet right through, Rahman has had a grand plan into which the singers and instrumentalists have mysteriously blended.

Nitin Desai insists that the village temple as a period structure, must not use a grain of cement. But, how are the eighty tonnes of stone in the temple to be held together? Danabhai and his workers have created self-supporting walls, by skillfully interlocking the stones so that they are held together by gravity. But how are the mammoth pyramidal roof and dome to be supported without cement?

Rao, along with Nitin's assistant, Sanjay Panchal, work with local carpenters to create huge wooden arches that are placed on the stone walls and stone tiles are then placed externally on the arches in an interlocking manner. The skill of the local carpenters and stone workers makes the impossible possible and the mammoth structure is created without the use of any modern material. It is only gravity, human ingenuity and perhaps a touch of divine grace that will hold the massive structure together.

I n London, Paul Blackthorne who is now playing Captain Russell, speaks to the Bangladeshi running the corner store about his role in Aamir Khan's film and becomes a celebrity among the Asians. A film with Aamir Khan has done more for him in these quarters than ten years of acting on stage and in European cinema. Paul finds a retired colonel from the British army to teach him nineteenth century army etiquette. The correct salute and other nineteenth century rules find their way into his repertoire. The realism bug is working its way overseas.

Rachel decides to educate herself about Hindi cinema and watches a couple of films. She cannot comprehend the logic behind the song and dance numbers. Why on earth would a grown man chase a grown woman around trees!

Eighty tonnes of stone, not a grain of cement

B ack in Kutch, the sets are ready, but something very important still remains to be done. With a four-month long shoot in a single location, the arrangements for meals, toilets, hair, wardrobe and make-up cannot be of a makeshift nature. On a typical outdoor shoot in India, at most the hero and heroine are provided with a make-up trailer, which will have an attached toilet and make-up area. Everyone else simply manages everything from changing their clothes to their toilet in the open.

Reena and Rao are determined not to let this happen on *Lagaan*. A massive ten thousand square feet structure is built behind the temple hillock, out of view of the camera. Half of it serves as a mess for the unit to eat in, while the rest is divided into areas for make-up, costumes, rest, toilets, a production office, a kitchen and rooms for the security guards to sleep in. On the cricket ground, the rear side of the British pavilion is used for providing these facilities.

Huge water tanks are constructed at a height on both the sets. These are then connected by a network of underground pipes to toilets that are fitted with water closets and showers. Half a dozen toilets are constructed on the village set by utilising the interiors of the huts on the periphery of the set. Externally, it is a Kutchi *boonga*, but open the door and voila, a modern toilet with showers! The toilets are in turn connected to drainage pipes emptying into giant septic tanks. In sum, Rao builds the facilities of a mini-township for the shoot.

Another township needs to be created – this one for animals. The village of Champaner is 'peopled' by cows, bullocks, goats and fowl. The animal farm will soon swell with the addition of horses, camels and an elephant. A huge area is created for them to live in just outside the main set. Like the actors, they will be brought in whenever needed for a shot and then returned to rest! A mountain of hay is purchased for the cattle. Over the next few months it will cost several lakhs of rupees just to feed them.

A amir is at a party with leading directors, Aditya Chopra and Karan Johar. It is a small gathering and the conversation inevitably veers round to *Lagaan*. Aditya and Karan strongly recommend that sync sound be dropped. "*Lagaan* is such a large film, with so many variables. Don't add to your load by using sync sound," is their considered advice.

Aamir stands by the decision. "If we fail, we should fail after having made an honest effort and on our own terms. Only then can we learn and go ahead."

The discussion ends, but Aamir realises that the eyes of the industry are on the *Lagaan* shoot. The success of the new work culture he wants to create — single schedule, First AD, sync sound — will to an extent depend on the fate of *Lagaan*.

20th December 1999 - 30th December 1999

T he *Lagaan* unit once again congregates at Aamir's house, this time for readings that will enable the actors to gear themselves for the shoot. Again, this is not a Hindi film tradition, but something that Aamir and Ashutosh insist on. Many of the actors present are from theatre and take to the method like fish to water. Aamir, however, stumbles and stutters through his lines for nearly two hours. He is not entirely fluent with the Devanagiri script and is uncomfortable with the long dialogues in Awadhi.

After an hour of stumbling, Aamir realises that everyone is eyeing him a little oddly. He stops and looks up from his script. "I know what you are thinking. That you need to re-cast for the role of Bhuvan." The actors have a good laugh, but Aamir is genuinely worried and a little upset.

Aamir had planned to spend the last three months before the shoot preparing for his role. He had wanted to stay for three months in the Awadhi speaking belt in Uttar Pradesh and use that period to interact with the villagers and internalise the Awadhi dialect with its peculiar music and points of emphasis. But the duties as the producer have prevailed over the needs of the actor. Never has Aamir gone into a shoot so unprepared. Aamir had turned producer to protect the creative integrity of *Lagaan*. Ironically, the actor Aamir Khan has to pay the price for this!

Immediately after the readings, Aamir calls up Javed Akhtar and asks him to suggest an Awadhi expert who could be a script tutor for him. Javed Akhtar suggests an actor-writer by the name of Raja Awasthi from Lucknow. He will join Aamir in Bhuj.

Less than two weeks before the unit leaves for Bhuj, there is a crisis. Mukesh Rishi who is to play Deva opts out of *Lagaan*. The eleventh hour pull-out upsets Aamir, but this is still far better than dragging an unhappy actor to the shoot. Pradeep Rawat is cast in Deva's role. Pradeep is willing to put everything aside to work in Aamir's film and to play the role of Deva. Pradeep belongs to a family of soldiers and as a child, dreamed of playing cricket for his country. The role of Deva the soldier, rebel fighter against the British and star cricketer of the Champaner team, is allowing him to play out on screen what he has dreamed of doing in his life. Pradeep shelves all other projects and signs on *Lagaan*.

There is still one last character left to cast – that of Goli. None of the actors auditioned had seemed quite right for the role. The actor Daya Shankar Pandey had called Ashutosh several times for a role in *Lagaan*, but Ashutosh had not even auditioned him, saying that he just did not look any of the parts. With a week left to go, Daya decides – to hell with courtesy. With his dark, almost black skin and earthy looks, he is convinced that there has to be a role for him in *Lagaan*. He berates Ashutosh on phone, "Don't tell me you have no role for me. If you don't cast me in *Lagaan*, is Yash Chopra going to make me a hero and take me to Switzerland?" Ashutosh sees Daya's logic and finally the Champaner cricket team has its Goli.

It is Christmas, but the printers and Xerox machine at the production office in Mumbai are working overtime. Apoorva has fed all the data into Movie Magic and the software has printed out lists for every department – property lists for art, actors' lists for hair and make-up, schedules for every unit member. There is a roomful of lists.

The production team is proud of the planning. Sometimes, it seems as if the lists hold the film together. I brag to my friends, "If you ask me what will be shot on a particular afternoon on a particular day in March, I can tell you everything – which scene will be shot, who will be acting, what the costumes will be, what time the actors will be in make-up…just about everything."

The lists are distributed to each department. Everyone has his or her folder of papers. Chest swelling with the pride of reflected glory, I take my folder and depart for Bhuj, even as the church bells chime for Christmas.

31ˢᵗ December 1999

I am the only member of the *Lagaan* unit from Mumbai in Bhuj. In the day, I wander around the village, entering the houses, lounging on the *khaats* and seeing the Kutch countryside from the temple hilltop. It looks unusually calm, as if time has stopped. It is difficult to believe that in two days, hundreds of people will be trampling all over the place.

At night, I watch Aamir on TV perform live at the Chowpatty beach in south Mumbai. Aamir is introduced as the star of the millenium and then proceeds to dance to the song *dekho 2000 zamaana aa gayaa*, from *Mela*. Watching his leather-clad form dance to a futuristic song welcoming the new millennium, it's difficult to imagine that just a few days later he will be performing the role of a nineteenth century villager.

I am a little embarrassed by the inanity of the song, but enjoy watching Aamir on the small screen in my room. In some way it reassures me that yes, there are a few hundred people out there preparing to come to Bhuj to finally shoot the movie. A juggernaut is rolling to Bhuj and as far as I am concerned, it cannot come fast enough.

Ashutosh spends the millenium night in Chennai, recording *ghanan*, the cloud song with Rahman. Despite all the pressure on Rahman, one song is yet to be recorded – the song which will ultimately be called *chale chalo* and also the music piece for the ballroom dance. Once the shoot begins, there is no way that Ashutosh can return to Chennai. The only way out is for Rahman to come to Bhuj. But, will the mountain come to Mohammed? By now Rahman has fallen a little in love with *Lagaan* and

Ashutosh. He repeatedly assures Ashutosh that he will come to Bhuj and the director must accept his assurance.

Ashutosh is thrilled with the music and lyrics of his songs. They now influence his vision of the entire film. Yet, the Chennai vigil has come at a price. Ashutosh has spent the past month working on the music, leaving him woefully short of preparation by way of his shot division for the shoot.

Considering that pre-production has taken over a year and considering the effort to make *Lagaan* a completely 'planned' film, it is a supreme irony that both the director and the lead actor are woefully short of preparation for the core challenges they must now face in the shoot. However, Ashutosh is not particularly disturbed in this regard.

If anything disturbs Ashutosh it is that in many ways, the fate of *Lagaan* is sealed. He has, by now, taken hundreds - nay, thousands of creative decisions that will determine what shall unfold on screen. Who the actors are, what costumes they will wear, how their hair will look, what and where the locations are, what properties will dress the set, what the music of the film will be...all this and more is settled and no changes can now be made.

In films made in the unplanned style of the Mumbai film industry, these decisions happen right through the shoot, giving rise to inconsistencies and lack of continuity on the one hand, but yielding flexibility and scope for correcting errors on the other. In single schedule *Lagaan*, all the pre-production decisions have been taken at one go. There will be no time for reflection or change.

Ashutosh can only hope that he has got everything right, because there will be no second innings. The die is cast and the film must now emerge from it.

Nothing works like example

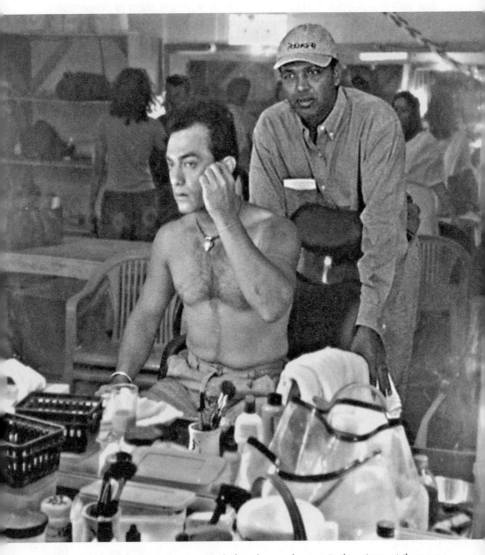

In the make-up room before dawn – the men in the mirror set the pace

BHUVAN: Chulhe se roti ko nikalne ke liye, chimte ko apna muh jalahik padi!
(If bread is to be removed from the oven, the tongs must suffer the heat!)
— LAGAAN

"Before coming to Bhuj, I hoped that since I was the heroine of the film, I would get special treatment. But here that was never the case. Everyday you had to get up early in the morning, at four o'clock, five o'clock, not just me – but Aamir as well."
GRACY SINGH (Gauri)

Nothing works like example

B huj Airport. A planeful of *Lagaan* emerges on the tarmac. Curious onlookers try to spot Aamir. Normally, film people look forward to outdoor shoots. In some ways they are extended picnics. A break from the Mumbai routine. An escape from their families. Perhaps an opportunity for a brief fling. Travel and sightseeing at the producer's expense. All this while earning fame and fortune. What more could one want?

Yet, the planeload that descends on Bhuj shows little sign of the picnic spirit. The faces wear a tentative, anxious look. They have bid farewell to their families in Mumbai, much like mountaineers leaving for an expedition. So much lies ahead that is unknown and uncertain. The only certainty is that they will not be home for another four months and that such a long stay in the searing heat of Bhuj is going to be great work perhaps, but no picnic.

The descent into Bhuj and the journey from the airport is in itself revealing. In fact, there is no civilian airport in Bhuj. What Bhuj has is a military airstrip belonging to the Indian Air Force, the civilian use of which has only recently been permitted. The tarmac is full of fighter jets emitting ear-splitting sounds, landing and taking off on sorties. It's almost like a war zone. For a moment, the *Lagaan* team wonders what kind of 'shoot' they have come for.

There is no airport building permitted near the landing strip. After the flight lands, like the other passengers, the *Lagaan* unit waits on the tarmac for an airline bus. It comes with an armed air force escort and takes them out of the air force complex to the tin sheds outside, which serve as airline offices. I welcome the unit members with a smile. They smile back, but without any conviction. I shepherd them into the waiting fleet of vehicles. The journey to Bhuj city begins.

Barring the air force quarters there are no buildings between the airstrip and the city limits. There is only barren land scarred by the cancerous green *babool* – then the city – two kilometres of houses and offices marking the city centre and then abruptly the city ends! In five minutes, the *Lagaan* unit has seen all of Bhuj! What kind of a one-horse town is this! How are we going to survive here for four and a half months? I can see the faces of the newcomers crease with anxiety.

On the Mandavi Road, just before the octroi check post, the fleet of cars stops at a building – Sahajanand Towers, at seven floors, obviously the tallest in Bhuj! The bewilderment on the faces of the actors deepens. Ashish and I hand out room and cupboard keys with a short letter of welcome from the production team, explaining the living arrangements. Among other things, the letter contains devastating news: "Kutch is a dry state. Possession and consumption of alcohol is a cognisable offence. Production shall take no responsibility for obtaining liquor or defending persons booked for liquor offences!" Shooting for so many months without liquor! This has got to be some kind of trap.

There is a buzz among the actors. Why are we put up in a building? Why not a hotel? What is this all about? Vallabh Vyas later recalls, "To me it was like buying a flat in a newly constructed building. You see your flat, you discover who your neighbours are. You see your neighbour's flat. You compare it to yours. After all you're going to be staying there for four months! Then, we were surprised, but pleasantly. Aamir and Reena occupy room no. 703 - just one room, like anyone else. No better, no larger – part of a flat shared with another unit member. I thought, maybe there is something in this method, which I have not realised."

The same afternoon, the actors see their village, the village of Champaner. The art department has put up signs lining the route from the highway pointing to Champaner. Nitin Desai is tense. This is the moment he has been waiting for. This is his litmus test. Will the actors feel they are entering a set or will they feel it is home?

Their actions speak. The actors do not congregate in groups. They enter their houses and sit there. They feel their tools.

Raj Zutshi playing Ismail, practicing on the potter's wheel

Raj Zutshi playing Ismail starts his work with clay and the potter's wheel. His hands are dirtied. Akhilendra Mishra playing the blacksmith, Arjan, blows air through the bellows and stokes the fire. A little iron is forged. Amin Hajee playing Bagha goes to the temple top and beats his drum. Dozens of eardrums resonate in protest. Gracy meets the girls who have built the village. Her shyness matches theirs. Guran strums his single-stringed drone, the *ektara* and sings. Or that is what he thinks he does. Everyone thanks Nitin for keeping Guran's house at a distance. Then the actors rest. In their houses. On their nineteenth century rope strung beds, the *khatiyas*. All without instruction.

This is no set. This *is* the village of Champaner. The village inspires belonging. Something very deep has been stirred.

Ashutosh forgets the names of all his actors. Henceforth, there is no Aamir; there is only Bhuvan. There is no Amin Hajee; there is only Bagha and Ismail and Bhura and…The actors leave their modern footwear behind and walk barefoot through the village. Aditya Lakhia, playing the 'untouchable'

Aamir who now only squats on the ground, using an unusual sun shade

Kachra hangs around on the set absorbing the atmosphere. Although his first shot is not due for another six weeks, Ashutosh has insisted that he camp in Bhuj with the others. He gets into character and sits alone, not speaking to anybody. Aamir begins work with his script tutor, Raja Awasthi, the Awadhi expert from Lucknow. Aamir stops sitting on a chair and only squats on the ground. He needs a lot of preparation and must pour himself into the role.

Ashutosh's dream location and the village that Nitin Desai has designed, possess that mysterious factor X – it is working on the minds of all the actors. Internally they have started a journey back in time to 1893 into the heart of rural India. The passionate commitment to realism in pre-production seems to be paying off.

Aamir meets Danabhai and hugs him. "We are fortunate to have found a man as good as you," he says. Danabhai beams. These words are more important to him than the money he has earned for constructing the village.

6th January 2000. Morning

The first shot or the *muhurat* shot is to be taken after the traditional *pooja* (religious rites). It is Ramzan. Aamir, Amin Hajee and several others are keeping their *rozas* and are fasting through the day. Aamir performs the *pooja* in the village temple with the fullest involvement. Guran is blowing on a conch. The brand new ultra modern Arri camera, imported from Germany is part of the *pooja*. It is garlanded and a coconut is broken before the camera rolls ceremonially.

Ashutosh has been tense all day. He takes me aside and confesses. "You know, till now I always felt in a sense shielded by the rest of the team. Now suddenly I feel like our close circle has fallen apart leaving me in the centre and everyone is looking at me for direction and I'm feeling like — suddenly why is everyone looking at me!"

A full house for the *muhurat*

The *muhurat* shot is the opening shot of the film after the credit titles. Bhuvan's mother Mai, is looking in vain for rain clouds while the narrator describes the drought in Champaner. Suhasini Mulay, playing Mai, looks up as the crane tracks forward and the crane arm tilts down. The crane keeps jerking and Anil Mehta, the director of photography, is unhappy. Yet, for the sake of morale, the *muhurat* shot is okayed. There is wild celebration thereafter. Bagha beats his drum. Rahman who is in Bhuj to attend the *muhurat* shudders at the quality of the drumming. Reena is overwhelmed. She can barely control her tears.

Aamir's family is present in full strength. His uncle Nasir Husain and father Tahir Husain, both industry veterans, are impressed at the level of organisation. They can sense the difference in the work culture and in the aesthetics of *Lagaan* and are extremely proud. Aamir had been an assistant director with Nasir Husain for a full four years. To now seek his blessings for his own first production is a big emotional moment and Aamir tries hard to control his tears. He is only now fully realising just how much the approval of his parents, aunt and uncle mean to him.

Although Ashutosh and Aamir are hugging friends and family, cast and crew, their expression is not one of celebration. The challenge has just begun and of all the persons present, perhaps only they have an inkling of the ordeal every unit member will go through before the shoot is completed.

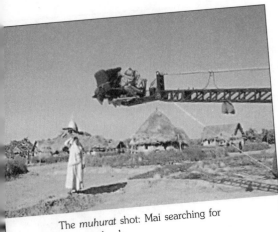

The *muhurat* shot: Mai searching for the rain clouds

The biggest challenge that Aamir faces is the task of team building – of creating a working atmosphere in which this mammoth unit fully accepts the leadership of Ashutosh and works as one body and mind to realise the director's creative vision. An outsider may well ask why this is so difficult to achieve. After all, Ashutosh *is* the director of the film and everyone is contractually bound to obey him. Yet, human beings are creatures driven by more than just contracts. They have opinions and emotions and judgments and Aamir knows only too well, that given Ashutosh's track record, the bulk of the unit has joined *Lagaan* because it is Aamir Khan's maiden production.

During the year long pre-production, Ashutosh has already demonstrated his command over film making and the depth and intimacy with which he has visualised his script. Yet, the commencement of the shoot takes the challenge to a different level. From his over decade long experience in the industry, Aamir knows how actors and major technicians soon form cliques that bitch about the director and his creative decisions. There is something almost inevitable about this. Perhaps every unit member is to a lesser or greater extent a frustrated director and having to constantly yoke one's creative judgment to the director is a contradiction inherent in the process of film making.

In the *Lagaan* situation, with a hitherto unsuccessful director, an unusual script being treated in an unusual manner, a long single schedule in a small town in hostile climatic conditions and a tough and exacting work culture, back-biting could completely sabotage the prospects of the film. Aamir must prevent this from happening, but without seeming to do so. More important, he must make the rest of the unit see what he is convinced about. The unit must genuinely believe as he does, that Ashutosh Gowariker is their creative leader!

So, from the pre-production days, through the method of casting where he remained out of the picture, to the insistence on signing on only those who believed in the script, Aamir has laid the basis for strengthening Ashutosh's hands. Over the past four days in Bhuj, since the unit arrived, Aamir has been continuing on the same tack. He is always but always formally respectful to Ashutosh to the point of deference. Any and every difference of opinion is expressed as, "Correct me if I'm wrong Ash, but…" and is never pressed beyond its first expression. No matter how great the difference in perception, they never but never squabble in public.

The other dimension of the challenges that Aamir and Ashutosh face is balancing time against creative requirements. The shoot must end on schedule. It must end on the 13th of May, 2000. This is crucial. Failure to finish the film according to schedule could lead to fatal repercussions.

Ashutosh at work

The British actors are booked for specific periods. If the shoot spills over, the Indian actors can be persuaded to complete the film, but the British actors who have no stake in a career in India, could simply walk away leaving the film incomplete.

Second, the schedule has been carefully planned so that the cricket match will be complete by early March, before the scorching summer heat fully sets in. A delay will mean that the Brits will have to shoot in the full blast of summer, which could potentially exceed their capacities of endurance.

Third and perhaps most important, the single largest item of expenditure is the shooting cost per day – the cost of transport, food, hotel rent and wages for the mammoth unit. The latest revision of the budget prepared by Reena puts the cost of the film at an intimidating sixteen crores of rupees. On paper, the film is already creeping into the red. Any further increase in the budget will make the film financially unviable. Aamir has repeatedly warned Reena to guard against the film becoming a runaway horse financially. The key to controlling costs is to finish shooting on time.

Yet, while meeting the challenge of keeping to the schedule, Ashutosh must make thousands of creative decisions correctly. He must do justice to his script.

It is hardly surprising then that in the midst of the *muhurat* celebrations, even on this happy day, both Aamir and Ashutosh wear grim expressions.

6ᵗʰ January 2000. Evening.

The shoot ends early, at five o'clock. There isn't enough light. This is bad news. The shorter winter days and the cloudy atmosphere are squeezing the actual shooting hours between nine and five, two hours less than estimated during the dry run in December and four hours less than the normal shooting day in Mumbai. The heads of department meet and discuss the situation. There is only one way out. Work harder and plan better. Every bit of preparation and set-up must be completed, so that the moment the light is adequate, the first shot is rolled.

Apu, the First AD and his assistants distribute a strange piece of paper to the entire unit. They refer to it as a 'call sheet'. It specifies the scene being shot, the actors required, the properties and animals required, the time at which the actors will be picked up…and worse…the time each actor has to be in hair, wardrobe and make-up. At night, Apu enters the dining area with a clock, which he proceeds to put up on the wall with great fanfare. He announces: "I hope everyone has received their call sheets. For those who can't read, let me repeat that the bus will leave at five a.m. sharp. To avoid controversy over whose watch has been set correctly, kindly treat the time on this clock as final. The bus will not wait even a minute for late comers."

The actors grin. Smart alec! We'll deflate him in two days. Just watch!

7ᵗʰ January 2000.

5 a.m. The parking lot at Sahajanand Towers. The dry winter air bites through the double layer of sweaters everyone is wearing. Surprisingly, everyone has turned up on time, cursing the weather and Apu. No one wants to be the first to break the rules. Raghuveer Yadav runs in limping as the bus engine revs up, the first of many such last minute runs. Production calls out the names of everyone who is supposed to be on the bus. Some of the irritated actors shout sarcastically, "present sir". It's back to school once more.

There is only one absentee. She is the heroine of the film, Gracy. The actors look at Apu mockingly. "*Ab kya karega bechara?* What option does the poor guy have but to wait?" At five sharp, Apu barks at the driver, "*Dekh kya rahe ho.* What are you waiting for? Move!" The bus departs minus the heroine of the film. Leaving her behind has a salutory effect on the rest of the unit.

The unit members wonder what's up with Production. Someone asks how Aamir is coming. Another wisecracks that his Mercedes will arrive later. Bagha points to a sleeping figure curled up on the last seat. It is Aamir. He has arrived early and continued his incomplete sleep on the last seat. The next day he will miss the bus by a minute and be humiliated, just as Gracy has been. That is the last occasion on which he will be late.

A point is made and a point is taken. The unit accepts the busing. Nothing works like example.

The bus slips out of Bhuj. The *gayatri* mantra is being played on the stereo. *"Om bhur bhuvah svah; Om tat savitur varenyam bhargo devasya dhimahi; Dhiyo yo nah prachodayat. Om"*. (Oh, Creator of the Universe! We meditate upon thy supreme splendour. May thy radiant power illuminate our intellect, destroy our sins, and guide us in the right direction!) Even the non-believers are moved. The mantra resounds through the silent wilderness between the city and Champaner.

The bus skims across twenty kilometres of road along the Bhuj-Khavda highway without seeing a human being. There are no streetlights and the sun is yet to rise. The headlights of the bus transfix a hapless jackal. Its eyes glint in the dark in a manner that horror film makers have yet to discover. The headlights are dimmed, the jackal escapes and the journey continues.

The bus turns past the sleeping village of Kunnaria - then hits the dirt track to nowhere. Out in the middle of a vast empty arid expanse waits the newly constructed village of Champaner. There's something intrinsically crazy about this – people from so many different parts of the world turning up in the middle of this desolate wasteland in pitch darkness!

The crackle of the walky-talkies breaks the spiritual air. The production team and Apu's team can't seem to stop their prattle.

"Are the toasts ready?"

"Please start breakfast NOW."

"You must be in the make-up chair in another two minutes."

" Please put your plates away NOW."

The walky-talkies never stop; the harangue never ends.

———————

There are sixty-eight speaking parts in Ashutosh's script. Each of them needs to be processed through hair, wardrobe and make-up. Yes, that's the word. Processed! Factory style. With a time specified for each activity. Because a make-up chair is precious. Because a hair assistant is precious. Because *every* minute of shooting time is precious.

Apu's assistants, or 'babes' as he calls them, are ruthless. Reema the seniormost, all of twenty-seven, pushes around men twice her age without courtesy or remorse. Kiran is slightly more polite, but barely so.

Priya is the softy. She has been assigned the Kutchis - the junior artists from Bhuj and the villagers. Priya is a psychiatrist practising in New York and has been 'smuggled' into *Lagaan* by Apu. She is using her sabbatical to study film. Only much later will she learn how closely film and insanity are related!

Reema bellows at Guran. He doesn't respond. She needs to get more aggressive. The method is to say the nasty stuff on the walkie line to Apu within the hearing of the person at whom it is aimed. It's a method reserved for the more stubborn actors. The ones who want to test how far they can stretch the limits and where the lines will be drawn. Guran is a classic case from day one.

The gang of four: (clockwise) Apu, Priya, Reema and Kiran

"Apu, Guran is irritating the shit out of me!"

"Reema, tell him we'll rewrite the script and cut him out of the scene if he doesn't get ready on time."

An alarmed Guran gets his act together, at least for the moment.

The next day Guran pushes his luck again. This time Apu really cracks the whip. Guran is made to give a shot holding his rather luxurious false beard with his hand, since it has not been stuck on his face. Guran gets the message.

Some of the senior actors are unhappy. Reema yells at Kulbhushan Kharbanda in her guttural Hindi, *"main tumko kitna time bolega ki* (how many times should I tell you) get ready on time". Kharbanda, veteran of over two hundred movies and a star in his own right, can't believe that this little wisp of a girl is really yelling at him. Embarrassed, he whispers to the other actors defensively, "She doesn't know who I am."

Aamir loves a huge breakfast and takes his time over it. Unfortunately, his make-up time is huge since his entire body needs to be stained brown —

his fair complexion is a liability for Bhuvan. Aamir doesn't have the time for both make-up and breakfast. Apu's babes hustle him over breakfast. Aamir gives up in frustration. "If you'll push me like this I won't eat breakfast," he complains. "If you're so keen on breakfast, you can come half an hour early," the girls retort. The breakfast plate is put away for the rest of the shoot. Better sleep than breakfast, thinks Aamir.

Bhuvan shaving on the way to work

In the days to come, the pressure on Aamir increases. Late night production meetings force Aamir to grab every available second of sleep till the bus departs. He starts doing his toilet and bath on set. Rao is relieved that he fitted adequate toilets and showers on the set. For the Bhuj juniors, Aamir emerging from the common toilets, towel wrapped around his waist is initially a curious sight. Soon it becomes routine.

For all the grumbling of the Mumbai unit, they have had much more rest than the Kutch actors. In Gandhidham, sixty kilometres from Bhuj, little Arjun, all of seven years, has been stirred from his bed at 3 a.m., by his father Pradeep Joshi. To reach Bhuj city at 5 a.m., they must board the state transport bus leaving Gandhidham at 4 a.m. From Bhuj there is the further journey to the set.

Arjun is one of Goli's kids who shout "lippit, rite, lippit, rite," as the British troops pass through the village square. A small, yet memorable role. His real life father, Pradeep Joshi, is part of the village background. By the time Arjun gets home at night he will have travelled over one hundred and seventy kilometres in the bitter cold of the Kutch winter. Yet, Arjun is excited and when the bus arrives in Bhuj, he is wide-awake. There he meets Ameya, Harsh, Ritu and so many other friends of his. Today he will see Aamir Khan. Today he will act in a film. Today he will do something he will remember forever. Even at the tender age of seven he knows that.

For sleepy, laid-back Bhuj, it is a strange sight. At ten minutes to five, sixty people of all ages and sizes descend in the stillness of the night into the town square. Almost magically, two buses emerge from nowhere. The Bhuj actors enter the buses and proceed to Champaner, while the rest of Bhuj continues to sleep.

Elsewhere, in the tiny village of Kotai, the women have risen at 4 am. Although their village is across the hills, just twenty kilometres from Champaner, they have duties to discharge before they may leave their homes. They must draw water from the village well, they must cook for the family and they must finish all the other household chores before they board Danabhai's tractors and trucks. For four months now they have followed the same schedule and the Champaner they built is a familiar sight. Yet, this morning, as their truck arrives on set they are nervous and apprehensive, as are the men who are travelling with them. Today, they will not be laying cow dung on the floors of Champaner. Today they will be acting in the film for which they built a village.

When they arrive, somehow everything seems different. There are hundreds of strangers all over *their* Champaner. Some are staring at them. Others chatter excitedly. Still others carry all kinds of strange machinery from here to there. Nothing seems to make sense any more. Then Rao greets them "Sitaram, Sitaram," the Kutchi equivalent of 'good day'. I smile. One more familiar face. Apu's assistant Priya is introduced to them and she gently explains what they have to do. Maybe things will be OK after all.

———————

At around six-thirty, the sun rises over Champaner. It is a glorious sight. For the Mumbaiwallas, always encircled by a concrete jungle, the opportunity of seeing the red-yellow glow rise over the hills is special.

By this time, the activity on the set is frantic. Dozens of Bhuj actors are being draped in *dhoti*s provided by Production. Even in small town Bhuj, the art of draping a *dhoti* has been relegated to history. The wardrobe assistant, Raju Syed demonstrates publicly with forty men following each action. It is a hilarious moment.

By seven-thirty, a small miracle has occurred. Three hundred actors have been fed, had their hair and make-up done, been clothed as per script, marched to set, and are in their positions, waiting for the camera to roll. Later in the shoot these numbers will rise to a peak of ten thousand and an average of around two thousand, during the shoot of the cricket match.

Ashutosh, Anil and Nakul are preparing to take a giant technological leap back in time by setting up for sync, that is synchronous sound. The decision to use sync sound means stringent specifications have had to be met: a load of sophisticated sound equipment, a blimped camera, the Arri 535 BL, silent light boosters, a silent generator. Yet, the worries remain. One can always buy or hire machines that are silent; the tough thing is — how does one get human beings to shut up?

The typical film set is like a Hindu marriage pandal. The entire function is ostensibly happening for the bride and the groom, yet barring the priest and the parents involved in the rituals, everyone else is pretty much doing their own thing. Similarly, on a shoot, barring the actors and technicians directly involved in the shot, the rest of the unit members entertain themselves in such manner as they feel fit – yacking on their cellphones, gossiping with friends, playing cards, flirting…anything is fair game. This is the tradition of the industry. In that sense the dubbing system is admirably in sync with the way we, as Indians, organise ourselves. For sync sound to work, this noisy tradition has to be broken. All the hundreds of actors and unit people will have to maintain PIN DROP SILENCE!

A lot of preparation has preceded the big moment. Thirty walky-talky sets have been purchased by Production. Each department has its quota of walky-talkies, including those with the security guards spread over the perimeter of the one hundred and twenty-five acre set.

Apu calls the shot, "Roll sound please."

His voice resonates on every walkie-talkie across the set. In the mess and make-up area a bell goes off and a red light is on indicating that a shot is being taken.

Pin drop silence in the unit as Raghuveer Yadav, playing Bhura, catches hens

Priya and Reema yell on the walkie-talkies, "Rolling, silence please!"

In the make-up area, Kiran echoes the call, "Rolling, Rolling, Rolling!"

Some wise guys in the make-up area lie down on the floor and pretend to roll, but no one makes a sound. Everyone shuts up. They have heard the language of Apu's gang. No one wants to risk Kiran's wrath.

The security guards stop all the cars in the region. A lone jeep driver outside the main gate, nearly a kilometre away, stubbornly keeps his engine on. Nakul, the sound recordist is upset. He shakes his head. His mikes are so sensitive that they can pick up even this distant sound. Apu bellows into the walkie-talkie. After some impolite exchanges, the jeep engine is silenced.

Nakul shouts, "We are at speed," indicating that his recorders are rolling and the sound is now clear.

"Mark!" barks Anil to Hassan Kutti, who is giving the clap.

"Scene 2 Shot 1 Take 1," yells Hassan and jumps out of frame.

"Background action," bellows Apu and on cue, women bearing bales of hay move in the distance and a man pulls his bullock through the village.

"And action," whispers Ashutosh – and Mai and Harikaka deliver their lines perfectly.

Ashutosh okays the shot. Everyone is mighty pleased. It is difficult to believe that such a mammoth campus can function with one mind and thought. It is difficult to believe that such a mega operation started as a tiny idea in the mind of one Ashutosh Gowariker.

None of the actors have seen such a silent film set in their lives. It seems startlingly simple now. Why did no one do this before?

The day goes on and shot after shot is taken. After the initial success of sync sound, come the problems. Every time an aircraft takes off from the air force base, the shooting grinds to a halt. The acoustics of the desert work against us, as even faint sounds carry over great distances. Five minutes before the fighter jet is visible and ten minutes after it disappears, its sound is audible on Nakul's headphones. In the afternoon, the wind is too noisy to shoot. There are so many actors in each shot and a fumble by any one of them means a re-take of the entire shot. After all, the shot must be good both for the camera as also for the dialogue delivery. The re-takes balloon. The actors swiftly realise the dimension of the problems and work hard with Ashutosh to cut down the fumbles and the re-takes. They have an added responsibility on this kind of shoot. There is far less scope for making errors.

The actors are thrilled with the idea of sync sound. It means the intensity of their performance on set is retained on the soundtrack. It means that all the ambient sound, including the chirping of the birds, the neighing of the horses and mooing of the cows, is captured on the soundtrack. Most important, it is apparent to all that sync sound has led to an unexpected benefit — there is tremendous focus and involvement of the entire unit. Every single person is following the shot. The wardrobe assistants are closely following continuity. The art department is looking for footprints of modern shoes. Everyone is on the watch for cigarettes stubbed on the ground or anything else that will give away the period look. Everyone is making a film together.

The shooting stops at five again. It is cloudy and the light is inadequate to shoot in. There is a peculiar dust haze in the air. Perhaps a great wind is blowing through the Rann or through the Banni plains. The buses head back to Bhuj. On a hilly turn, a herd of buffaloes blocks the road, exaggerating the dust haze, scattering the rays of the setting sun. In the golden hour of dusk, when it is neither day nor night, the refracted rays of the sun create a magical look that never fails to move me. The cattle plod on unconcerned as the buses pass and enter Bhuj city.

Outwardly, a shoot has begun – one more film to add to the hundred-odd Hindi movies churned out each year. Yet, many have begun to sense that this is more than just another film — not consciously, for there is no time to think, at least for the moment. The next day's pick-up is at five in the morning and it is important to get to bed on time. Even as night falls, from the village of Kotai to the cities of Gandhidham and Bhuj, hundreds of *Lagaan*ites go to sleep.

When the going gets tough

An exhausted Captain Russell snatches forty winks in the make-up room

Kathinayi se takra jaa tu

Nahi haar maan le tu, mitwa...
(Go forth to meet hardship head on,
Don't ever accept defeat, my friend...)
— Song from LAGAAN

"If I were to have left the film and gone back to
Mumbai, what would have happened to the film? I
decided, come what may, I'll shoot. I'll die with my
boots on."
A. K. HANGAL (Shambhukaka)

When the going gets tough

9

8ᵗʰ January 2000

Mela released yesterday. Aamir is unusually tense – more so than for his other releases. *Mela* co-stars his brother Faisal whose career prospects hinge greatly on how the film fares. The entire *Lagaan* unit wants to see *Mela*. Tonight, the last show at Modern Talkies in Bhuj is reserved for the *Lagaan* unit. Dozens of fans hang around the theatre to catch a glimpse of Aamir. As the lights go out and Aamir's name appears on the opening credits, the unit goes wild with cheers and whistles. Even here, Apu is orchestrating the action.

Within half an hour it is clear which way the wind is blowing. The unit has fallen silent. In the interval the mood is glum and when the end credits come on, the atmosphere is one of mourning. Faisal has acquitted himself well, but the movie! No one has the heart to meet Aamir's eyes. Aamir sits alone in the bus on the way back. As we get off, he asks me, "That bad?"

10ᵗʰ January 2000

Notwithstanding the *Mela* debacle, on the *Lagaan* set, the atmosphere is joyous. The shooting of *ghanan*, the cloud song, has begun. The unit is in love with the song, but there is a major problem. Barring Aamir, none of the other actors have performed songs on screen before and between Rahman's complex rhythm patterns, Javed Akhtar's unusual lyrics and the need to dance to the beat, the actors are fumbling again and again and again. Choreographer Raju Khan and his assistants are infinitely patient, but Production is desperate. At this rate the song will take forever to shoot.

That night, Ashutosh comes to the mess with a tape recorder and plays the song. He asks the actors to listen carefully and then SING out their respective lines aloud. Despite the apparent simplicity of his directions, the actors fumble initially. It is only with much practice that they finally get the hang of the beat and the lyrics. Now they are enjoying the song again. The entire village cast yells out the song, creating a cacophony, much like collegians on a picnic. Half of Bhuj resonates to their voices. Their confidence has returned. "Sing, don't just sync your lips," is Ashutosh's mantra.

11th January 2000

A shutosh's mantra has worked its miracle. Lakha, Arjan, Goli, Ishwarkaka, Guran, Mukhiya, Ismail and the others have shed their inhibitions and are dancing and singing with gay abandon. The scene on the set is hilarious. Most of the Mumbai actors are not really dancers and the villagers are…well, villagers. Each person raises his or her arms and legs in a different direction. There are over a hundred and fifty villagers in each frame and in each take at least a quarter of them do something really bizarre. By the standards of Hindi films, where slickly choreographed, highly synchronised movements are the order of the day, the song could be a write-off, but Ashutosh is not worried, neither is the choreographer Raju Khan. "The more raw it is, the more natural it will look," says Ashutosh.

A rehearsal of *ghanan* in full swing

The villagers are delighted. Many are dancing for the first time in their lives – directly for camera. From a remote village in Kutch to screens worldwide – some journey that, though most don't realize it. They are curiously uninhibited. They don't even stare at the camera, the main error of the uninitiated. Their advantage is that most don't understand what exactly the camera does. They don't even understand why they are being asked to do what they are being asked to do. They view it as one more job given by Danabhai. It is much better to dance, than slog in the sun building a road.

12th January 2000

T he Mumbai unit is in a state of shock! The Kutch soil is imporous and a poor conductor of electricity, so the kinetic energy created by any movement accumulates as a static charge on the body. Touching good conductors of electricity like taps and car doors discharges the electricity and gives one a shock. Curiously, some people face this problem more than others. Aamir carries a huge static charge and a handshake with him in the dry morning hours is literally electrifying. People start greeting him from a distance.

More important, the generator cannot be earthed properly. Moolchand, the gaffer, creates a huge earthing pit, which consists of a metal bit buried under charcoal and salt, into which the earthing wire is led. Unit members are requested to pee into the earthing pit, as the salts in urine carry electric charge effectively. Despite the elaborate toilet arrangements on set, dozens of male unit members stand on the edge of the path leading to the set, peeing into the earthing pit. This has got to be the strangest method of controlling the power of electricity!

13th January 2000

The night temperatures have been falling steadily and for at least twelve hours, the mercury does not rise beyond single digits. The actor most affected by the deepening cold wave is Avtar Kishen Hangal, who plays Shambhukaka, the oldest character in the film and at eighty-four, is the oldest member of the unit. Nursing age and a bad back, Hangal just can't seem to get the Kutch cold out of his bones. Yet, the cold turns out to be the least of his problems.

This evening, Aamir receives a call in his room. Hangal has had a fall in the bathroom injuring his back. He is in agony and needs to be hospitalised immediately. An X-ray reveals no fracture, but the jolt received by the spine has irritated the nerve endings. He is unable to even move without excruciating pain. Shooting is out of the question.

Ashutosh is petrified. Hangal is locked into continuity and his big scene in which he warns of having to leave the village if it does not rain, is yet to be shot. The schedule is changed and the scene postponed by a week.

14th January 2000

The choreographer for the *ghanan* song, Raju Khan spends a lot of time on the set alone – sometimes on the temple top, sometimes in the fields. For someone who directs dance, he is curiously immobile. Initially, many attributed his love of solitude to an aloof temperament. As the song shoot has proceeded, it has become clear that Raju Khan has been soaking in the ambience of the village and its geography. He has designed complex shots with long takes spanning an entire verse, which richly exploit the beauty of the village and its periphery. From the ground to the bullock cart to the roof tops to the temple hillock, the dancing villagers are seen in every plane.

Raju has taken pains to allow the village and its ambience to speak to him. Now he expresses himself through its spaces and beauty.

15ᵗʰ January 2000

I n the film, clouds are seen at the beginning of the *ghanan* (cloud) song, travelling towards the village. In the middle of the song, these clouds are overhead and cover the sun, putting the entire village and surrounding areas in shadow. The shadow was to be generated by using a giant white cloth to cover the entire village. But, when nature's bounty delivers cloudy weather at the start of the *ghanan* song, Rao on behalf of Production requests Ashutosh to finish the middle part of the song first instead of relying on man-made means. Ashutosh declines, preferring to stick to plan.

By the time Ashutosh starts shooting the middle part of the song, there is not a cloud in sight and only human ingenuity can create a cloudy effect.
Moolchand starts stringing up the mammoth cloth to cover the village. He builds rostrums, giant towers from which the cloth can be strung so that the entire village is in shadow. So huge is the cloth that it requires twenty men just to carry it. The giant towers are rapidly erected and the lightmen start stringing the cloth from tower to tower. Everyone is thrilled by the simplicity of the solution and the ease of its execution.

A vain attempt to create a cloud shadow

From the west, a breeze starts blowing even while the unit watching the stringing of the giant cloth is enjoying the weather. Then suddenly, almost as if a switch has been pressed, the pleasant breeze turns into a gale, screaming through the village. There is something unreal about this. The gale picks up the giant cloth and there is a ripping sound as some of the stitches give way. Moolchand grimaces, but the wind is not done with the cloth yet. It lifts the cloth still higher. The cloth balloons. It is now a sail. The huge metal towers shake briefly although they are anchored with weights consisting of dozens of gunny bags filled with mud. Sixty feet of metal quiver. If even a single tower falls, it will be a calamity for the set and any life trapped beneath. Moolchand abandons the grand plan summarily. The cloth is hastily unstrung and hauled away, never to be used. Nature has shown who the real boss is.

The wide shots in which the entire village is seen in shadow can now be shot only in the few minutes after sunset, when the light is still adequate to shoot. The execution must have military precision. Through the day the shots are designed, rehearsed and perfected and the shots are actually canned in less than twenty minutes after sunset.

16ᵗʰ January 2000

The difficulty in obtaining liquor in 'dry' Gujarat has seriously irritated the unit. Today is Sunday and the 'dryness' of the atmosphere creates more friction than on other days. Some of the unit members have tried to obtain a permit, but the rules are so ridiculous and the procedure so tedious that it is better to pay the hundred percent premium and buy liquor from the now flourishing underground market. Aamir, Ashutosh and Rao, committed teetotallers, are secretly delighted at the problems the 'boozards' face.

Production adds to the drinkers' woes by insisting that they eat on time. A circular is put up in the dining area stating that dinner will not be served beyond ten at night. The reason: the caterer's men rise at four in the morning to prepare breakfast and need at least a few hours of sleep at night before the grind of the next day begins afresh. The circular is strictly implemented.

Tonight, Arjan demands dinner at ten-thirty. "If I'm not shooting the next day, why should I be required to eat early?" he harangues me at full volume.

Aamir's man Friday, Aamos appears at the opportune moment and bellows at Arjan. "Last night, Aamir saab couldn't get dinner because he was late. Do you think you are so special that the rules do not apply to you?"

Arjan backs off. Despite being 'high', he realises that no one can demand privileges.

As days go by, the mumbles at Sahajanand Towers are becoming grumbles. Unit members complain to Production about leaking taps, geysers that don't heat water, air conditioners that keep tripping the fuse, televisions with missing remotes...the complaints are endless and are made at all hours of the day and night. Some of the damage is in part because unit members are being less than careful with the appliances. The hapless production staff has been trying its best, but in tiny Bhuj, facilities for repairing gadgets are scarce. It takes ages to get even minor jobs done.

Reena sends out yet another letter to the unit. "Sahajanand Towers is not a hotel. It is your home. Please maintain it like your home...!"

These letters will become famous before the shoot is through as 'the matron's missives'!

The letter is well received. The unit is now more careful with the use of fixtures and more patient with the maintenance efforts of the production staff. The word 'home' replaces the word 'hotel'. More important than the change in the word is the change in attitude. The Lagaanites start decorating their 'homes' with rugs, photographs and paintings. Some hire a refrigerator and gas and start cooking to avoid the monotony of the caterer's food. Unit members become familiar sights at the vegetable and fish markets. Apu cooks not only for himself, but also for his 'babes', winning their loyalty in the process. Now you know the way to a woman's heart is through her stomach!

All in all, the unit is getting domesticated in Bhuj.

19th January 2000

Elizabeth, or rather Rachel Shelley is the first Brit to arrive. She lands several days in advance of her first shooting day so that she can get used to riding side saddle on her horse. She was to have had lessons in England, but getting side saddle lessons, where the lady rides with both legs on the same side of the horse was next to impossible in modern England. "Lots of women ma'm, very few ladies left," she's told.

An English lady learns to ride side saddle in Bhuj

So, now Rachel is in Bhuj, trying to learn how to ride as genteel British ladies did a hundred years ago.

In December, during the dry run, Ashutosh had identified a horse for Elizabeth. A gentle, pretty brown horse from the police stables with an appropriately filmy name: Rekha. Even if the rider were inept, Rekha would always follow her master's oral orders.

Production had handed over a side saddle to the police riders at least a month in advance of the shoot, so that by the time Rachel Shelley arrived, Rekha would be used to the idea of being ridden side saddle. This was very important, because when a horse is ridden side saddle, the weight is decidedly on one side of the animal and this makes the horse uncomfortable.

But Rekha has never been ridden side saddle till our Elizabeth, that is Rachel Shelley, arrives. The reason is simple. The police riders were too ashamed to do so. It would have been as embarrassing as a champion male cyclist riding a ladies bicycle! So, when Rachel arrives, the police riders put out the fantastic story that the only reason why they did not ride side saddle was for the noble cause of protecting the precious saddle and assure her that she will pick up the technique in a couple of days.

Rachel is upset that Rekha has not been trained, but fortunately there is time for both the rider and the ridden to get used to the side saddle. I take Rachel for riding lessons to the police grounds. Hundreds of kids turn out to watch the 'white goddess'. Some even ask for autographs. Rachel is amazed. She is a star in India without having shot a single frame!

The star leads her life on the edge. Sometimes she nearly rides into the crowd, sometimes the saddle nearly slips off, sometimes, she nearly falls off. Even Rekha is exasperated and Rachel feeds the horse huge lumps of sugar to make up. I warn Aamir that if the lessons go on for much longer, we will have a champion rider with cuts and bruises, but no heroine.

21st January 2000

Aamir is an excellent rider and in the evening takes Rachel riding in the village. He tells her that the slower trot is more difficult than the faster canter and gallop where the movement of the horse is smoother. They gallop through the village with Aamir demonstrating on the side saddle. Rachel gains confidence. Ultimately, she will give her riding shots well. With some courage and lots of luck, a major hurdle is being ridden out.

22nd January 2000

The mood among the Mumbai actors is upbeat. They have settled into the demanding work culture. Raj Zutshi, playing the potter Ismail, is enjoying his innings with pottery and produces quaintly shaped objects from time to time. Daya Shankar Pandey, playing Goli, is gradually learning the art of flinging stones with his *gofan* (catapult) and Yashpal, playing the woodcutter Lakha, has been driving his axe into sundry trees until he was reminded of the Forest Act and the penalties under it. Only one actor, Raghuveer Yadav, playing the hen-keeper Bhura, is a little unhappy.

Raghuveer started life in a small village near Jabalpur in central India, doing little else than farming. By the time he was fifteen, he was convinced that there was more to life than ploughing the soil and weighing the crop and that something more was music. With his father hostile to his musical prospects, there was only one way out. Raghuveer ran away from home and found food and shelter in a travelling drama troupe, which enabled him to feed himself once a day in return for rabble-rousing performances in the itinerant company.

After six years of such 'survival' in the most literal sense of the word, Raghuveer Yadav was miraculously admitted to the National School of Drama, where he learnt a different form of acting and much else. A few years later he made his film debut in *Massey Saheb*, which led to a National Award and within a few years, he established himself as one of the finest actors in the country.

The down side of this rather incredible journey was that music was sacrificed at the altar of acting. One of the big reasons why Raghuveer agreed to do *Lagaan*, was that with a long schedule in a quiet town, he hoped to have lots of time in which to work on a music album. In the early days of the shoot, Raghuveer would sit in the make-up room and play heavenly music on his flute as the rest of the unit listened mesmerised. But the silence required by sync sound and the endless hours on set have made Raghuveer realise that making music in Bhuj shall remain a pipe dream. Again, the actor in him will continue to prevail over the musician and he must simply accept it.

28th January 2000

The next Brit to arrive is Paul Blackthorne. He travels by train so that he can "see the countryside on the way". Glimpses of Mumbai and then the countryside, have exposed him to India's poverty. Paul is deeply disturbed by what he has seen.

The entire unit is keen on meeting the villainous Captain Russell. When he arrives, they cannot believe what they see. They behold an enormously tall man with sleepy, squinty eyes, hair like a hippy's, an overgrown, unkempt fungus-like beard, wearing a navy blue vest, a traveller's haversack and mauve cotton trousers folded up above the knees and sagging way below the waistline. This has got to be a practical joke, everyone thinks. He just can't be the villain of *Lagaan*!

I take Captain Russell for a tour of Champaner. Russell is mumbling to himself. To me it appears as if he is speaking in Spanish. The mumbling grows louder and I realise that he is speaking in Hindi – Russell has learned all his Hindi dialogues by heart and is speaking them out aloud on location. Obviously, he has waited for this moment.

The village is deserted – the unit is shooting at the practice field, some distance away. It is 2 p.m. and Russell suffers under the searing heat. He throws off his haversack. The mumbling grows louder. The walk proceeds. Russell removes his vest. He is bare-chested and his trousers hang ominously lower. The mumbling grows still louder and Russell now removes his trousers. He is down to his briefs and shouts out his big dialogue: "*Hum tum logon se itna lagaan vasool karega ki pahenne ke liye kapda bhi nahi rahega.*" ("We will extract so much tax from you that you will not have any clothes left to wear.")

I cannot bear the irony any longer. I hold up his clothes in my hand and mock, "Have you realised Captain Russell, that it is you who have no clothes to wear!"

Hair designer, Pina Rizzi, transforms a 'hippy' into a military officer

The next day, Paul receives a hair cut from the principal hairdresser, Pina Rizzi. He shaves and dresses in his military costume. As his appearance is transformed, Paul begins internalising Captain Russell. The twitch of the facial muscles, the menacing lift of the eyebrows, a stiffness and iron in the walk and unpredictability mark his behaviour. That evening, Paul reads his lines for Ashutosh, his voice almost a whisper.

There is none of the shouting and screaming that characterises villains in most Hindi films. Yet, his soft undertone reeks of menace and bite.

"It's no use playing the villain in a villainous sort of way," Paul tells me in his disarming manner. "Russell is basically a nice guy driven up the wall by Bhuvan and the rest of the lot." Paul has constructed an elaborate back story about what kind of parents Russell must have had and what the circumstances that led to his capricious cruelty are. He is trying hard to play the villain 'inside out', rather than 'outside in'.

I soon realise that I had been deluded. Behind the hippy façade, is a thinking actor with poise and craftsmanship.

24ᵗʰ January 2000

Hangal has been recuperating at Dr. Rao's hospital. The doctor couple, Gyaneshwar and Alka fuss over Hangal as if he were a part of their family. Hangal who has lost his wife and his daughter-in-law in the past two years is touched by their affection. This evening, a busload of *Lagaan*ites descends on Dr. Rao's hospital on their way home and sings for Hangal. Half of Bhuj collects outside the hospital. Hangal, lying flat on his back and still in great pain, is visibly moved.

Aamir and Ashutosh realise that Hangal is in no position to shoot and discuss contingency plans. Aamir tells Hangal that they will make alternate arrangements, but is taken aback by the ailing actor's response. Hangal tells him that if Production sends an ambulance to bring him to the set, he will shoot. Aamir tries to persuade Hangal that his back is more important than a film, but in vain. In the autumn of his life, Hangal may have lost his health, but not his determination.

Hangal has loved life and been a great survivor. As a child he had narrowly escaped as British troops massacred civilians in the streets of Peshawar. As a young man during the partition days, he endured detention in a Pakistani jail for his refusal to accept the two-nation theory. In the evening of his life he braved the wrath of Bal Thackeray and endured a crippling work boycott. To run away from duty now would be out of character.

25ᵗʰ January 2000

I arrive at Dr. Rao's hospital with an ambulance to fetch Hangal to the set. When I enter, I see a shrivelled-up man huddled on a hospital bed. Hangal smiles when he sees me, but is unable to make the slightest movement. I wonder how on earth he will shoot today. Hangal's assistant

Gopal and I gradually lift him on to the stretcher. The process of shifting him from the bed to the stretcher takes fifteen minutes, as every movement of his body has to be carefully planned and gently executed. Despite all our efforts, Hangal cringes with pain right through.

The ambulance crawls as slowly as it can on the bumpy mud track to Champaner. Production has a cast iron rule forbidding the entry of vehicles into the shooting area to avoid the risk of tyre marks finding their way on screen in a period film. An exception is made for Hangal. As his ambulance enters the set, a stunned unit breaks into applause. The stretcher is eased out and Hangal waves to the cheering crowd. The pain is as intense as ever and Hangal goes through the process of having his beard trimmed and being dressed for the shoot, with agonising moans.

An injured A. K. Hangal being carried to the set for his shot

Then comes the big moment. A huge shot with the camera snaking past seven characters, until it halts before Hangal for his finale: *"...Nahi Nahi! Is saal jo anaaj hai usi mein gujar basar hoi jaye, lekin agale saal agar yahi haal raha to gaav chhodne ke ilava kauno hi rastaa naa bachi, kauno hi rasta naa bachi."*(No! We will survive this year on our existing stocks of grain, but if the drought continues next year, then other than to leave our village, we have no alternative whatsoever.)

The shot goes into five takes. Once, Goli fumbles, once Anil is unhappy, once Nakul; but on every single occasion, Hangal's take is perfect. Not once does he forget his lines, not once does he moan in pain, not once does his performance fail.

That night at dinner the air is sober and reflective. Everyone knows they have been privileged to see something special. They have witnessed the triumph of the spirit over the flesh.

26ᵗʰ January 2000

It is Republic Day. Aamir is invited to the flag hoisting ceremony at the tiny school in Kunnaria village. Aamir unfurls the national flag and Ashutosh, Gracy and a few others from the unit join in singing the national anthem. An hour of precious shooting time is lost, but going to a tiny village school and singing the national anthem with the people of Kunnaria is a beautiful moment for the *Lagaanites*, a slice of Bharat they will not easily forget.

27th January 2000

The hair and make-up processing is turning into a nightmare. With such a large number of actors whose hair and make-up must be carefully attended to, the work needs to start really early and the hair, wardrobe and make-up teams typically leave for the set at the unearthly hour of 5 a.m. The two Canadians, Nicole heading the make-up department and Pina heading the hair department simply hate leaving in the bitingly cold morning hours. Both have done a good job with their work, but the sharpness of their skills is well matched by their tongues.

The actors have taken to the factory-like processing rather well. The make-up room does much more than change the look of the actor. It is also the place where they start getting into character. As Guran's beard is pasted on, he becomes crazier than he generally is, the boisterous Suhasini transforms into the sober, motherly Mai and the sharp and witty Goli is reduced to a simpleton. With twenty make-up stations filled by twenty actors getting into character, the atmosphere, to put it mildly, bears a close resemblance to a lunatic asylum. With all that, or perhaps because of it, the make-up room also bonds the actors together as a common space where they go through a similar journey together.

Guran's beard is so wild that it is impossible for him to eat without desecrating it. For the next four months, he must survive through the shooting shift on soup and juice sucked through a straw.

The only discontented soul among the actors is Rachel Shelley (Elizabeth). 'This is not the way we do things back home,' is her general tack. Rachel is unhappy with the way she has been welcomed, she is unhappy with the welcome provided to the other British actors who are arriving. She wants a kit provided to *every* British actor, with a map of Bhuj and Kutch, a list of the tourist spots, how one gets there, how long it takes and so on. She has even gone to the extent of writing out a model letter of welcome to the other Brits and giving it to Production for further processing and printing.

Somehow, nothing seems to work for her. The food is not right. The clothes are not right. The shooting timings are not right. She asks Production to organise a copy of *The Guardian* of London to be delivered in Bhuj and they don't and that doesn't seem to be right.

Rachel is free with expressing this discontent, especially with the British actors who are just arriving. I am deeply alarmed and can see a crisis brewing, but am not quite sure what can be done.

28th January 2000

High noon in Champaner

Rachel has been constantly testing the limits to which she can push Production. Today she goes a step further. Rachel arrives on the set and charges towards Sanjay Dayma, who is also handling wardrobe responsibilities and screams shrilly at him. The entire unit is stunned. This is the first time in four weeks that *anybody* has raised his or her voice.

Aamir calls for Rao.

"Why is Rachel yelling? Is there something that we have done wrong?"

"She's upset because she doesn't have hat pins," Rao quietly replies.

Aamir walks up to Rachel and assures her that she needn't shoot without hat pins. After a while Rachel calms down sufficiently for the shoot to proceed, but now Aamir's mind is in turmoil. A tantrum on the set so early in the shoot bodes ill for what could follow. Aamir has sensed that Rachel is engaging in an unethical power game and wants to test the limits of how far she can go. He calls for a meeting with her.

"Rachel you have every right to insist on having hat pins before you shoot. What I am upset about is the manner in which you expressed it, which disrupted the atmosphere of the shoot."

In his characteristically calm voice, Aamir continues, "Rachel, on this set, only two people have the right to raise their voices – one is the director and the other is the producer. As it happens, even they do not raise their voices. That is the way we work here. If you want to work in any other way, then you are free to leave."

Even as Aamir says this, he knows that re-casting at this late stage would be nothing short of a disaster. There would be incalculable loss of time, money and energy, endangering the entire *Lagaan* project. But *Lagaan* is going to be made the proper way or not at all and the earlier this is established the better.

Fortunately, this contingency does not arise. Rachel apologises and at least outwardly, that closes the chapter.

11th February 2000

Danabhai has been asked to mobilise 800 villagers. Today is the first day on which we need large crowds to shoot. As it happens, they have been called for a twenty-four hour shoot, starting on the late morning of the 11th and continuing till dawn on the 12th.

This is probably not a good way to start with such a large group. These are people who have no bond with the *Lagaan* unit and are coming to shoot for the first time. How they will fare is anyone's guess. The entire unit is on red alert.

The crowds arrive in their trucks and tempos. They are counted. Production is relieved to find that the eight hundred called for are all there. Feeding them and getting them into *dhotis* and *kurtas* is a huge logistic operation that would have been beyond the resources of the Mumbai team. Fortunately, by now the Bhuj actors are more than just actors, they are multi-purpose unit organisers. Pankaj Jhala, Anand Sharma and others queue the newcomers for various tasks. Jayantibhai Jethi teaches them how to drape the turban and the young men from Bhuj help put on the *dhotis*. With this massive army of volunteers, all eight hundred are processed and made ready for the shoot inside an hour. So far so good!

What happens thereafter, is far more fractious. After being prepared for shoot by twelve-thirty, the crowds are made to wait a mile away from the shooting area for nearly three hours till their shot comes up. The crowd grows impatient. "How on earth does one explain to them that such waiting is inevitable in a shoot?" asks Rao in exasperation.

By late afternoon, the restive army is marched to set. The heat is searing and the crowd is irritable. They have been placed on the hill around the practice field and Aamir Khan is a small dot in the distance. This is far less interesting than they expected it to be.

'Apu's gang is in full swing, getting the crowd to remove sunglasses, plastic footwear and other modern accoutrements smuggled onto the set, as these will betray the period look. The heat is relentless. Some of the young men don't like the way they are being ordered around by the second assistant director, Reema.

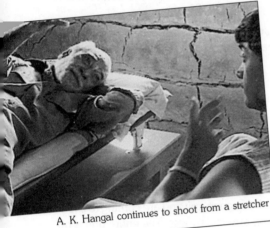

A. K. Hangal continues to shoot from a stretcher

At a corner of the hill, an argument is simmering. The polite difference of opinion becomes less polite and Reema orders one of the village youth to leave the set. He retorts that he will take all his friends with him. He has around a hundred and fifty friends here. If they all leave, the shooting day will definitely be lost. I rush over and work out an uneasy peace between Reema and the mutineers, that leaves Reema simmering. She complains to Apu.

By five in the evening, the day shoot is over, but the patience of the crowd, especially of the youth, has run out. Some want to leave without waiting for the night shoot. There is utter panic in the unit. No crowd means no shoot. Apu loudly announces to whoever will care to hear that Production has tricked people into coming; that they were called to see Aamir Khan, not to shoot.

Production is appalled at Apu's allegation. They have spared no effort to build a relationship with the Kutchis based on mutual respect. This could well be undermined by arrogant behaviour with the villagers. A meeting of Production, Apu and Danabhai is swiftly called. The wardrobe area is converted into a council of war. Danabhai clarifies that the crowd has been called for a shoot, for which they are being paid and that the villagers are only too aware that it is a twenty-four hour shoot. Apu's allegations are clearly without basis.

Danabhai then discloses the reason why the youth are anxious to escape.

"The youth are only upset at being ordered rudely. 'Sit here. Stand there. Remove your *chappals* (footwear).' They just aren't used to it. No amount of money will make them accept what they perceive as an insult to their honour."

Danabhai plants himself at the main gate of the set. Ruffled feathers are smoothed and hurt egos are assuaged.

As the night shoot starts, a horrible realisation begins to set in. The village crowd had been called in the early afternoon when it was unbearably hot, so they had dressed lightly, with no sweaters or shawls. Now they have nothing to protect themselves against the deepening chill. By ten at night the desert winds begin blowing and Paul and the other Brits in the scene are unable to keep the cold out of their bodies or their minds. Universal central heating has destroyed their resistance to cold. Mercifully, the scene requires the village crowd to hold flaming torches, *mashaals* in their hands. The heat of the flame keeps them going, but between shots, the torches are extinguished, leaving them to the mercy of the biting wind. The crowds instinctively huddle together.

The scene being shot is the one where Bhuvan and his team are practising cricket at night under the light cast by *mashaals* held by the villagers and appears at the end of the *chale chalo* song. The village team is in their usual garb. Aamir is wearing his thin vest. Kachra and Bagha are bare-chested and the others are wearing the thinnest of *kurta*s (shirts). Apu moves around in shorts and T-shirt. His assistants are also uncomplaining. The actors have no *mashaals* and are completely exposed to the bitterly cold wind and yet, they shoot through the night. The villagers watch them admiringly. If they can do it, so can we, is the sentiment.

Just a few hours back, they had threatened to walk off the set. Now they are our partners in adversity. We are together in the middle of a desert, the only persons for hundreds of miles together who are at work at this time of the night – watching cricket being played in the light cast by *mashaals*. There is something inspiringly insane about the whole idea and that spirit infects the villagers too. The bitterly cold wind is giving birth to a new warmth and a new bond.

12th February 2000

The entire British cast is now here – all eleven cricketers and over thirty extras. The unit is genuinely multi-national now. There are the Canadians Nicole and Pina, there is one Dutch and one Polish girl and a Frenchman among the 'British' extras. The unit from Mumbai is itself drawn from the four corners of India. Even the usually unrepresented north-east has an important member – Reema Kagti from Assam.

It is Saturday night and the unit is rocking. Location: the terrace of Sahajanand Towers. A local music group soulfully sings some *ghazals*. The

An e-mail from 1893: Suhasini Mulay (Mai) works on her laptop

Lagaanites listen patiently, but only just so. The entire audience consists of performers and they can't wait to get started. The moment the Bhuj artists finish, Aamir gets hold of the mike and acts as Master of Ceremonies. Most of the Indian actors fancy themselves as singers and render their favourite numbers. Aamir does his '*Aati kya Khandala*' to loud applause. It is a picnic atmosphere.

Then the unit starts with the *ghanan* song. This is *their* song. They are singing it now before the rest of India will. It is a secret they are privy to and they share it loudly with the residents of Bhuj. Rao comes up to the terrace looking anxious. What if the neighbours complain? He whispers something in Aamir's ear. But Aamir is no longer in producer mode. He is one of the boys and too lost in enjoying himself.

The Brits enjoy the atmosphere, looking on from various corners of the terrace, nursing such alcohol as they have been able to lay their hands on in dry Bhuj. The Indian actors pull the Brits in. Paul is asked to sing. He squirms with embarrassment. The Indian gang thinks he is being shy and it is only after much persistence that they discover that in the songs department Paul's reportoire is empty.

Suhasini Mulay, playing Bhuvan's mother Mai, is the life of the party. The contrast between her screen and real life persona is startling. Now she seductively croons, *"Raat nasheele hai, bujh gaye deeye, aake mere paas, kaanon mein mere, jo bhi chaahe kahiye, jo bhi chaahe kahiye."* ("The lights are dimmed and the night intoxicates. Come close and whisper in my ears, anything, just anything!")

Ultimately, the spirit infects the Brits too. Jon House and Ray Eaves sing a few numbers. The Indian gang cheers lustily. Several dozen 'happy' people sing loudly and their voices resound for miles around. The party is but the first of many such that will follow and which play no small role in bonding the culturally diverse unit.

14th February 2000

Today the Brits will be shot playing cricket. The period cricket equipment that Aamir and Reena had bought in London from Shawn's shop is unveiled. The British cricketers approach their work with heightened respect. They pore over the photographs in the nineteenth century book of British cricket, soaking in batting stances and bowling actions. They too journey back a hundred years. The effort taken in creating a realistic look is now paying rich dividends.

15th February 2000

A problem has been looming which most members of the unit are oblivious to. Despite all efforts, the pace of shooting is slow. Ashutosh is ten days behind schedule. Much of the time has been lost for reasons completely beyond his control. He has lost two shooting days because the weather was too cloudy. He has lost precious hours waiting for jets to pass and winds to die down, because he is shooting with sync sound. He has spent hours trying to choreograph the movements of his giant cast, using golf tees as markers to ensure that each actor is exactly where he is supposed to be.

Considering the odds he is battling, Ashutosh's performance is nothing short of magnificent. The mood in the unit is almost euphoric as everyone knows that something quite extraordinary is being captured on celluloid. Everyone is on a high…everyone except executive producer, Reena Datta.

Reena is in Mumbai. She has been to Bhuj twice during the shoot, but there has been so much to do in Mumbai. Coordinating the departure of the British actors from London, receiving them in Mumbai, ensuring their foreign exchange payments, overseeing their travel from Mumbai to Bhuj, ensuring the movement of raw stock from Mumbai to Bhuj and guaranteeing the safe passage of the valuable exposed negative from Bhuj via Mumbai to the laboratory in Hyderabad…all this and more is being managed by her in Mumbai, with help only from the versatile Clementina Santos and Akram Shah from the production team.

Every night she receives a report from Rao and every night Reena's blood pressure rises. Ashutosh, Aamir, Anil, Nakul, Apu, all seasoned professionals, have prepared the schedule and declared it 'locked', 'sealed', 'frozen'. They have had the opportunity to do a dry run, rehearsals and readings, make-up tests…the works. No cost has been spared in making actors, technicians, even make-up artists available in advance of the shoot. A mountain of paperwork has been generated and everything planned to the last detail, only so that the film may be shot according to schedule. Now, the schedule is falling apart and nobody seems to be doing anything about it.

Reena is experiencing nightmares. She sees the film going way beyond schedule and cost-wise becoming a runaway horse. She imagines the British actors walking away after their dates are exhausted, the monsoons arriving and causing the shoot and film to be abandoned. She shudders at the prospect of repaying debts for years to come,

The dark dreams haunt her night and day. These are not far-fetched anxieties, they are more than likely possibilities. To her, it seems as if Ashutosh and Aamir are sanguine, almost euphoric. Reena needs to do something drastic. Fast.

Reena arrives in Bhuj without notice and heads straight for the set to check things out. Aamir and Ashutosh are pleasantly surprised to see her and greet her warmly. Reena barely acknowledges them. After pack-up, she calls for a meeting with the heads of department. In the meeting, she can barely contain her anger.

"I am giving you guys one week to get your act together. If even in this period, you cannot keep to the schedule, I'm shutting the film down. Whatever money has been spent so far, I'll absorb the loss, but I don't want to continue in this manner."

Ashutosh turns pale. Aamir tries to explain why they have fallen behind schedule. Ashutosh is confident that the lost time will be made up during the shoot of the cricket match.

Reena is not impressed. "You guys are the experts. You are the creative minds who have planned the film, prepared the schedule and locked it. Now if you can't keep to it, as the executive producer, I am going to decide what I think is right, no matter what Aamir might say."

The meeting ends awkwardly. There are no smiles, no spirit of – 'I'm just pushing you, but don't worry I'm not serious.' So far as Reena is concerned, her job is not about being nice, it is about getting the job done – well and on time. For the next five months, Reena will continue in this mode and earn a fearsome reputation as the real power at Aamir Khan Productions.

Aamir can scarcely believe the transformation in Reena. Although he cannot openly acknowledge it, secretly he is admiring his wife. She had started work on this, her first film, less than a year back and now she is ably confronting a highly acclaimed creative team. Phew!

However, at a professional level, Aamir must restrain Reena and begin a balancing act between his executive producer and director, a delicate task he must perform through the production of the film. He must get Reena to believe in Ashutosh's genius and appreciate the difficulties in shooting *Lagaan*. He must on the other hand get Ashutosh to realise just how stark and real Reena's concerns are.

19th February 2000

An air of desperate urgency hangs over Champaner. Everyday Ashutosh hands over a written shot breakdown before the shoot starts. Sometimes he finishes his list of shots for the day, but sometimes he does not. Even before Reena's one-week deadline passes, the film is behind schedule by one more day. Reena keeps up the pressure with her unsmiling, grim look, but no further meeting is called and the shoot continues.

———————

In the privacy of Room No. 703 at Sahajanand Towers, Aamir tries to persuade Reena, "Trust my judgment. We're going as fast as we possibly can. This is the *only* way to make a film like *Lagaan*."

One floor below, there is a midnight knock on the door of Room No. 603. Aamir visits his director. "Ash, make the film as you've visualised it. Don't compromise. I'm with you."

Ashutosh is reassured. Being tough is part of Reena's job – taking her tough talk in his stride is part of his job. What is unsettling is the challenge looming up ahead – the first day of shooting of the cricket match with a crowd of ten thousand. To execute the most critical and expensive day of the shoot, Ashutosh has an army at his disposal; yet, the general must bear his burden alone. His mind is racked by the thousand and one creative decisions he must make to translate his ambitious script to celluloid.

Back in Room No. 703, Aamir tosses and turns, tortured by the weight of his responsibilities. Never in his twelve years in films has he felt more vulnerable. He keeps telling himself hypnotically, "If you want to make a great film, you need guts!"

———————

Ten thousand actors

A crowd of ten thousand performs on cue

Toot gayi jo ungali utthi,
Paanchon mili to, ban gayi mutthi
Eka badhtaa hi jaavey, chale chalo!
(If a finger rises, break it will
When all five join, a mighty fist forms!
Let our unity grow.
Come on, walk ahead!)
— Song from LAGAAN

"I felt like a general in battle. I had mammoth
regiments and commanders all over the place, but
getting this army to charge in an organised manner
was a daunting task."
ASHUTOSH GOWARIKER
Writer-Director

10
Ten thousand actors

14th February 2000 – 20th February 2000

Ten thousand people are required for the first day of shooting of the cricket match. The plan is to take dozens of wide-angle shots with the use of five cameras that will cover the entire cricket ground. It is only by seeing the ground and even the surrounding hills full of the people of Champaner province, that the audience will appreciate just how high the stakes in the cricket match are. Having shot with ten thousand spectators on one day, for the rest of the cricket shoot, the camera will see only specific sectors, not the entire ground. The shoot with the full crowd will enable Ashutosh to estimate just how many people he will need to populate each sector.

At the daily meeting of departmental heads held in the centre of the cricket ground, Rao reports on the lukewarm response to the mobilisation efforts. "I don't think we can get more than three thousand people," he concludes.

A dismayed Ashutosh asks, "But how can we shoot the cricket match without ten thousand people on at least one day?"

Before Rao or Reena can say a word, Aamir interjects, "Ashutosh may think he can manage with ten thousand, but to make this ground look full, I think we require at least twenty thousand people."

Reena and Rao look skyward. Ashutosh and Aamir have either not understood what Production is saying or they have lost their heads. Rao has a reputation for being calm under pressure and Reena is blessed with a naturally calm temperament. Yet, there is a time to be calm and there is a time to express shock. "Where on earth do you expect us to get so many people from?"

Aamir is not interested in any arguments. The crowds are a make or break issue. For *Lagaan* to work, at least ten thousand people must be produced. By asking for twenty thousand, he hopes that Production will manage at least half the number. He rapidly concludes the meeting with an uncharacteristic diktat.

"Mr. Rao, I don't care how you do it, but do it. We must have at least ten thousand people on Day 1!"

Reena and Rao are in a state of panic for very good reasons. The task of mobilising a large crowd for the cricket match has always haunted the production team. In the pre-production days, Rao, Ashish and I travelled extensively through dozens of villages in Kutch. At each village we stopped over at numerous houses for tea, distributed sweets to the kids and got to know dozens of people not just by sight, but by name. We even learnt a smattering of Kutchi. The network we created was more than adequate to ensure a smooth supply of carpenters, masons, plumbers or even vets and doctors, but six months after first setting foot in Kutch we know that mobilising ten thousand people for the shoot is way, way beyond us.

The geography and demography of Kutch are against the mission being a success. For one, the entire population of Kutch is just over thirteen lakhs. From this figure exclude those whom the census enumerates in Kutch, but who have migrated to Mumbai and other cities around the world. While hunting for properties, the production team has seen that over half the houses in every village are permanently locked. Further, exclude the very old and the very young. The number available for the shoot actually lies between two and three lakhs. Mobilising ten thousand of these means that something like five percent of the available population of the entire district will need to turn up for our shoot.

To add to Production's woes, people are spread over a mammoth area. At 45,612 square kilometres, Kutch is geographically a fourth the size of the state of Gujarat and larger than Belgium, Denmark or the Netherlands! Worse, there is no way to contact or mobilise people in such large numbers at one go, because most live in villages, really tiny hamlets, separated from each other by miles of arid semi-desert. Many live in areas so remote, that television and film culture are yet to penetrate. A shoot has far less lure here than it has in an urbanised area.

In sum, the star-producer may want ten or twenty thousand people at his shoot, but whether so many people want to come for the shoot is a wide open question. Not surprisingly, Rao refuses to commit himself to a figure. All he says is, "We'll try our best."

Ashutosh and Aamir had banked on a direct approach. An advertisement had been placed in the local newspapers offering a decent sum of money, food and transport to all volunteers and urging people to register for the shoot. The response was miserable – barely a few hundred registered.

This was bound to happen. We had tried the Mumbai method – offer a good price and get good service. But we were in Kutch not Mumbai. To wake up at 3 or 4 a.m. and travel hundreds of miles to reach Champaner for a few hundred rupees just didn't make sense. What is a film? What is a shoot? What do we have to do with it?

Considering where the Kutchi villager comes from, the whole thing just didn't make sense.

––––––––––––––

The only way out now is to use the existing network among the Kutchis and the trump card which Rao has is Danabhai Ramji Ahir. Born into the house of a humble Kutchi farmer, in the tiny drought-stricken hamlet of Kotai, Danabhai had dropped out of school early and earned a reputation as a street smart, go-getting, unruly youth. With agriculture completely unviable, Danabhai had latched on to the trucking business then booming in Kutch after the discovery of major deposits of lignite. The truck business brought with it brawls, tension and violence and young Dana showed he was as tough as it gets. However, over time, the gentle Kutchi blood in him pushed him to the relatively less rugged and more peaceful line of construction, where Danabhai rapidly earned a reputation of being a highly quality conscious contractor. Both trucking and construction had taken Danabhai into the far-flung corners of Kutch where he developed the relationships that we are now banking on.

Rao had sensed the extent of Danabhai's contacts when he was building the village. A week before D-Day, he puts all his eggs in Danabhai's basket. "My *izzat* (honour) is at stake, Aamir Khan's *izzat* is at stake. You have to get all ten thousand people by yourself."

Danabhai laughs.

"No, no, I'm serious Danabhai, do what is needed, but get them."

Danabhai is still unconvinced. Rao gets Aamir to meet Danabhai.

"Danabhai, this is the single most important day of our entire schedule. We are depending only on you. If you don't get the crowd, we cannot either. We just will not be able to make the film properly," Aamir puts all his cards on the table.

Never in his forty years did Danabhai Ramji Ahir imagine that the fate of a film will one day depend on him. Never did he foresee that one Aamir Khan will plead helplessness before him.

Honour is a strange thing. You put a man on honour and he will give his life for you. So far as Danabhai was concerned, now that Aamir had put all faith in him, his personal honour was at stake, the honour of Kutch was at stake. Come hail or high water, ten thousand people have to be produced. The shoot has to be carried out successfully.

In distant Kutch, the telephone if it exists in a village, is largely an ornament. The only way to get one's message across is to get oneself across. Danabhai climbs into his little Maruti car and hits the highways criss-crossing Kutch, going as far as Rapar, hundreds of kilometres away on the rim of the Great Rann of Kutch. For over two weeks Danabhai keeps up a punishing schedule, leaving his home at dawn and returning well after midnight. He visits ninety villages and extracts a promise from at least one leader in each village on the numbers that he will mobilise. The villagers are curious. A few have heard that an actor called Aamir Khan is shooting a movie in Kutch, but the more remote villages are completely disconnected from the modern world and nothing that Danabhai says makes sense. As far as they are concerned, Kutch's honour is at stake. The honour of Kutch needs to be protected.

As Danabhai mobilises the crowds, Rao and his team are making the production arrangements. Every detail has been calculated. It will take ninety-five trucks and forty trailer-tractors to carry the villagers. The entire crowd needs to enter Champaner in one hour between five and six a.m. But the dirt track leading from Kunnaria to Champaner is only wide enough to accommodate single lane traffic for trucks. Portions of the road are relaid and strengthened. The thorny *babool* is trimmed to make the road wider.

Food is a mammoth issue. At least ten thousand food packets are needed for breakfast and another ten thousand for lunch. Rao selects the biggest hotel in Kutch, located at Gandhidham, for the job. It is more expensive than the Bhuj caterers, but they seem to have the requisite infrastructure. Rao warns them that food can be a make or break issue for the shoot.

Serving water individually to ten thousand people is impossible. So, a network of underground pipes is laid all around the cricket ground, carrying water to dozens of taps concealed in the surrounding bushes of *babool*. Yet, even this might not be enough, reckons Rao. A 'period' solution is found. Hundreds of earthen pots, *matkas* are placed all over the ground. These will be seen in the film as the *matkas* the villagers carry with them to the match.

Although Danabhai has been instructing the villagers to come in traditional clothes, even in sleepy Kutch, the younger generation of men has replaced the traditional *cheni-kediya* with the ubiquitous shirt-pant. Akram from Production is sent to distant Ahmedabad to buy two thousand *dhotis*, *kurtas* and *gamchas* (headwear).

Other than ten thousand people, Ashutosh wants a large number of transport animals including thirty bullock carts, three camels, twenty horses and one elephant. The other animals are easily procured; the missing beast is the star: Raja Puran Singh's elephant. I am despatched to Ahmedabad to procure an elephant suitable for a king.

In Ahmedabad, Aditya (Kachra) Lakhia's father takes me to a massive temple complex with an elephant. I see the elephant standing alone and bored, tiredly chewing on the hay laid out in front of her. Her skin has turned pink in large patches and the folds hang loose. "She's shot for *Mughal-E-Azam*," the *mahout* (keeper) tells me, but clearly the pachyderm has seen better days. I hire a video camera and shoot the elephant. Back in Bhuj, Ashutosh sees the 'audition'. My hunch is right. Ashutosh's casting zeal is undiminished. The 'beauty' from Ahmedabad fails to impress him. Puran Singh's elephant has simply got to be majestic. Think big, Ashutosh tells me for good measure!

I'm back on the elephant trail, setting off at dawn on the Saurashtra road. With six days left for the elephant's first appearance, I am now desperate. I pull off the highway into every adjoining town to ask people on the road whether they have seen an elephant. Some think I'm mad, others think I'm pulling their leg. After some time I think that life is pulling my leg. A year back at this time I was arguing weighty matters of life and death in the high court of judicature and now here I am on a dusty highway in Gujarat searching for an elephant.

In the afternoon I pull into Rajkot and have lunch at a tiny hotel where inevitably I veer round to my favourite question, "Do you know where I can find an elephant?" Amazingly, the manager nods confidently and gives me an address with detailed directions. His confidence makes me suspicious and as his directions lead me to a large congested colony of chawls, I am convinced that the manager having sent me on a wild goose chase must be chortling away. I ring the doorbell tentatively, terrified at the prospect of having to ask the occupant whether there is an elephant inside.

My problem is miraculously solved. The doorbell rings and an elephant trumpets in response. A man in the saffron attire of a sadhu opens the door and eureka, just about fitting within a tiny open courtyard is a majestic elephant, also named Lakshmi! The sadhu tells me that the place and the elephant belong to a religious institution, which regularly hires out Lakshmi for weddings and other functions, so shooting for a film will be a very pleasant change, thank you. An hour of haggling later, the deal is sealed and I head back to Bhuj with the thrill of a unique conquest. Thus is Raja Puran Singh's elephant obtained!

21ˢᵗ February 2000

A full day has been set aside for the technical rehearsal. A hundred things have to be worked out. The five-camera set-up covers every square inch of the ground and the cameras will constantly see the shooting crew. A decision is taken that the entire crew for the D-Day must also be dressed as nineteenth century villagers.

Anil has the mammoth task of designing the five-camera set-up with his additional four camera teams. Fortunately, each of the four additional cameramen, Mohanan, Rafe Mehmood, Joginder Panda and Sudhir Palsane have assisted Anil earlier and they are well tuned to one another. Ashutosh has prepared a list of the shots to be taken. These are basically the shots where a wicket falls or some other major event in the match has taken place and hence the reaction of the crowds is important. Various angles are tried before finalising the position for each camera for each shot. Ashutosh and Anil generate a mountain of drawings while finalising the camera angles.

The technical rehearsal for the big day

Directing the background action will be crucial. This is Apu's big day. Other than his three assistants, he has five crowd controllers from Mumbai and five of the production staff at his disposal. For a crowd of ten thousand, these are clearly insufficient. The sixty Bhuj actors who have been coming in daily, double up as volunteers.

Aamir holds a marathon meeting with the cast to discuss the production arrangements for the day. The wardrobe continuity is worked out. Shooting instructions are given and all questions of the actors and technicians addressed. On D-Day, not a minute should be wasted on discussions. Then, all the major shots are rehearsed. On paper, the day has been planned with military precision. Now, only the execution remains.

22ⁿᵈ February 2000

The wake-up call goes off at 3:30 a.m. Many have not slept all night out of excitement. The production team has not had the time anyway. Ashutosh wakes up and peeps out of his window. There are no clouds in the sky – an encouraging start – the cricket match can only be shot in harsh sunlight that will accentuate the agony of drought-stricken Champaner.

The entire main unit is on the cricket ground at 4 a.m. before the crowds arrive so that the smooth movement of the trucks carrying the crowds is not interrupted. Everyone from the make-up men to the spot boys are in rustic, period costumes. Even Nicole, the Canadian make-up artist is dressed in *salwar kurta* with a colourful turban to conceal her blonde hair.

All the camels, horses and bullocks are tethered to their positions. Lakshmi, Maharaja Puran Singh's elephant (my find!) is looking aptly royal with her silk cloth and impressive *howdah* (seat).

Some of the production staff and the Bhuj volunteers take up positions along the highway to direct the trucks and ensure there is no traffic jam. The breakfast packets arrive from Gandhidham. They are counted out. All ten thousand of them. So far so good. All the water tankers have arrived. Ten will provide water for the crowds and ten for the rain machines that will be used for the shoot.

By 5 a.m., the trucks carrying the crowds start arriving. We wait with bated breath to see if the required numbers will turn up. First, it is just a couple of trucks and then a relentless roar as truck after truck drives in. The crowds pour out in waves. It seems as if half of Kutch is in Champaner. Danabhai has upheld the honour of Kutch and of Aamir Khan! Rao and Reena heave a huge sigh of relief. Half the battle has been won.

The breakfast packets are handed out as fast as hands can carry them. There is more freshly fried *papadi* and *jalebi* inside than most can eat. Many of the young men are in trousers and need to be dressed in *dhoti-kurta*. The wardrobe exercise starts in right earnest. Most do not know how to wear *dhoti*s and the wardrobe team and the Bhuj juniors conduct a mass sartorial exercise. Most of the men are rolling up their trousers legs and draping the *dhoti* on top of the trousers. Priya tries to persuade them to remove their trousers, as they may show in the shot. After much laughter on their part, she realises why they are unwilling to take their trousers off – they are not wearing any underclothing!

The crowds are instructed to leave their footwear in the trucks they came in and to put their watches in their pockets. Both these would give away the period look. They are confused and unhappy about this instruction.

The crowds are alighting at the village set, where there is place for the trucks to pull over and park and for the crowds to be served breakfast and dressed for the shoot. Now, ten thousand people must walk two kilometres ahead to the cricket ground. Those dressed in appropriate outfits are being walked to the set. It is soon apparent that the walk to the cricket ground is tougher than anticipated, because the crowd is walking barefoot and the thorny undergrowth hidden in the sandy soil makes its presence felt, slowing down their movement. There is loud cribbing in a section of the crowd. I swiftly remove my footwear and join the barefoot brigade. The cribs subside.

Dressing the shirt-pant brigade in *dhoti-kurtas*

Meanwhile, another problem looms up. The number of people who would arrive on set dressed in modern clothing has been grossly underestimated. The two thousand *dhoti-kurtas* are exhausted in less than an hour. There are now a few thousand young men on set who are not wearing the correct outfit. The production team had brought up this possibility earlier and the decision taken had been that all persons wearing inappropriate clothes would be concealed behind rows of appropriately dressed people. The decision now haunts everyone involved in controlling the crowd.

Thousands of young men are 'detained' in the village while others are being marched to the cricket ground and placed around the ground at the appropriate spots by Apu. Those detained are unable to comprehend why they have been made to wait for hours doing nothing, while others who have just arrived are heading for the set. They begin to suspect that they are missing out on something exciting on the cricket ground and nothing that is said, can persuade them to believe otherwise.

A few hundred youth in modern clothing at the village decide to bolt towards the cricket ground. Ronit Roy, who is in charge of security, physically blocks them and pushes them back. Reema, Ronit and I face an increasingly hostile crowd, which has now swelled to over a thousand angry young men desperate to go to the cricket ground set. The problem is that they are all inappropriately dressed for the shoot and they can only be taken in once everyone else has been positioned. After desperate pleas to Apu, the hostile crowd is released. It soon becomes clear that there is no way to prevent the correctly and incorrectly dressed sections from mixing. Ten thousand people, complete strangers to a shoot, being kept in position by a few dozen people is an absurd situation.

The crowds grow increasingly restive. Earlier, as the crowds had arrived, Apu had successfully primed small groups to shout "*re bhaiyya chhoote lagaan,*" after him. But the difference between a few hundred and several thousand is more than just the numbers. There is a subtle change in the balance of power and the crowd senses it. People move around, shifting their positions freely. They now feel like an audience at a show, not like

Difficult to control

actors at a shoot. Apu, dressed as a British soldier tries to yell at a particularly rowdy group. The move backfires as a group of aggressive youth shout right back. A skirmish develops and Apu has to be rescued by security.

Maharaja Puran Singh's elephant, the gentle Lakshmi, is upset by the noise of the crowds. Should she stop listening to her *mahout,* she could well become aggressive.

After the initial success in terms of the crowd size, everything else seems to be going wrong. To Rao, it appears as if the sheer size of the mobilisation will destroy the production effort.

Then, the tide turns dramatically. There is a hush and then a roar as ten thousand pairs of eyes focus on a single man who walks out of the British pavilion, clad in the *dhoti* and vest that will later be known as Bhuvan's costume. Aamir strides out and greets the crowd, first in broken Kutchi and then in Hindi.

"I thank you all for travelling hundreds of miles to participate in our shoot."

The crowd cheers in response. At last things have started happening!

"Your performance is crucial for the success of this film," Aamir continues as he walks around the perimeter of the ground, smiling and waving to people placed in every section of the mammoth cricket ground.

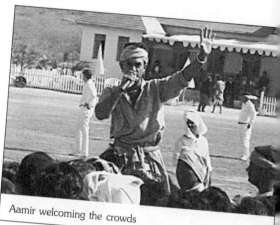

Aamir explains that Apu will be giving them instructions regarding what they have to do and then hands over the baton to Apu. At last the shooting begins, a full three hours behind schedule.

Aamir welcoming the crowds

The first two hours of shooting proceed smoothly. Five cameras roll in unison as valuable footage is canned. Nakul has wired the entire ground with his sound cable connected to hidden microphones. Many of the British actors hear the massive roars on Nakul's headphones and are awestruck.

By twelve o'clock, the crowd is restive. They have had enough of the heat and enough of acting. They could hardly be blamed. What they are watching is not a cricket match played in the usual manner. They are viewing specific shots, tiny parts of a match. To them these appear to be a bizarre series of actions. A ball bowled here, a catch taken there, a six hit, a catch dropped … random disconnected shots that make no sense. To compound it, there is this awful man called Apu who exhorts them to endlessly shout and cheer. Not surprisingly, the crowd is restless, even distracted and refuses to perform enthusiastically.

Once again, Aamir must work his magic. Aamir has worked out a plan with Ashutosh. Aamir goes close to the audience – very close – he sings "Aati kya Khandala" with a wiggle of his hips. The audience gives an almighty roar. Five cameras roll rapidly. The shot is canned!

B y twelve-thirty, the lunch trucks roll in from Gandhidham. The production team is relieved. They feel their big challenge is behind them. Ten unit members are on each truck to hand out the food parcels. Suddenly, the crowd notices the trucks. It is difficult to say what exactly happens, but the effect of seeing the food packets is such that hundreds and hundreds of people rush towards the trucks and climb on to the sideboards and grab two, even three food packets. Danabhai tries to explain that there is more than enough food for everyone, but it is a lost cause. A 'we will be left out' insecurity has taken over. Within ten minutes, the packets are 'distributed'. There are still two trucks on stand-by full of food, but logic has yielded to mob psychology.

The crowds ring the cricket pitch

In a corner of the ground, one of the Bhuj city juniors is angrily complaining about the food. Production rushes over. She complains that the food has gone bad. I smell the food and taste it. It is not bad, but it is not fresh either. The caterers are called in. They explain that in order to get the food ready on time in such large quantities, they had started cooking the previous afternoon. For those used to eating freshly cooked food, there is a problem. For the Mumbaiwallas, used to eating food refrigerated for over a week, the food is just fine. Akram and I climb into a truck and in full view of the crowds eat the food to reassure everyone. The lady from Bhuj is unconvinced. She throws away the food packet and instigates others to follow suit. Fortunately, the villagers eat the food without complaint, though with little enthusiasm.

Huge barrows are being moved around in which the crowd is to throw the empty food packets. But the concept of a dustbin is alien to the Kutchis, or for that matter to villagers almost anywhere in India. Despite a hundred requests, they throw the food packets on the ground, often with uneaten food spilling out. Within no time, the entire cricket ground and the hill are dotted with food packets, yellow *bundi laddoo*s and *dal*. Mercifully, Rao had insisted that the food packets should be brown so that their colour merges with the colour of the soil, but the uneaten food is a hopeless giveaway. There is no way that the shoot can proceed without cleaning the ground. But how are thousands of food packets spread over such a massive area to be cleaned in half an hour?

The production team is desperate. Rao, Reena and I start on the work ourselves. The few spot boys not otherwise engaged are also mobilised. Clearly this is not going to be adequate. There are over forty jeeps hired for the day. Many of the drivers have been with the film for some months now. Seeing us on all fours picking up food with our hands, they too spontaneously join in. The cleaning detachment swells to around fifty. A tractor-trolley is driven in. There is an insane frenzy in picking up food packets and throwing them into the tractor-trolley. In an hour, the impossible is accomplished. The ground is not spotless, but shooting can proceed. A disaster has been averted through sheer will power.

Shooting starts after lunch with the pre-lunch chaos compounded by sluggishness and inertia. Dozens of people have climbed the hills around and dropped off to sleep. Many have removed their *dhoti*s at lunchtime and are now freely moving in shirts and trousers in positions that will be prominently picked up by the camera. So much for the p-e-r-i-o-d!

Aamir moves into another gear. He climbs up on a tall black horse and directs the action from his vantage point. Aamir is a master at handling the crowds and the audience responds well. He keeps them entertained with one act after another - sometimes with a song, sometimes shaking hands with dozens of villagers, sometimes by appreciating their work with applause. Aamir does it all genuinely and with complete involvement. His transparent honesty and passion about his work communicates and carries

Aamir, on horseback, directing the crowds

through to them. He befriends the villagers. They feel he belongs to them while he draws them into the world of the shoot and of *Lagaan*.

Providing rain to drought-stricken Champaner

By four in the evening, Ashutosh is ready for the last shot – the winning shot in the film, where the crowd runs on to the field to celebrate – looks up – sees the rain clouds – it pours. The rostrums have been built and the rain machines readied. Aamir and the village cast perform a rehearsal for the crowd, showing them what they have to do. It is not an easy task giving instructions to ten thousand actors at one time. It is impossible to even know whether they have understood the instruction until the shot is taken. A rehearsal is out of the question, since getting ten thousand people to run on to the field and back to their positions could easily take upto an hour.

Apart from getting the shot right, Aamir is concerned about the safety of the British cricketers. After the winning shot in the film, the villagers run on to the field while the British cricketers run off it. If the villagers get carried away, the British cricketers could get hurt. Aamir calls the British cricketers on the field and introduces them as cherished friends and guests of whom special care must be taken.

The shot is taken. Ten thousand villagers run on to the field as the British cricketers safely exit. It is a magnificent shot, ruined by one single youth in black trousers and purple shirt, who positions himself right in front of the camera! The shot has to be taken again.

It is the end of the day and Aamir thanks 10,000 actors for their efforts. Despite the trials, the crowds know they have done something quite extraordinary. They depart in high spirits.

It has been a day of mixed results and mixed emotions. Despite the meticulous planning, the results are less than perfect. Without the planning, it would have been a disaster. Ashutosh is pleased. He knows that a lot of valuable shots have been canned today. A glass is either half full or half empty. He chooses to see it half full.

Aamir is less satisfied. Production has substantially delivered what had been asked for, but the creative team has not been able to utilise the opportunity fully.

Anil is unhappy. He knows only too well the number of shots ruined due to people wearing modern clothes.

Apu is thrilled – he plans to go back to America and show his film pals the call sheet for the day, with the list of ten thousand people, camels, horses, cattle, elephant *et al*.

The British actors are awe-struck. They have never witnessed anything like this before. In the eyes of most, *Lagaan* now has an epic quality.

The Mumbai actors are ecstatic. They have made history. This is a tale worth passing down to grandchildren.

Rao has felt the edge of the numerous problems through the day, but his overwhelming sentiment is that of relief. After organising such a mammoth day, the rest of the shoot should be a cinch.

That night there is a small celebration in Bhuj. Everyone feels that Everest has been climbed — only the descent remains. No one but no one has guessed how wrong they are. The unit sleeps peacefully that night, oblivious of the trauma that awaits them.

Climbing a mountain

The glorious uncertainties of cricket: Fun one moment...a nightmare the next

11

BHUVAN: Ek baat aap sab logan ka phir se yaad dilai doon: yeh sirf khel nahi hai jo hum kisi ke mauj manoranjan ke liye khelat hain. Yeh ek ladhai hai jo hamka jeetni hai.
(Let me remind all of you of one thing. We are not playing this game for fun or entertainment. This is a battle, which we have to win!)
— LAGAAN

"Logistically, it was a mammoth task and the fact that we held out for those six months was because Production made it possible for us. I tell you any crew, anywhere in the world, would have cracked up."
ANIL MEHTA
Director of Photography

11
Climbing a mountain

23rd February 2000

S hould the cricket match be of a single inning or should it be a two-innings game? A simple question, but one that can make or break *Lagaan*. When Ashutosh first wrote the script, he visualised a two-innings match, as the greater length of the game would accentuate the suffering and pain of the villagers as also the difficulty of defeating the British team. Yet, on second thoughts, a single-inning match might be dramatically more lean and effective.

During the year long pre-production, Ashutosh and Aamir couldn't make up their minds. They flipped and flopped endlessly, until the list of shots for the ten thousand crowd day was finalised. The most expensive, important and difficult day of the schedule was used to film isolated shots of a two-innings match spread over four days!

With the ten thousand crowd day done, Aamir now insists that Ashutosh put down on paper the entire list of shots for the cricket match before continuing the rest of the shoot. "It doesn't matter if it takes two days, four days or even a week. Let's continue only after we write down every single shot we require."

Aamir, Ashutosh, Kumar and Sanjay sit together on the deserted cricket ground and work out the detailed story and score card for the cricket shoot, while back in Bhuj, a three hundred and fifty strong unit at full wages sits idle. The waste of two shooting days more than pays for itself. Ashutosh and Aamir realise that the two-innings story just doesn't work. Showing thirty-nine wickets fall is too repetitious, time consuming and tiresome.

In the evening, Anil Mehta, Reena and Rao visit the 'cricket sub-committee' to check out the progress. A discussion is sparked and the director of photography, the executive producer and the chief executive - production all plump for a single-inning match. Finally, the only open portion of the script is sealed. The climax of *Lagaan* will be decided in a single inning. One decision that will save *Lagaan* from disaster.

The change has come at a price. A fair number of the shots taken with ten thousand extras are on the assumption of a two-innings match played over four days and must now be junked. Yet, the consensus is that it is better to accept that one was wrong earlier and cut one's losses, rather than continue further down the road to disaster.

24th February 2000

Now, every intricate detail of the cricket match is finalised. The number of runs each player will score, who will dismiss him and how, is locked. On this basis is scripted the number of batting shots required of each player as also the fate of each of the shots. Does the stroke go on the offside or on the legside; is it fielded or does it cross the boundary; every one of these details is put on paper. Similarly, the number of shots of each bowler at each bowling end and the fate of each ball are committed to writing.

A little before midnight, the paperwork is complete. Reena has a look at the number of shots with what can only be described as horror.

"One thousand two hundred shots!"

Reena's mental calculator starts whirring. Within four weeks, the British actors' contracts run out. After deducting the holidays and the days required to shoot the cantonment portion, that leaves 20 days to shoot the cricket portion. 20 days for 1200 shots means that an average of around 60 shots must be canned on every shooting day, if the match is to be shot within schedule.

"Impossible," says Reena, "you'll never finish within time."

"It's possible," says Aamir, "Our planning and paperwork will help us save time."

It is difficult to tell how much conviction Aamir has in this assertion, but the mammoth paperwork which has now enabled axis shooting is certainly going to save some time. Axis shooting means that when the camera is facing the British pavilion, all the shots where various batsmen, whether Indian or British, are at the British pavilion end, will be shot without having to move the camera, crane and the rest of the shooting gear, saving enormous amounts of time. Similarly, the shots where the camera is facing the makeshift Indian pavilion can all be shot at one go.

Axis shooting creates one major problem. Continuity. Take for example, a ball being bowled from the British pavilion, which is hit by the batsman towards the Indian pavilion. Axis shooting means that the bowler delivering the ball would be shot on one day, while the shot of the batsman playing it, which would be from the opposite axis, could end up being shot even fifteen days later. For the playing action to look authentic on screen, continuity of fielding positions will have to be strictly maintained. Ashutosh cannot have Bhuvan fielding at slips when Deva is bowling and mysteriously appearing on the boundary line when the ball is hit towards the Indian pavilion.

To enable continuity, Ashutosh has painstakingly worked out the fielding continuity for every single bowler and sketched it out on several diagrams.

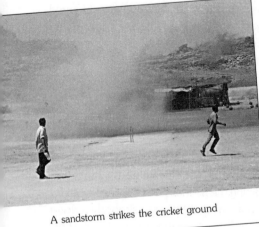

A sandstorm strikes the cricket ground

The problem of continuity is not limited to just the players. It must also be worked out for the spectators. Something like two thousand villagers will shoot every day through the cricket match. Continuity of their seating arrangements, clothes and expressions has also to be kept in mind.

Ashutosh has also worked out the reactions of the spectators in the British pavilion, the village actors in the Indian pavilion and of the villagers for each shot. Do they clap from the beginning of the shot? Do they start clapping and then fall silent? Do they start silent and then sigh with disappointment? Do they say something?

A huge amount of paperwork has been generated, no mean achievement under other circumstances, but a bare necessity in *Lagaan*. Ashutosh cannot afford to miss anything. A patchwork shoot for an omitted shot will be impossible, because neither the cricket ground nor the British cricketers will be available later. There simply is no room for errors of omission.

The cricket match now only remains to be executed. Given that a lot of the cricketing action will be 'cheated', in the sense that the audience sees only what the camera shows them, the shoot should be over within the scheduled three weeks.

At any rate, this is what Ashutosh and Aamir claim.

25th February 2000

At four-thirty sharp, Ashok Shinde from Production reaches the set with Sadruddin, the generator operator. It is the dead of the night and the jackals howl as their jeep bumps along the dirt track to Kunnaria. The generator is switched on and the magic of electricity illuminates the Kutch desert. The unit can now work.

The cooks arrive close on their heels. Breakfast must be cooked for two thousand villagers before they arrive on the location. The smell of freshly fried *puris* and well-spiced potato *bhaji* wafts through the air. As if on cue, at 5:30 a.m., two thousand Kutchi villagers pour in. The breakfast is served and enjoyed. A meal so early is odd, but what the hell, so is the idea of coming to a nineteenth century British cricket ground and acting in a film!

The Mumbaiwallas arrive on the set sporting a 'we made history' swagger. The ten thousand day shoot has resulted in a few hundred inflated egos.

The shoot starts with the British innings, with the shots of Deva bowling to the British opening pair. One of the shots demands that Deva bowl on the legside for Smith to sky the ball towards Lakha at square leg, who deliberately drops the catch. For this shot to be executed, Deva must bowl on the legside, at a length that will make it possible for Smith to sky the ball towards Lakha. But Deva, really Pradeep Singh Rawat, is an actor, not a cricketer. He just can't bowl to a plan. Either he bowls way off the stumps, or he bowls on the offside. Ben Nealon, playing Smith, is a good batsman, but this is calling for skills beyond the call of duty. It requires re-take after re-take for the shot to be canned, by which time, Ashutosh is a worried man.

Lunch is taken at 12:30. There are fifteen buffet counters for the villagers. After the problems with the food on the ten thousand crowd day, Production has kept a hawk's eye on the quality of food being served. The *shrikhand* (sweetened curd) is delicious. It is not easy serving a buffet for two thousand people. Ashish, Ashok, Akram, Ranjeet and I stand at the lunch counters personally serving the food, urging everyone to eat well, exactly as one would at a wedding party. Like an

Operation lunch time

army, a film unit marches on its stomach and Production is determined not to lose the battle.

Post-lunch, Arjan is at the crease. Per script, in his brief innings, Arjan must hit two boundaries before being dismissed. Arjan bats at number three in the Champaner side, yet in real life he has NEVER played cricket. This is soon evident.

Take 1: The crowd being primed by Apu roars on cue as Smith runs in to bowl. The cameras roll. The ball, at amiable pace, is bang on the middle stump and asking to be hit. Arjan misses by a mile.

Take 2: Again the crowd roars. Again the cameras roll. This time Smith has been told to ease off. Yet, he is no match for Arjan's cricketing talent. Again Arjan misses.

Arjan plays cricket without a ball

Take 3: This time Ashutosh wants to take no chances. He decides there will be no bowler. The camera will see Arjan in midshot and the ball will be tossed to him from next to the camera. He only has to make contact. The ball is tossed up. Arjan unleashes an almighty heave. The ball dollies past him.

Ashutosh grimaces inwardly. Apu curses openly.

Takes 4 to 14 all meet the same fate as Take 3. Arjan just cannot connect. Ashutosh has a sinking feeling. There are two cameras rolling with two different magnifications and angles exposing valuable stock, all of which so far is a complete waste. But a shot is a shot is a shot and if bat does not touch ball, it cannot be okayed no matter what the pressure is. Clearly, Arjan and cricket *ka janmon janmon ka bair hai* (they are enemies from their previous life).

Ashutosh now plays his last card. He removes the ball from the frame. Arjan is asked to heave with his bat while the camera sees his facial expression in close-up. This is cricket without a ball. Overjoyed at this wonderful sport, the actor Akhilendra Mishra takes over and the shots are swiftly okayed.

The first day has been a disaster, but many shrug it off. Who doesn't have a bad shooting day? Tomorrow is bound to be better.

1ˢᵗ March 2000

Four tomorrows have come and gone since the first shooting day of the match. They have all been frighteningly similar to Day 1. Guran, Ishwarkaka, Goli... all non-cricketers doing their very best. What they do best is acting, not playing cricket. It takes them time and several retakes to get it right. And time is something which *Lagaan* just cannot afford.

Reena and Rao are anxious. The date crisis looms larger than ever. If the match is not shot in three weeks, then fresh dates will have to be booked for the entire British cast. If even a single British actor refuses to give dates because he or she has been committed elsewhere, or even out of pique, then the shooting of *Lagaan* will grind to a halt. Ashutosh of course knows this. Reena 'helpfully' reminds him. Externally, Ashutosh is confident that he will finish in time. Internally, only he knows what he is going through.

Ashutosh had cast the Champaner team strictly on the basis of the suitability of a particular actor for each character, without any regard to their cricketing ability. As a result, over half of the team is completely cricket illiterate and the remaining half has played the game years ago at school and college. Creatively, this was a correct decision because the Champaner team wasn't supposed to be cricket savvy; their awkwardness in playing cricket would give the film a more realistic feel. But in terms of shooting time, there is obviously a huge price to be paid and there is nothing in the world Ashutosh can now do about it. One thousand two hundred shots have to be taken and they have to be taken properly.

Meanwhile, the production saga continues. Daily, two thousand villagers are trucked to set before dawn. Daily, food and water are arranged. Fortunately, at least half the villagers wear their traditional clothes, which are acceptable, but the remaining half, the pant-shirt brigade, must be dressed every day for the shoot by the wardrobe department.

At dawn, as the villagers arrive on set, Raju Syed and his wardrobe team have just folded the *dhoti-kurta-gamcha*s they washed last night. The drying area is the size of the cricket ground. Raju Syed murmers "tarchur, tarchur" ("torture, torture") even as he hands out the clothes. He warns the villagers that if they don't put the clothes back exactly where they took them from, they will get no clothes tomorrow. The villagers are already used to his fuming and fretting. The older ones replace the clothes correctly, but some of the youth enjoy teasing Rajubhai by leaving their *dhotis* in the bushes.

Raju Syed has worked with Aamir's father, Tahir Husain, for several decades. He is now working with Aamir whom he has seen as a little boy playing on set. Raju Syed is overworked and under-appreciated – yet he cannot get over his awe at the magnitude and scale of the film or his pride in being part of it.

The elephant, Lakshmi, is most unhappy. She is not used to the sound of jackals baying at night and by dawn she has yet again destroyed her shelter. Clearly, she cannot be asked to stand in the heat all day. Rao sends for workers from Kunnaria village to rebuild the elephant's shelter.

One of the horses from Mumbai has fallen ill. I go to the nearest agricultural village, Sumrasar, and source a vet. Five men hold the horse's mouth open as the medicine is poured in. The horse sneezes. The medicine is obviously bitter and the horse is complaining. He is old and weary with a hundred shoots and a thousand falls. Fortunately, in *Lagaan*, no stunts are expected of him. He has only to stand around in the distant background, barely noticed. Yet he must be looked after like any other unit member.

The chartered accountant for the film, Bimal Parekh, comes to see the set. He is most curious about the toilets. He cannot believe that so many lakhs of rupees have been spent on toilets. I show him round the relevant spots. He is horrified by what he sees. Not only are there several toilets, but also they are spotless!

"Why on earth are you spending so much on toilets? The distributor is not going to pay you more money for your film, because you had clean toilets. As if this unit could not use the open as all other film units do!" Bimal is indignant at this waste of valuable resources.

Reena laughs off Bimal's comments. Every decision cannot be made with an eye on the bottom line. What is correct must be done for its own sake.

The shoot starts on the dot at 8:30 a.m. The day starts superbly. Goli is to be clean bowled. His cricketing 'talent' ensures an effortless single-take shot. There are smiles all around. Ashutosh looks a little more relaxed.

Then, Ben Nealon playing Smith comes in to bat. The Brits are all regular players at the club level and have been cast in part for their cricketing ability. At least this portion should go well, hopes Ashutosh. Ben is an excellent cricketer and a fine actor and shot after shot is picked off with ease.

Then comes the shot where Ben is run out by a throw from Bhura/Raghuveer Yadav. Ben must receive a ball from Aamir, which he can hit near Bhura, yet not directly to him. This is easier said than done and the problems never seem to end. Either Ben cannot connect with the ball or he cannot hit it near Bhura or Bhura fails to field it, so the ball goes to the boundary. The list of problems is endless.

Then, completely by chance, Aamir bowls and the ball is hit near Bhura who picks it up cleanly. Ben starts for the run, reaches half way... realises that he is not going to be able to make the run and desperately tries to make his way back, but the Champaner team has switched into another gear. For a moment one feels it is the finals of the World Cup Cricket. Ben charges back to the crease as though his life depends on it. As he approaches the crease he realises that it is going to be a direct hit, so he throws himself full length at the crease with the bat outstretched. Alas, the bat digs into the ground and the entire weight of Ben's falling body is levered via his outstretched arm onto the shoulder, yanking out the arm from the shoulder socket, dislocating it.

Bhura's throw hits the stumps directly with Ben out of his crease. The Indian actors forget the film and go mad with joy congratulating each other. They have learnt cricket after all! On screen joy and off screen joy merge, but in all this excitement, no one has realised that Ben is hurt and is in genuine pain. Ashutosh seeing the agony on Ben's face is impressed by the 'performance' and holds the shot waiting for Ben to get up and leave the frame. Like everyone else, he is oblivious of Ben's dislocated shoulder and thinks he is still acting. Ben is turning blue with the pain, yet he refuses to ask for help for fear of spoiling the shot. Finally, by a supreme act of will, Ben gets up and staggers out of frame. It is only then that Ashutosh calls "cut" and Ben falls to the ground crying out in pain.

All the actors surround Ben, full of concern. Production rushes to organise a doctor. The walkies are buzzing and within minutes an ambulance is on the way, but Ben cannot wait. He is in agony. Then he does something unbelievable. With his left hand, he bangs the dislocated arm in place and magically the pain diminishes. Everyone is awe-struck by Ben's fortitude and commitment. All this for a film which cannot possibly do anything for his career in England!

Later, Ben's shoulder is bandaged and slung by an orthopaedic surgeon. There's a wonderful shot in the can, but the accompanying drama as also the need to reschedule Ben's shots for a few days have not helped Ashutosh's schedule crisis.

With Ben temporarily indisposed, Ashutosh turns to the shots of the monster fast bowler Yardley, played by Chris England. Chris is the Harold Larwood of the movie, the nasty fast bowler who destroys the batsman if he can't get his wicket. Chris is a competent batsman at the club level, but is not a fast bowler by any stretch of imagination. When he does bowl, he delivers a gentle variety of offspin, that too, only as a last resort. Ashutosh however cast Chris for his look. He was convinced that with the addition of sideburns and a handlebar moustache, Chris would have the menacing look of a brutish fast bowler. The look perhaps comes naturally to Chris, but now the time has come to deliver with the red cherry.

Ball 1: Chris approaches the bowling crease at great speed, but the ball leaves his hand well before it reaches the highest point of the overhead arc. The ball shoots thirty feet in the air flying over the head of what would have been third leg slip and hurtles towards the boundary.

Ashutosh grimaces and the Indian actors snigger. So, this is the weapon with which the Indian team is to be demolished!

Ball 2: Chris approaches the bowling crease snorting with rage and hurls the ball angrily. Again, the ball misses the batsman, the wicketkeeper and the leg slip cordon and crosses the boundary.

Ashutosh sighs inwardly. Such a perfect look! If only he knew how to bowl.

Ashutosh knows there is no shortcut. Dozens of shots of Yardley must be canned. His nastiness is the lynchpin of the British bowling. Ashutosh knows he has a similar problem with Paul. Per script, Captain Russell scores a century, which means that dozens of his batting shots are required. But Paul, playing Captain Russell, is a stranger to cricket and though every member of the unit has volunteered advice and coaching, Paul continues to be a novice. Shooting with the two 'best' British cricketers will cause Ashutosh as much grief as will the shots of the cricket-illiterate Indian actors.

The day has been yet another disaster. Instead of gaining time, Ashutosh is a further three days behind schedule. The total of 1,200 shots looks ever more intimidating. Ashutosh is running out of time and he feels it intensely. He feels as if each shooting shift is a one day game which he wins or loses depending on the number of shots he completes. Yet, each shot must be carefully okayed, for the audience is not going to be concerned about the conditions and compulsions under which the film was made.

Go faster he must and Ashutosh's best bet is in the shots involving Aamir, who is excellent at cricket. Aamir's shots form nearly a third of the shoot and it is these shots which are coming up.

4ᵗʰ March 2000

At Sahajanand Towers, Reena's mood is grim. Whether or not Ashutosh admits it, she can see that the cricket shoot will go wildly beyond schedule. Reena leans on Aamir, "You're not pushing Ashutosh hard enough."

Aamir is walking a tightrope. Although Reena and Ashutosh are pulling in diametrically opposite directions, both are right. Aamir must defend Ashutosh when he is with Reena and protect Reena when he is with Ashutosh. He must be the creative person in the day on the set with Ashutosh and the producer at night with Reena. Aamir is not playing games with either of them. He is telling them what he genuinely believes.

Aamir explains to Reena that with so many characters and the tremendous difficulties in shooting a sport, Ashutosh requires time. Constantly pushing him will shatter his morale and affect his creativity.

With Ashutosh, Aamir must tread a more delicate course. He tells Ashutosh to make the film as he has always seen it, but to constantly remain aware that every creative decision has commercial implications.

Both Ashutosh and Reena can see Aamir's point and yet being true to their work also means being blind to it partially. Ashutosh, making his third film is to some extent inured to the pressure and at any rate faces no personal complications. However, for Reena, doing *Lagaan* as her first film, the tensions of interacting as executive producer with her husband in his producer *avatar*, are driving her up the wall.

The production team has socially separated itself from the rest of the unit. They stand together separately on the set. They travel separately. Each night after dinner they meet separately in the production office on the fifth floor where they let off steam (really bitch) about the day's events. Even Aamir is not spared in these nightly sessions. Aamir, by pitching his lot with the creative camp has excluded himself from these sessions and the close-knit production team headed by his wife.

It is a strange, intense experience. Reena had joined *Lagaan* and films in part to do something together with Aamir. Yet, even as *Lagaan* is filmed, their separate and often antagonistic compulsions are forcing them in opposite directions. Reena must maintain her distance from Aamir as much as she must from Ashutosh. She must criticise Aamir and push him into hastening the shoot as much as she must do so with Ashutosh. It is a new dimension of being husband and wife, which is both beautiful and full of danger.

7ᵗʰ March 2000

The climate is simply unbearable. The hot winds of summer have arrived. Every ten minutes, the hot wind blows through the cricket ground lifting the sandy soil in round twisters and depositing it in the hair and eyes of the actors. The worst affected are the villagers sitting on the ground in the desert soil with nothing to protect them. With fortitude and perhaps by dint of habit, they survive the heat and dust.

Muslin masks to beat the heat

The British actors are least capable of handling the elements. Although the heat is still mild by the standards of the Kutch summer and despite their relative comfort on chairs placed in the British pavilion, they just cannot cope. To add to it, they cannot handle the Indian food and upset stomachs are the norm. One of the cricketers, Ray Eaves, has already been hospitalised twice for dehydration and daily, at least one of the Brits sees Dr. Gyaneshwar Rao, who now threatens to open a dispensary on the set.

The Mumbai actors sitting on the ground or on the *khaats* in the Indian pavilion are more resistant to the heat and dust, but their morale is low. The real problem is the waiting. Most of the actors are busy doing soaps on television and are accustomed to rushing from one shoot to another, constantly giving shots. Here, most of the time they are either waiting for their shots or are in deep background, unsure of whether or not they are really being seen by the cameras. Ashutosh has warned them that one of the cameras is fitted with a telescopic lens picking off their reactions to the cricketing action, but as the days pass, they have begun to doubt the truth of this claim.

To handle the terrible wait, two days back, they have begun playing cards in the pavilion between shots, but Ashutosh has clamped down and banned cards, further provoking their ire. Raghuveer Yadav promptly vents his resentment in verse and pens a lament titled: *"Yeh kaisi lagaan!"* ("What kind of tax is this?") The poem labels Ashutosh a sultan for banning the card games and generally bemoans the misery of the actors.

Production recognises that the poem is nothing more than a creative outlet for the privations the actors have been subjected to. Instead of taking offence, they produce hundreds of copies of the poem and circulate it with the daily call sheet. This morning, Raghuveer Yadav is reading out his diatribe to a large crowd of admirers including the victims of his ire, who are guffawing at every punchline.

By 8 a.m., the crowd is marched to the set and Apu and his team place them around the ground. It is Guran's turn to bowl. Rajesh Vivek has merged perfectly with Guran – rather it appears as if Guran was created with Rajesh Vivek in mind, at least, that is what the unit feels. Rajesh Vivek does exactly as he pleases. To hell with what Ashutosh has written, Rajesh Vivek is constantly trying to write his own script. Colleagues have warned Rajesh Vivek that he will not get a credit line as the writer of the film, but he is not deterred.

The crowd enjoys the Guran shots. His wildness is so much more interesting than the discipline of the rest.

The shooting makes no sense to the crowds. They are not watching a cricket match. What they are witnessing instead, are senseless swings of bat and ball, repeated randomly without apparent design or purpose, while they are keyed by Apu to manufacture various reactions. Their throats grow hoarse with senseless cheering, their facial muscles hurt with trying to put on the interested expression of spectators in the midst of a nail-biting match. They cannot understand the purposelessness of it all, the utter waste of time, money, resources, to shoot the same thing over and over again. They are bored, they are annoyed and it takes all of Apu's antics to keep them humoured.

The shooting makes no sense to the crowds

Apu and his assistants Reema, Kiran and Priya are incredibly effective. Apu follows two key rules. The first is that neither he nor his assistants sit even once throughout the shooting day. By punishing their bodies, they ensure that none of the actors can complain about physical discomfort. The second rule Apu follows, is that he makes the crowd laugh half a dozen times daily. The methods are infinite. Sometimes he says something funny in Kutchi, but more often he relies on the slapstick method of jumping around to motivate the crowd, tearing a hole in his T-shirt, and doing just about anything that is crazy and unpredictable. His muscular physique and the energy he exudes, all go towards commanding obedience from the crowds. It is a heroic effort and one that holds the cricket shoot together.

After lunch, the scheduled shot is that of Aamir being hit on the ear by Yardley's bouncer. It is important that the bowler hit only the ear, because shots of the bleeding ear have already been canned. But how on earth is the ball to strike Aamir's ear? Even a test level pace bowler would not be able to bowl with such precision and then Chris England playing Yardley is no bowler at all. The only solution is for someone at close quarters, but unseen by the camera, to throw the ball hard at Aamir's ear. Ordinarily, this would not be difficult, but the shot also requires Aamir to duck, trying to avoid the bouncer.

Takes 1 to 10: Apu positioned fifteen feet away throws the ball hard at Aamir who ducks. The ball sometimes hits Aamir's cheek, sometimes his head, sometimes his chest...but never his ear. Although the ball is not a real season ball, it is still fairly hard and thrown at great speed from close range, it leaves Aamir smarting all over. Apu announces to whoever will care to listen: "I have the privilege of hitting India's number one star as often as I like!" He is promptly taken off the task.

Apu tries his luck at hitting Aamir's ear

Takes 11 to 15: Ejaz, the assistant fight master, tries his hand at hitting Aamir's ear, again with no success.

Take 16: I have great pride in my aim and try my hand with a gentle throw, but Aamir's ducking motion is most distracting and I miss by an embarrassing mile as the unit twitters.

Takes 17 to 19: Aamir is now worried that the entire unit will queue up to try their hand. His ear has become a prize target like the balloons to be shot in a fair with an air gun. Try your hand and win a prize! His body is already bruised with the missed tries. Aamir insists that only Apu throw the ball.

Take 20: Apu finally connects with Aamir's ear. Aamir collapses in agony as the take is okayed.

A shutosh is distraught. It's now clear that the main problem with shooting a cricket match does not lie in the cricketing ability of the actors. The problem is much deeper.

The problem is playing a cricket match according to a script. How do you make bat and ball act according to a script? How do you ensure just the right kind of delivery visualised in the script, the right kind of shot from the bat, which must go at a particular speed to the right fielder, who will then field or misfield it, and then throw it with the right aim, to get a run out! All this while the camera is rolling.

The problem is not with any particular actor; it is with the requirements of shooting any sport. On the one hand, it must look completely spontaneous and natural, yet on the other hand it must be played in strict accordance with a script.

This result can only be achieved with repeated re-takes. One thousand two hundred shots of cricket played by the diktats of a script just cannot be canned in three weeks. In the shadow of this realisation the date crisis looms larger than ever.

8th March 2000

D espite going faster each day, Ashutosh has fallen a further five days behind schedule. It is absolutely clear that there is no way this lost time can be made up. Morale is now running desperately low in all quarters and a few kind souls are thinking up ways to raise depressed spirits. The Bhuj juniors sing old Hindi film songs during their long waits. Sanjay Dayma concocts an innovative way to get the British extras dressed on time - through a 'dressing competition'. Kiran and Priya have a gala time urging the men to get their pants on. Yet, not all the zany games can maintain the sagging morale.

The match is being shot with sync sound. Nakul has buried miles of sound cable all over the ground and connected it to concealed mikes. In addition, he has three boom mikes capturing the sound of the bowlers' run up, the batsmen's reactions and the exclamations of the fielders. Gulam, his boom man, moves with the players on the field like a dancer executing a complex ballet step. Nakul has been capturing some really incredible sound, yet now he is deeply worried. The heat and dust are making it impossible for his digital recorders to survive. Already, two of these have had to be sent to Mumbai for repairs. Now, only two are left.

Nakul asks Production for an air-conditioned vehicle so that he can cool his DAT recorders during lunch time and the tea breaks. The request is swiftly met. So, while the DATs chill in air-conditioned comfort, the sound recordist roasts in the heat.

9th March 2000

The Production camp is desperate about the collapsing schedule. For a long time, Aamir and Ashutosh have been feigning confidence in their ability to finish within schedule. Now, they must accept the inevitable, so that fresh dates may be booked with the actors and the rest of the unit. Production quietly prepares a fresh schedule that extends for five more weeks, shifting the last shooting date from 13th May 2000 to 18th June 2000. Before the schedule is made public, Production runs a copy by director of photography, Anil Mehta and sound recordist, Nakul Kamte.

Anil is in no mood for an extension of the schedule. As the cameraman, the physical demands on him are enormous. The scorching heat has burnt his skin black. His equipment continues to suffer. The zoom lenses of the camera are so full of the fine dust of the desert, that Nakul now hears a grinding sound on his headphones when the zoom lenses are used. More than the physical exhaustion, Anil is mentally drained. Shooting day after day without an opportunity for rest or reflection is eating into his creative reserves. Perhaps what is most trying for Anil is far more personal. Anil and wife Jenny have wound up their home in Mumbai and shifted to Bangalore to enjoy a more settled life. Before they can settle into their new home, he is off again, spending half a year away shooting a film. Ironically, *Lagaan* initially excited Anil because of its single schedule shoot. Now, the single schedule has turned into a nightmare.

Anil reacts strongly to the idea of extending the shoot. He urges Ashutosh not to shoot beyond the last scheduled date of 13th May and to shoot the rest of the film six months later, after the monsoon. Anil is convinced that unless this is done, the mental fatigue of the unit will affect the quality of the shoot. For good measure, Anil informs Ashutosh and Production that he will not be available beyond the last scheduled date of 13th May 2000.

Ashutosh is appalled at the prospect of Anil leaving the film and informs Aamir about Anil's intent. Anil leaving the film would greatly damage the creative integrity of *Lagaan*. Aamir knows this and yet has respect for the personal and professional crisis Anil faces. Aamir has little idea how he can persuade Anil Mehta and has even lesser time to figure it out. Even as he tells Reena and Ashutosh, "Let's discuss the schedule extension at the meeting of departmental heads this evening," he adjusts his headgear and walks on to the cricket field for his shot.

Anil Mehta on the crane

The shoot starts with Bhuvan (Aamir) bowling to Captain Russell. A couple of shots are taken swiftly. Then, in the third shot of the day, Aamir wobbles just a bit on the follow through. The shot is okayed, but Aamir hobbles off the pitch. His face is calm, but one foot leaves a bloody mark as he walks off. A chair is rushed to him. He sits and turns the foot up. The upper portion of the sole of his foot is a raw mass. A piece of skin, roughly two inches in diameter has come off, a result of extensive barefoot movement and of the thorns hidden in the sandy Kutch soil.

It is a horrible sight. More frightening is the thought of what this will mean for the shoot. Aamir is strangely calm. Nicole Demers, the Canadian make-up artist, has a piece of medicated false skin in her kit. After cleaning the wound with an antiseptic, the false skin is affixed and Aamir continues to shoot without displaying any outward signs of pain. The shoot continues while the wound is dressed. The whole process is over in less than half an hour.

The unit accepts Aamir's fortitude as a matter of course. Everyone will be taxed for *Lagaan* to be shot!

At the end of the day's shoot, before the meeting of the department heads, Aamir has an impromptu conclave with Ashutosh and Reena. "Ashu we simply have to complete the shoot in one go. If we break the schedule now, the film will never be completed. Trust my judgment on this and back me in the meeting."

"But what if Anil refuses to stay on," an anxious Ashutosh asks.

There is a pause before Aamir reluctantly replies, "If we cannot persuade Anil to continue, then we should complete the film without him."

Ashutosh urges an impassive Aamir, "Please do something that can make Anil change his mind."

Ashutosh is terrified at the prospect of shooting the film without Anil Mehta, but he knows that *Lagaan* is now in deep trouble and no one is as well equipped as Aamir to handle this situation.

After pack-up, the rest of the unit has returned to Bhuj city and rest. On the centre of the cricket ground, Aamir, Ashutosh, Reena, Rao, Nakul and Anil are all alone. Everyone can smell the crisis. Without waiting for Anil to play his hand, Aamir proceeds to address him. Even as he does so, Ashutosh freezes. Will Aamir directly tell Anil that he will go ahead with or without him?

Aamir does exactly the opposite.

"Anil, this film will not be made without you."

Anil is taken aback.

Aamir continues, "For emotional reasons, if you feel that you cannot continue in the film without the schedule being broken, then we will break the schedule. But remember one thing. If we break the schedule now, it is my overwhelming feeling that we will never be able to complete the film."

Aamir then explains how the financiers and prospective distributors will lose confidence in the project if the schedule is broken. He then puts the ball in Anil's court.

"Anil, it's up to you. Do we break the schedule or do we pull it through. I think it's a case of now or never."

Anil is in a cleft stick. He must make a tough decision and Aamir is not going to make it easy for him.

There is an interminable silence. Ashutosh and Aamir look at each other and at Anil anxiously. An emotional Anil throws in the towel. "I won't leave *Lagaan*."

Aamir and Ashutosh heave a sigh of relief. A major creative crisis has been averted - by a hair's breadth!

12th March 2000

For the first time since the shoot started, the unit works on a Sunday, to make up for lost time. At night after pack-up, the production office on the fifth floor of Sahajanand Towers is buzzing with activity. Aamir has called for a meeting on the terrace with the entire Indian cast. The actors enter gingerly. They know that something explosive is afoot. Aamir places all his cards on the table.

"We are desperately behind schedule. There is no possibility of completing the film by 13th May as planned. We need another five weeks of dates from all of you."

The actors are aghast. Doing *Lagaan* has been a gamble for most. Television is their bread and butter and in order to do *Lagaan*, they have all chosen to give up a very large amount of work. In the TV industry, out of sight is often out of mind. Professionally, *Lagaan* could be a poison pill – who can predict what its fate at the box office will be.

At a personal level, the prolonged absence from home is getting to be trying. Vallabh Vyas, playing Ishwarkaka, has not been around when his eleven-month-old daughter first said "papa" – in itself a small thing, but it happens just once.

Daya Shankar Pandey, playing Goli, faces a serious problem. His wife is having a difficult pregnancy and has been advised complete bed rest.

The boy actor Tipu, will probably be unable to appear for his final examinations because of the delayed schedule and his mother is desperately trying to persuade the school authorities to promote him nevertheless.

Suhasini Mulay, playing Mai, was to have joined a family reunion in Canada, which is now jeopardised by the change in dates.

These and a hundred other thoughts flash through the minds of the actors, as they troop out of the meeting. They cannot let Aamir or *Lagaan* down. Yet, not in their wildest dreams had they bargained for such a prolonged shoot.

The meeting with the British actors is held immediately after the meeting with the Mumbai team. The Brits have been expecting this. They are understanding and sensitive to the situation and immediately agree. The extension of their contracts must however be confirmed by their agents, with whom they have had no contact since leaving England. Reena now has the herculean task of communicating with each of these agents and completing the paperwork from Bhuj, where the telecom network is at best primitive.

14th March 2000

Aamir's birthday on set

Yet another birthday is celebrated on set. This time it is Aamir's. Because of the trying conditions, even the smallest reasons to celebrate are not being relinquished. Wedding anniversaries are being celebrated even in the absence of the spouse! Production has given standing instructions to a hotel in Gandhidham to deliver a cake to the set every day.

Sometimes it appears as if we are all growing old in Kutch. The sunburn caused by the relentless desert heat makes everyone look at least five years older. The birthday celebrations emphasise this.

15th March 2000

The Mumbai unit smiles a little less when they see each other. The smiles in Ashutosh's direction are drying up completely. The director can feel a hundred accusing eyes boring into him, a hundred eyes saying we have a life other than *Lagaan*. In the name of God, when are you really going to finish?

Ashutosh can feel the resentment building up. At times, he overhears snide remarks aimed at him. Yet, he must not let the unit's morale affect his own. Through all the travails of the shoot, he must protect his creative vision.

Barring the actors, people's appearances are falling apart. At the start of the shoot, the unit would come to work in bright, well-ironed clothes. Now, despite the generous laundry allowance paid by Production, clothes are crumpled, hair is overgrown, beards are growing wild and unkempt.

The scorching heat has tanned faces black. Earlier in the shoot, Amir and Raj Zutshi had to be stained brown to look like villagers. Now, the sun has done its work and their dark tanned bodies need no further staining.

The tension has taken a toll on everyone. Ashutosh had shaved his head in the first month of the shoot. The hair never quite grew back and it is evident that the bald will be the most visible scar that *Lagaan* will leave him with.

The Bhuj actors after the initial enthusiasm are holding on through sheer grit. They have taken leave from their jobs or holidays from school and college based on the original schedule. Now, the schedule looks like it is stretching interminably. More important, with the initial thrill exhausted, it has become routine 'work' in every sense of the term.

The shoot has acquired a monotony that will make the most diehard cricket fan hate cricket. Today is no exception. Bats have been swung in the air, balls have been thrown at no apparent target...and the list of one thousand two hundred shots shrinks at an imperceptible rate.

J ust before lunch, Ashutosh rises from his chair and a sharp spasm of pain shoots through his back. It is a pain he has never felt before and it frightens him. He has worked without respite for the past fifteen months and has survived essentially on nervous energy. Now, the body is hitting back. Ashutosh needs to see a doctor immediately. While the rest of the unit has lunch, Ashutosh and I leave for Bhuj.

Dr. Patel examines Ashutosh carefully before pronouncing his grim judgment. "We'll confirm it with an X- Ray, but I am quite sure that you have a slipped disc. You will need to take complete bed rest for at least three weeks."

I am aghast, but Ashutosh is curiously calm, almost relieved as he hears this. I watch with increasing consternation. Has Ashutosh understood what the doctor has said? Is he relieved at the prospect of bed rest? Will he break the schedule and stop the shoot? Has he simply lost it? There is no way to know and Ashutosh's reactions make no sense to me.

X-ray done, Ashutosh heads back for the set. I rush to Sahajanand to send the news to set via the walky-talky and then hurry back to the set in another vehicle. Just outside Bhuj, I notice that Ashutosh's car has stopped. I wonder whether there is an emergency. It is only when I pull up next to Ashutosh's car that I realise what is happening.

On the highway leading to the set, is an old woman with withered stumps in place of legs slithering along the ground. Everyday, the unit sees her making a journey back and forth. Who is she? Why is she on the highway, miles away from habitation? How does she survive? Where is she headed? These questions have probably passed through a hundred minds daily, yet no one has had the courage to stop and ask. Sometimes, answers are just too painful. Yet, on this terrible day, even as the fate of *Lagaan* hangs in balance, Ashutosh has stopped his car to feed the disabled woman.

I wait silently for Ashutosh to finish and then join him in his vehicle. As the car gently moves forward, I hesitantly ask, "Ashu, what will you do now?"

Ashutosh answers without batting an eyelid: "I'll direct the shoot from a portable bed."

Within an hour, the carpenters on set put the bed together. Ashutosh lies down on the hard wooden surface. The video assist monitor that enables him to see the shot is tilted down as in a hospital room. Then, mike in hand, the director continues to shoot *Lagaan*.

17ᵗʰ March 2000

Ashutosh continues shooting on his back. Apu makes unkind references to Ashutosh's 'hotel' and even announces it as such on the mike. Any instructions by Ashutosh are called 'room service'. But Ashutosh has taken it all in his stride. Whatever must be absorbed to make *Lagaan* shall be absorbed.

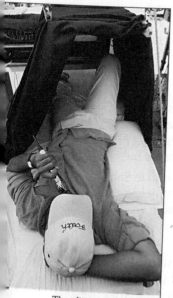

The director continues to shoot from a bed

Today should be better than others. His buddy Amin Hajee, playing the mute Bagha, is before the camera. Ashutosh has been banking on canning Bagha's shots at express speed. Bagha is supposed to connect with the ball with a massive heave, sending it over the ropes for a six. Bagha fancies himself as a cricketer and has been waiting anxiously for this moment.

Take 1: Bagha pumps himself for the shot. The veins on his forehead are showing. Apu stationed ten feet away from him throws the ball towards Bagha's bat. Bagha shrieks loud enough to give the unit goose-flesh and at the same time there is an almighty heave. The ball bounces past him mockingly. Bagha laughs at himself — a useful quality in this situation. "It was thrown too fast," he complains.

Take 2: The ball is thrown a little slower and almost on to the bat. Bagha shrieks even louder, but the bat and ball do not meet.

Takes 3 to 17: The ball is almost lobbed up and yet again there is the same result: no contact between bat and ball. It is hardly credible that a full-grown man with all his faculties intact cannot connect with a ball practically lobbed on to his bat. Bagha so badly wants to do well – both as an actor as also for his bosom pal Ashutosh, but somehow, the pressure of the rolling cameras, the need to be hundred per cent in terms of his expressions and shriek, the roar of the crowds and the hand of heaven have contrived against him today.

Take 18: Bagha who has been pumping himself for the shriek, yells "Aaargh!" and the bat slips from his hand as he falls to the ground. The massive striker of the ball is himself stricken. The constant rush of blood to the head from the shriek has taken its toll and he is almost unconscious. Were it not for his genuine distress it would have been funny.

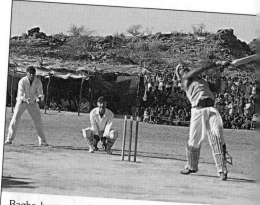
Bagha heaves and shrieks but just cannot connect

Take 19: There is an interval of fifteen minutes for Bagha to recover. Bagha wishes he never knew Ashutosh Gowariker. Ashutosh also wishes he never knew Amin Hajee. From his hard wooden bed, he is now sledging his buddy with unprintables. If only those could work, but alas!

Take 23: The law of probability finally justifies its existence. Partly aided by an impeccable throw right on to the bat, Bagha finally connects with the ball and it sails over the boundary ropes. A genuine six! Ashutosh heaves a sigh of relief.

If it takes 2 hours for 1 shot, how long will it take for the rest of his 1,200 shots? The schoolboy maths problem entrenches itself in Ashutosh's head. Again and again and again he thanks god for giving him the good sense to restrict the match to one inning. The very *thought* of having to get these shots for two separate innings is depressing.

I n the afternoon a strange smell envelopes the set. The stink gets stronger. Investigation reveals that the septic tank has overflowed and the sewage has seeped up above the ground level. The Kutch soil is imporous and the water has not seeped below as it should in a septic tank. With the shoot proceeding endlessly and a massive unit using the toilet facilities, the shit has hit the ceiling both metaphorically and literally! A fresh tank is urgently built for the balance portion of the shoot.

19th March 2000

Notwithstanding the wide differences in culture and background within the multi-national unit, adversity has brought understanding, it has brought everyone closer. At least four separate cultures are rubbing shoulders: forty British actors; a half westernised three hundred strong unit from Mumbai; sixty-odd actors from the tiny town of Bhuj; a few thousand Kutchi villagers.

A couple of British actors have a jaundiced view of most things. Jeremy Child playing Major Cotton tells me that his most enduring memory of India will be the pigeon shit outside his flat at Sahajanand Towers! The issue though is not one of nationality. Child is one of a handful of unit members, both British and Indian, who are unhappy with what they are doing. Most *Lagaanites* believe this is a huge film that requires effort, dedication and sacrifice. In a hundred large and small ways they are creating and building the spirit of *Lagaan*.

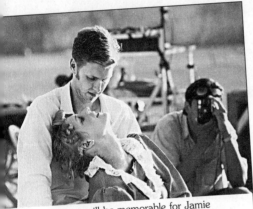

Lagaan will be memorable for Jamie and Katkin

One such British effort is reaching its climax today. The finals of the table tennis tournament organised by Barry Hart, one of the British cricketer-actors, are being played. The tournament, played over two weeks has comprised sixteen doubles teams – one Indian and one British player in each. Every night after shoot, dozens of unit members have got together in the dining area to watch the game and cheer the players. Pairing the British with the Indians has built a lot of camaraderie. Sometimes, the camaraderie is more than desired as Rachel/Elizabeth, who was paired with Rajesh Vivek/Guran, discovers in the post-match smooch from her partner.

The finals are between the Aditya Lakhia – Chris England combination on the one hand and Aamir and Charlotte on the other hand. Aditya has played table tennis for the state of Gujarat and his ability tilts the scales against the Aamir-Charlotte combination. Handsome prizes have been announced for the winners – not by Production, but by some British actors. The entire table tennis tournament has been a British baby, nurtured to foster greater team spirit in the *Lagaan* unit!

Meanwhile, another game is underway, this one uniquely Indian. Rajendra Gupta aka *mukhiya* has infected the actors with his enthusiasm for playing cards. Every night at eight sharp, the actors assemble in either Gupta's room or Pradeep Rawat's room and start a gambling session which continues late into the night. Aamir loves gambling and even the otherwise austere Ashutosh joins in occasionally. A few Brits also try their hand.

Playing cards is really an excuse for getting together and enjoying themselves. The gambling involves stakes, but these are not taken seriously. There is an unwritten rule that players are not supposed to win and retire. A victor is expected to gamble more recklessly and lose his winnings.

The players have named this activity the LPCC: the **L**agaan **P**laying **C**ards **C**lub. Membership and loyalty are taken surprisingly seriously. Players are expected to turn up on time and not absent themselves from duty.

Reena, 'the matron' turns a blind eye to an activity she otherwise dislikes. "At least they are keeping out of trouble," she says.

20ᵗʰ March 2000

The heat is unbearable and at pack-up there is a rush to get home. As the actors head for their buses, a now somewhat recovered Ashutosh stands in their path with the rain machine hoses in his hand. He signals, the pumps are turned on and the spray begins. It is Holi and shoot or no shoot, it must be celebrated. The Brits have heard about Holi and are dying to experience it. They plunge in with glee. There is a mud bath

Holi revelry: Rachel and Paul with Ashutosh

of sorts. Unit members are dunked into the water tanks turn by turn. There is wild laughter, shouting and screaming.

Various couples are identified by who is playing Holi with whom. The Apu-Rachel pair is noticed, as is the romance between Paul Blackthorne and a female crew member.

The less romantic majority have fun too, forgetting for a moment that it is nearly three months since they left home and loved ones to make a film. It is a release of a lot of pent-up emotion. Clearly some very deep thinking led our ancestors to devise this festival. Rarely must Holi have played such a therapeutic role in shooting a film!

24ᵗʰ March 2000

A shutosh comes to the set lying on the rear seat of his jeep, shifts to the set bed and shoots all day on his back as he has for the past ten days. As the shots reduce in number, the condition of his back seems to improve. He stands up more often and the smile has returned to his face.

Ashutosh's wife Sunni and their kids are in Bhuj. The actors and unit members too have been calling in family and the trains and planes to Bhuj are full of *Lagaanites*. Wags in the unit ask Production to start a *Lagaan* Express and solve the train booking problem once and for all.

The last British actors' contracts have come through the previous evening. Provided the additional weeks are adequate, actors' dates are no longer an issue.

Reena's anxiety, however, has moved beyond the date crisis. A large chunk of the film will be shot at the height of the desert summer, in the months of May and June. The exhaustion of the unit could become evident on screen. Already, the heat is unbearable and to hold the morale of the unit together, Reena and Rao have taken to standing out in the open without any umbrella to shield them or chair to sit on. Punishing their bodies is a form of *tapasya*, a self-inflicted punishment, which the unit members respect.

The physical demands of the film pale before the financial crisis. With every shooting day, the cost of the film is going up by at least a million rupees. Reena must maintain this gigantic unit with nearly two thousand junior artists and a contingent of over three hundred and fifty from Mumbai, day after day without the end being in sight. In every way, the film seems to her to have become a runaway horse, with Production being dragged in its trail.

Lagaan is in grave danger of being financially unviable. The budget has now crossed two hundred million rupees. When Aamir last asked Reena for the estimated total cost, she has told him that now she does not even know how much over two hundred million it will come to – this after having started work on the project with an initial budget of 80 million rupees! The producer couple decides that they will now try not to think of the budget. Perhaps that is the only way to maintain sanity and morale.

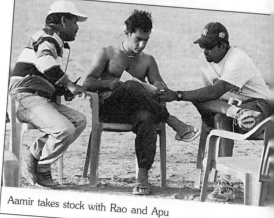
Aamir takes stock with Rao and Apu

Their anxiety is heightened by the fact that no one has the slightest idea as to whether the market will accept 'the weird story about villagers in the British Raj'. Yet they must keep the flow of money going. They must hold the shoot together without allowing their anxiety to affect the other unit members. Aamir and Reena's morale is sustained in no small measure by the unquestioning support of the film's financier, Jhamu Sughand, perhaps the most unrecognised contributor to the *Lagaan* story. Not once has Jhamu raised an eyebrow or expressed concern about the escalating schedule and budget. He has believed in *Lagaan* as much as have the producer and the director.

25th March 2000

The heat, dust and privations have only made the unit more determined. The Brits are more and more Indianised by the day. Every evening they can be seen roaming through the Bhuj market with their Indian buddies. Some have even befriended the local shopkeepers. Paul is particularly famous on account of his obsession for taking photographs of cattle and kids. He has absorbed the Indian passion for feeding cows and carries bananas with him to feed them.

The Brits are great travellers and most of them know more about Kutch than the Mumbai actors ever will. Paul, despite being the second male lead in the film is more than happy to use the public transport and Sunday sees him headed to different parts of Kutch with his camera and a

Paul bonds with Kutch

small bag of essentials.

John Rowe playing Colonel Boyer, has researched the life of John Grey, an English clergyman-poet who was stationed in Kutch in the early nineteenth century. Rowe visits the Protestant cemetery in Bhuj to visit Grey's grave, discovers it is locked and age notwithstanding, climbs over the wall to get in and photograph the grave. Rowe seems to have inherited the admirable spirit of enquiry and adventure his ancestors possessed. He has also been a pillar of support through the trying shoot.

A s the shoot stretches endlessly, relations of the unit members with near and dear are strained to breaking point. The unit has been away from home for nearly three months. For those in Production and the art department who have been in Bhuj since the pre-production period, their exile has exceeded six months. Wives wonder what their husbands are up to, children miss one parent and lovers feel neglected.

Already, while the unit has been in Bhuj, Shobha from the hair department has lost her husband in Goa due to heart failure, the son-in-law of Syed Raju from the wardrobe department has been stabbed in Bihar, Nakul's wife has been suffering from emphesyma, a serious lung ailment and Raja from the crowd handlers was unable to remain present when his father passed away in Mumbai. My wife, Svati, is barely on talking terms with me as she heroically handles two young children and a hectic job single-handedly. All this plays on our minds even as we suffer under the scorching sun. It almost feels as if we are on the frontline of a war zone and hence no personal tragedy can be more important than the fight at hand. Without winning the war we cannot return.

Anil Mehta with his penchant for philosophising, calls this a process of creative destruction. As the film is being created, it demands human suffering as its fodder.

26th March 2000

The British cricketers in England have been demanding a cricket match, a real one against the Indians. The logic is simple. The script forces the Brits to lose and they know there isn't a thing they can do about it. This has injured their vanity. Now they want revenge – off screen. For many days there has been talk of the 'grudge' match.

Production has repeatedly postponed the 'grudge' match because of the anxiety of exposing so many of the actors to still more heat and exhaustion. With the cricket stint due to end, no one can now keep the cricketers away from their moment of glory. The match is scheduled for today. We are all surprised at just how much this match means to the Brits.

It seems utterly mad. After six weeks of being roasted on the cricket field, instead of resting, half the unit heads back for some more cricket - this time for real. Aamir, competitive as ever has put together the best possible team, consisting of the lightmen, some from the art department, some technicians and his star weapon, Apu. The British team on account of sickness and casualties has only ten players, so the Indians loan them Aditya Lakhia aka Kachra, to loud shouts of "traitor, traitor" from the Indian camp. The rest of the unit comes to cheer.

When the captains, Aamir and Chris England go out for the toss, the atmosphere is electric. It could well be England versus India. There are cheerleaders, there is a running commentary, there is a giant scoreboard, there is a cameraman (me) filming the event and there is some serious competition...or at least that is what the Indians think.

The game takes all day, but the competition is a non-starter. The Brits are regular club players, some have even played cricket at the county level, whereas the Indians are novices at best. The British win the game without being seriously pushed. The Indians give the winning team a standing ovation. A day of rest 'wasted' in playing a 'grudge' match has brought everyone closer.

27th March 2000

The last shot with the British actors on the cricket field is canned. The balance cricket shots where the British actors do not feature have been left for June. The unit shudders at the idea of coming back to this furnace in June, but are relieved at the thought that their ordeal is over, if only for the moment.

A function is held to distribute the prizes for the 'grudge' match. Apu has prepared wonderful trophies for each of the participants and in particular for the winning British team. They are touched by the gesture.

In the second part of the function, Aamir and Ashutosh on behalf of the unit felicitate the spot boys for their tireless work. In a country where those who perform menial physical tasks are looked down upon, this is an important moment. Apu has been the guiding spirit behind this initiative. Over the past fortnight, he has asked all those who have played in the cricket match to contribute to the spot boys' fund. Apu hands them the envelopes, while Aamir and then Ashutosh embrace each of them.

Felicitating the spot boys

The spot boys are moved by the gesture. It is a recognition of the services of the least paid section of film workers who do the largest amount of menial work. Serving water and tea, hefting around heavy equipment and doing hundreds of jobs that keep a unit going in the terrible heat of the cricket ground has been gruelling. At least on the sets of *Lagaan*, nobody can say it was a thankless job.

The unit breaks out into its war cry: "*Re bhaiyya chhoote lagaan!*" and the hills resound with the echo. Sharad, from the make-up department is carried away and unexpectedly proclaims, "*Inquilab zindabad!*" ("Long live the revolution!") There are a few surprised smiles all around at Sharad's outburst. But something about what we are striving for inspired it.

E motionally, star and spot boy, technician and actor, Kutchi and Mumbaiwalla, Indian and Brit have all come together in the blazing heat of the Kutch desert. *Lagaan* has become a melting pot. A melting pot for different cultures, for people coming from diametrically opposite parts of the world, literally and metaphorically.

For the entire unit, *Lagaan* has ceased to be a film, or rather, that we are shooting a film has become incidental or secondary to our life experiences. Somewhere, a sense of wonder has been awakened, a sense of pride in doing the impossible has been aroused.

Why does a man climb a mountain? Not just to get to the top, but to experience the challenges of the climb. As the shoot enters its fourth month, what is happening off screen has become larger than life, more so than what is happening on it. Solidarity and struggle have made everyone a few inches taller. We are not just making a film together; we are climbing a tall, steep mountain called *Lagaan*.

A set becomes a temple

Memories of a memorable wedding

Jo panchhi gaayengey, naye din aayengey
Ujaale muskura dengey andheron par
Prem ki barkha mein bheegay bheegay tan man...
(The song birds will sing
Of the new days that are to come
Light shall smile at darkness
Love's rain will drench hearts and bodies)
— Song from LAGAAN

"I believe in only one God by whatever name you call
it and that God was there in the temple."
KATKIN
British actress, about her marriage in the Champaner temple

12

A set becomes a temple

29ᵗʰ March 2000

The first sight of Mandavi town is dramatic. Nothing prepares you for this. A sharp turn of the road, then on to a narrow bridge and suddenly one is surrounded by the sea. One savours the moment. The sea. One savours the word. Vast, infinite, cooling. The sea. Something the unit from the island city of Mumbai has always taken for granted, but after nearly three months of desert, the sight of the Arabian Sea is stirring.

The driver rattles on along the narrow roads oblivious to the emotions of his passengers. He passes the shipyard where wooden dhows are being built, a reminder of a lost world. Then, a brief glimpse of modern windmills along the beach generating electricity, a circuitous passage along the winding walls of what was once a fortress and before we know it, the bus is out of Mandavi town.

Instantly, the landscape turns bleak, arid, more typical of Kutch. Everybody's heart sinks as the bus drives on.

The unit has shifted from the cricket ground to shoot at the seaside town of Mandavi for the next three weeks. The change in the shooting location from the blistering cricket ground to coastal Mandavi had raised hopes of better climes. Now, however, the *Lagaan* unit is convinced that they are in for another desert siege.

Six kilometres out of Mandavi town, the bus takes a sharp left turn onto a narrow and bumpy road, revealing a strange, almost eerie sight. On both sides of the road, the land is barrren, sandy and saline, bleached white; yet a kilometre up ahead are thousands and thousands of trees, mostly dead. So intimidatingly barren is the soil, that no one can believe that trees could ever have grown here. Yet they exist – headless stumps, shrivelled remains, bearing testimony of what must once have been a lush green plantation.

The bus approaches a massive iron gate. An ancient gatekeeper emerges, wizened with age, possessing a single eye and in some sad way, a relic from other times. The gate is opened and the bus drives through to a narrower gate, which reveals a well-maintained walk with a lush green, perfectly trimmed hedge...one more turn and you see it — the Vijay Vilas palace, a massive yet beautiful structure, the summer resort of the rulers of Kutch. It is now to serve as the British cantonment in *Lagaan*, residence of Captain Russell, oppressor of Champaner.

Beyond the palace is a narrow sandy path leading to the beach and the Arabian Sea. With access to this section barred by the Maharao's six hundred hectare plot, the beach is empty, except the last flock of flamingoes yet to return to Siberia. The waters are cool, clean, transparent and inviting and for a moment, it is painful to remember that there is work to do and a film to be shot. The contrast between the arid semi-desert around Champaner and the environs of the Vijay Vilas palace couldn't be more stark.

Anil Mehta hangs precariously to catch a lady in love

The palace is controlled by the eldest son of the last ruler of Kutch, His Highness Maharao Pragmulji III, Sawai Bahadur of Kutch. Thus doth he write his name and thus doth he perceive himself. The Mumbai actors and even the Brits are impressed by the mention of 'royalty', but the Kutchis in the unit refuse to even call him Maharao, saying to the Mumbaiwallas, "He may be your king, he certainly isn't ours."

The Maharao had visited Champaner during the shoot at the cricket ground and memories of his visit are still fresh, especially for me. Aamir had sent me to the Maharao's palace in Bhuj with a number of vehicles, to bring him and his guests to the set. What happened next was straight out of another epoch.

The Maharao's right-hand man, Dilipbhai, refuses the use of the vehicles. "The Maharao cannot travel in another's car," he explains in a shocked whisper. Evidently, this has been a breach of protocol. I apologise and we proceed.

The Maharao's travelling companions are an eclectic mix – a former inspector general of police, a surgeon's daughter, Dilipbhai, his sister, wife and daughter Rudrani and of course the Maharani. The cars stop at the Bheed Naka, a dirty and dusty outpost of Bhuj.

Dilipbhai conspiratorially informs me, "We are waiting for the convoy. The Maharao cannot proceed without a convoy."

The Maharao awaits his 'convoy' for ten minutes. It arrives. Two cars belonging to a local ice cream manufacturer. One of the cars is laden with ice cream which will be served on the set. The 'convoy' is now complete and a 'fleet' of six cars leaves for Champaner.

The road to Champaner passes through Kunnaria village where once again the Maharao's car stops. The 'convoy' grinds to a halt. I am intrigued. The set is at least a couple of kilometres away. The Maharao emerges from his car with Dilipbhai and heads for the village temple. The only 'subjects' who follow are a group of curious children. Dilipbhai educates me with a knowing whisper, "Maharao *saab* will listen to *firyads* (petitions) in the village."

Advance word of the visit has probably been sent, for a little girl emerges with a clay pot and performs a small *aarti* (ceremonial welcome). The Maharao and his guests seat themselves on a few chairs in the village temple. Dilipbhai tells the only adult available, to call the village people to meet the Maharao who has come to hear their difficulties. Five minutes later, a couple of adults join the makeshift 'durbar'. Dilipbhai urges them to tell the Rao Bawa as the Maharao is known in public, their *takleef*, their difficulties.

The villagers are silent. After much prodding by the gentle Dilipbhai, half the adults present, which is to say one villager says, "It hasn't rained for the past two years."

The Maharao looks skyward, despairing at the futility of the petition. Five minutes into the process and the Maharao gives up. There is just so much he can do for his 'subjects'! The 'convoy' proceeds to the set.

The journey from Kunnaria to the set at Champaner takes the Maharao into much friendlier environs. Aamir welcomes him with heartfelt warmth and introduces the royal couple to all the actors. Many are delighted at the opportunity to meet 'royalty' and the Maharao signs several autographs with his full name and title: His Highness Maharao Pragmulji III, Sawai Bahadur of Kutch. The actors love the sound of the name and the feeling that they are mixing with blue blood. The Maharao appears pleased. Finally, royalty gets the recognition it deserves!

30ᵗʰ March 2000

The shift to Mandavi has a special significance for me. I am relieved of my duties in the production department, so that I may direct a film, the yet to be titled, making of *Lagaan*, a task I had hitherto dabbled in, alongside my production duties. I am excited at the opportunity to direct, but know that with over half the shoot behind us, reconstructing the story on film will not be easy.

Coming to Mandavi to shoot the cantonment scenes does wonders for both body and spirit. The change in the environment gives the entire unit a second wind. Ashutosh's back miraculously recovers. Appearances improve – hair is cut, clothes are ironed and the unit members make a quick journey back to civilisation.

Parenting on set: Aamir with son Junaid and daughter Ira

The relief from the searing heat of the cricket field and its accompanying tensions creates a different frame of mind. We are like an army during a ceasefire. We have the mental space to remember that we have a life other than *Lagaan*; that we have other needs and others have need of us; that a world exists back home, wherever that home might be. The men remember their wives. Wives miss their husbands. Fathers think of their children. In some cases, they are forced to by circumstance.

Ashutosh's children, Vishwang and Konark, are in Kutch along with his wife Sunni. Aamir and Reena's children, Junaid and Ira, too are camping in Bhuj. Now, my wife Svati calls to say that she must go abroad for a week for some work and the only place she can leave the children is…yes, Bhuj!

The idea of *meeting* the kids is wonderful, but the idea of *working* with my boisterous four-year-old in tow is terrifying. I have barely begun my innings as director and here I am being asked to parent on the side. One part of me does not want to accept that there is a life other than the task at hand. Another part recognises that this is the very least I can do by way of fulfilling long-neglected responsibilities towards my family. Reconciling the two parts is traumatic.

My situation and the experiences of hundreds of colleagues around compel me to examine the realities of film making. It just does not allow for a 'normal' life. Either one is out of work and therefore on edge or one is doing so much work that one lives life on the edge. One is a war of the mind and the other a war of the mind and body. Both are war zones and only the hardiest warriors survive. It is no coincidence that so many film marriages end on the rocks.

This, however, never stands in the way of film romances for which the atmosphere of Mandavi is most conducive. There are peacocks in the bushes cavorting with peahens. The night shoots have started and as Elizabeth twirls around to Rahman's music sighing, "I am in love," it would be a wonder if romance did not bloom. Rachel and Apu exchange 'secret' notes, Paul finds an Indian girlfriend. The Indian couples are more discreet or hypocritical, depending on how one views it.

For the first time since the shoot began, the Kutch villagers are not with us, neither are the Mumbai actors, barring Lakha. The rest of the actors have returned home to Mumbai for much needed rest and perhaps to finish assignments of desperate producers.

The unit has shrunk dramatically and the bulk of the shoot is with just two actors: Paul playing Captain Russell and Rachel playing Elizabeth. Ashutosh's look is transformed. The tense expression of the cricket ground has been replaced by his characteristic assurance. To me this underlines the mammoth effort he has poured into directing hundreds and even thousands of actors over the past three months. It suddenly strikes me that the man has been directing the shoot without a break since the sixth day of January!

The smaller unit also provides relief to the beleaguered production team. The arrangements for food and transport are a little more manageable and back at Sahajanand Towers the 'hotel' is running at less than full occupancy. Rao and Reena are just a wee bit less tense and there is hope that Reena will smile again.

R ahman has arrived by the morning flight and promptly fallen asleep. He must rest so that he may work at night. That is how his body clock is tuned. Fortunately, his body clock gears well with Ashutosh's needs. Ashutosh and Rahman must work through the night to finalise the music for the ballroom dance. A lot of the groundwork is complete, but Ashutosh must have the finalised soundtrack by the morning,to shoot the ballroom dance the next day.

Rahman is a one-man orchestra. His keyboard is a violin, a flute, a lute…you name it and he performs like a virtuoso. By the morning, the miracle has occurred. A fifty instrument orchestral piece is composed and the genius is fast asleep.

31st March 2000

A. R. Rahman in Bhuj with Ashutosh, Aamir and Vijay Singh of Sony Music

There is good news from Mumbai. Daya Shankar Pandey aka Goli's wife delivers a baby boy, who will be named Jayaditya. Serious complications had arisen during pregnancy and the baby who is delivered by caesarian section spends the first twenty-four hours in the intensive care unit. Fortunately, the baby's health stabilises and the entire unit shares the joy of the new arrival.

8th April 2000

Aamir has a short break in his shoot and has returned to Mumbai. Most of the scenes are between the Brits and the dialogues are all in English. It almost seems like we are making an English film. The smaller number of actors enables Ashutosh to step up the pace and the unit gains a couple of days in the schedule. Ashutosh's look changes almost by the day and the morale of the unit rises like a buoy released in deep waters. There are strong rumours that yes, some day the shoot will end and everyone will go back home, though not everyone believes them.

The British cricketers and extras have been leaving through the week. Today, the last of them finish their shoot and tomorrow they shall leave. We will miss them all. Howard Lee, an accomplished juggler entertaining kids in Bhuj, Neil Patrick, always spotted on the hill at the cricket ground watching the sunrise, Jon House with his guitar, the reserved Alex Shirtcliffe, the jovial Simon Holmes, Barry Hart with his deceptively effective offspin bowling, my table tennis partner Ray Eaves…each leaves his memories. They have stayed on for over twice the period they were originally contracted for. They have suffered sunstroke and dehydration, upset bellies and hospitalisation and yet, there is a smile on the faces of most. It is sad that they have seen little of India that is not dry, dusty and physically exacting, but perhaps, in part, that is why their *Lagaan* experience has been so intense.

Two of the British extras, Jamie and Katkin, are planning to stay on

Goodbye – posing with the Brits after the ballroom dance

along with Jamie's sister Charlotte. Jamie and Katkin are engaged and plan to be married in England after their return. For the past two weeks they have been toying with the idea of a small romantic marriage ceremony in a temple, maybe in Pushkar, Rajasthan. Aamir has, however, persuaded them to get married in Kutch, in the Champaner village temple. "What's the point in getting married all alone? Your marriage belongs to all of us," he has urged.

13th April 2000

The Mumbai actors return to Kutch looking rejuvenated. Ranjeet from Production suggestively asks a few how it felt to end prolonged celibacy and receives a satisfied sigh as answer.

Strangely or perhaps not entirely strangely, many of the actors complain that they were utterly restless during their two weeks in Mumbai and were dying to get back to Kutch, though they did not dare mention this to their families. Despite all the hardships, the feeling of overcoming adversity in this insane shoot in the middle of a desert is intoxicating.

14th April 2000

The terrace at Sahajanand Towers is brightly lit for the traditional *sangeet* (musical night) preceding Jamie and Katkin's wedding. The men in one corner and the women in another sit on rugs hauled up to the terrace for the occasion. In the centre of the male group sits Jamie looking out anxiously for Katkin who sits concealed in a *ghungat* (veil) among the women. The proceedings could well have descended into caricature had it not been for their seriousness. For over four hours, the bride and groom are teased, cajoled and initiated into the customs and rites of a traditional Hindu marriage. Slowly but surely, they get into the spirit of it.

Jamie and Katkin have been living together in Bhuj. Now, the Indians demand that they spend at least the last night before the wedding ceremony in separate rooms. They agree. They want their marriage to be as similar to a traditional Indian wedding as possible. Their only request is that they may be permitted to see each other, but the *baraatis* (groom's accompanists) are firm and Katkin is shielded from Jamie's searching look.

15th April 2000

Jamie and Katkin – "To love and honour you all the days of your life"

The temple hilltop is transformed. There is a *hom* (holy fire) lit up into which the priest constantly pours *ghee* (clarified butter) even as he chants the sacred hymns. This is not for screen; this is for real.

Everyone is dressed in their very best. Faces hitherto not washed and shaved in weeks are barely recognisable in their decent *avatar*.

The marriage has been taken with complete seriousness by the entire unit. Production has taken as much trouble to organise the evening with food *et al* as they would each day of the shoot. Production head Rao is dressed in a *lungi* and *kurta*, traditional wedding clothes of his native Mangalore.

One of the issues the wedding faced was: who would perform the *kanyadaan,* the ceremonial handing over of the bride to her husband? Ordinarily, the father of the bride does this, but Katkin's father is not here. Katkin requests Aamir to 'give her away'. Now, Aamir and Reena are fulfilling that role with gravity and a sense of responsibility.

Amin and Aditya Lakhia help Jamie select his clothes. The wardrobe-in-charge for *Lagaan*, Shakti Siddhu, dresses Katkin with great enthusiasm.

Jamie is the first to arrive. As he approaches the temple, he sits on the bonnet of the jeep while his *baraatis* dance, Hindi film *ishtyle*. Jamie joins in for a bit. I ask Amin whether Jamie has studied tapes of Amitabh dancing. I'm told he hasn't. He has only seen lots of Indian actors trying to dance like Amitabh at the Saturday night parties on the terrace. Someone, not Bagha, is playing the drums. The dancing of the *baraatis* (groom's accompanists) grows more frenzied. Accompanied by raucous cheers, Jamie climbs up the temple steps. A elaborate Indian wedding is underway.

Half an hour later, a jeep appears and a tall woman in a gracefully draped red sari steps out. The *ghungat* covers her face completely. She is slightly uncertain in her manner of walking, the only indication that she is perhaps unused to her dress and situation. Shakti and Kiran Rao escort her on either side as she walks up the temple steps, head resolutely lowered. As she approaches the temple hilltop, the head is raised fractionally, revealing the blonde hair of Katkin, but her eyes are coyly lowered as if so trained from childhood. It is an incredible transformation.

Blessing the bride: Reena with Katkin

The sacred chants are recited in Sanskrit. Jamie and Katkin perform the rites with complete involvement. It is a strange sight – a white couple from England sitting in this beautiful temple in the middle of the Kutch desert becoming husband and wife with the blessings of an Indian film unit.

It is time for the *saat pheras*, the seven rounds the bride and the groom will take around the sacred fire. The priest chants the Sanskrit *shlokas* (holy verses) and explains the significance of each to Aamir in Hindi who in turn translates into English for the couple. The rays of the setting sun and the flames of the holy fire create a strange luminescence around the couple as they circle the holy fire seven times. The final exchange of *malas*, the garlands of flowers and the marriage is complete, or well almost.

No priest in India is going to tell the groom, "You may now kiss the bride." Yet, for Jamie and Katkin, the marriage would be incomplete without that. The bride and the groom kiss, freely and unabashedly, Katkin clinging to Jamie to cheers from everyone present.

Everyone is moved by the simplicity and beauty. Jamie and Katkin speak of how this has been a dream marriage. Though they are both born and raised as Christians, they have poured their souls into performing the Hindu rites. Somewhere, there is a spirit for which names and titles and rites do not matter. It is a spirit that recognises the union of souls and it is to this spirit that the couple have surrendered themselves this day.

They candidly confess, "Earlier we had looked on the temple marriage as a private moment for the two of us, a rehearsal as it were for the real marriage in a church in England. But the spirit in which everything has been done…now we feel that this is the real marriage and the one in England will be a formality."

A shutosh does not attend the wedding, rather he cannot. Javed Akhtar and A.R. Rahman have flown down to Bhuj once again to complete the unfinished sixth song of *Lagaan*. Even while the others celebrate the marriage, Ashutosh, Rahman and Javed Akhtar have spent the day working on *'chale chalo'*.

This is Rahman's third trip to Bhuj. He cannot believe he is here again. Never in his entire career has Rahman visited a set so often, not even for his debut film. Every trip has meant a mammoth effort. Packing a tonne of music equipment and carting it from Chennai to Bhuj, living with the rest of the unit in the relatively austere Sahajanand Towers and most important, enduring the continuing power failures. No electricity has meant trudging up and down seven floors, it has meant no air-conditioning, it has meant a spiked hard disk and being unable to work. Yet, Rahman is drawn to Bhuj, in part by a sense of professional commitment, in part by his love for *Lagaan* and in part, by Aamir's repeated caveats before he started work on the film. Like everyone else, Rahman too must pay his share of *lagaan*.

Tonight, however the god of electricity has submitted to the god of music. It is the night for Javed Akhtar and Rahman to receive tribute. The entire unit is in love with their songs and is dying to show it. All the actors pile into Ashutosh's living room. They sing *ghanan*, not a perfect rendition, but the spirit is stirring.

Then Ashutosh and Javed Akhtar sing the bhajan: "*o palanhare nirgun aur nyaare, tumre bin humra kauno naahi*" ("O Beloved Saviour, You are our only hope"). It is the first time that the unit is hearing the song and they are deeply moved by the lyrics and the music. There is a quiet spirituality. The entire unit, atheists included are in tears. Rahman is a little embarrassed by all the attention. Characteristically, he says nothing. The presence of Javed Akhtar and Rahman has lent an enchantment, a magical feeling to the evening.

18ᵗʰ April 2000

I bump into Aamir in the dining area at 4:30 a.m. and wish him. Aamir looks confused. He has forgotten it is his wedding anniversary. He presses the panic button. Let alone buying a present, he has not even wished Reena. He must act and act soon. Aamir gets hold of Amin (Bagha) Hajee who is not shooting, and requests him to buy silver jewellery that he may present to Reena in the evening after returning from the shoot.

Amin goes to the silver market in Bhuj and buys exquisite Kutchi jewellery. Aamir thinks he has the perfect gift, but Reena is not deceived. Later at night, she thanks *Amin* for 'his' present.

"Why couldn't Aamir personally buy a gift for me?" she enquires.

Aamir asks Amin, "Tell me, was it possible for me to go to the Bhuj marketplace and buy the gift without being mobbed?"

Reena retorts, "Couldn't you have asked some jewellers to come to Sahajanand Towers and show you stuff? Aamir, where there's a will there's a way."

The producer has been clean bowled by his executive producer. Aamir dives for Reena and the two tumble on to the bed, while Amin beats a hasty retreat.

19ᵗʰ April 2000

I t is over a hundred days since the shoot began, but the demands are as intense as they were on Day 1. Today, Rachel's call time was 4:30 a.m., while Aamir left for the set at 5:15 in the morning. All this, for a romantic song sequence in the rays of the rising sun! Vaibhavi Merchant is the choreographer for this song, "*Ori Chhori*". The dates have worked in such a manner that she has had to shoot it in three separate trips to Bhuj. Every time Vaibhavi returns to Bhuj she faces a time warp.

On Mumbai's glitzy sets, she is shooting ultra modern twenty-first century songs with funky dance steps, whereas for *Lagaan*, she must yoke her sensibility to rural India, the bullock cart and the *dhoti-kurta*. She must swiftly sense the aesthetic of each director and blend with it.

For Vaibhavi, this is in part second nature and despite being in her early twenties, she has the confidence of a veteran. Her grandfather, Master Sohanlal had choreographed several songs for Vyjanthimala, including the famous '*piya tose naina lagey re*'. Her grandfather's brother, Master Hiralal choreographed the '*hothon pe aisi baat*' number to which Gracy and the other girls danced for their *Lagaan* audition. Now, Vaibhavi directs a song that she hopes will live as long as her forefathers' classics have.

Despite starting the day well before sunrise, the rest of it is no less exacting. An important scene - Russell's journey back from the British Headquarters to the cantonment is to be shot. In the blazing heat of the afternoon, Paul gallops through the dry, cracked earth of Banni. This is where Kutch first beckoned to Ashutosh. This is where Paul now ends his journey in *Lagaan*.

His last shot done, Paul shaves his head. The ruthless military officer is gone, the sensitive and lovable actor returns. Once more, the shorts hang perilously. The freaky traveller look returns. Moment by moment, we can see Paul driving Russell out of his mind. His transformation underlines the preparation and method that had gone into his performance.

Like so many others, Paul too has paid a price for *Lagaan*. It is while he was in Bhuj that he separated from his British girlfriend. The mental and emotional space created by this shoot in an Indian desert lent Paul a different lens through which he viewed this relationship

Amin (Bagha) Hajee has returned a few days back from Mumbai after setting in process the end of his marriage with actress Reena Roy. Amin cannot stop speaking of the good times he had with Reena and his respect for her, yet, the distance enforced by this prolonged shoot has irrevocably changed Amin's perspective on life.

A film is being made and hundreds of relationships are in turmoil, a turmoil engendered by the innards, the very process of creating an image. The whole process is inherently transient. It is there and then it is gone. It is an illusion, a fantasy generated by the persistence of vision when an image is changed at the rate of twenty-four frames per second. The change creates the illusion of permanence. What is real is the transience. In some strange way, the optical illusion plays itself out in the lives of those that make the film.

As the longest single schedule Indian film, *Lagaan* is wreaking havoc and weaving magic at the personal level. The one cannot exist without the other. Fantasy and reality go hand in hand and we must exert ourselves to stay on the right side of both.

Goodbye to Kutch

Celebrations on the set after the last shot

BHUVAN: ...aapne humre liye jo kiya hai hum kabhi nahi bhoolenge.
(...we will never forget all that you have done for us.)
— LAGAAN

"It's strange how this big unit, this big sort of family thing gets together, gets so close you are almost in each other's pockets 24 hours a day, staying, living, working in the same place...and then everybody goes home...and you may never see each other again."
PAUL BLACKTHORNE (Captain Russell)

13
Goodbye to Kutch

23rd April 2000

T he Mandavi stretch has finished ahead of schedule and we are back at Champaner. Despite the beauty of the Vijay Vilas palace, it is the humble village in all its austerity that feels like home. Danabhai's villagers from Kotai are back as are the regular Bhuj extras. 'Ram Ram Sitaram' is exchanged as also 'hello' and 'hi'. The unit size swells and so do our hearts. The family is together once again.

26th April 2000

W e are into the night portion of the shoot. Sunrise is at 6:21 a.m. and sunset at 7:08 p.m. The days are long and the nights are short. For a night shoot, the early sunrise and late sunset mean shorter working hours. On a sync sound shoot, the pre-dawn chirping of birds from around 4 a.m. creates an auditory illusion of sunrise and further curtails the shooting hours.

Tonight, Yashpal playing Lakha, runs up the temple steps to escape the wrath of several hundred villagers. The long gap has meant that the villagers have returned to shoot with renewed vigour and enthusiasm. When Yashpal flees up the temple steps, they chase him so ferociously, that I fear for his safety if they do get their hands on him. As it happens, Yashpal manages to beat them to the safety of the temple, but barely. The villagers pound on the closed door and the walls of the temple with such conviction that the set department interrupts the shot and warns them that there is not a grain of cement in the temple. Bang away at your own peril!

Ironically, the villagers who are pounding away on the temple walls are the very workers, who a few months back, built the structure. *"Us time pe hum mazdoor they, ab hum actor hain,"* ("Then we were construction workers, now we are actors,") they tell me in stumbling Hindi.

Nonetheless, the warnings are given due regard. The thought of eighty tonnes of stone held together only by gravity and human ingenuity is sobering. The villager-actors pound on the temple door in a more restrained fashion.

28th April 2000

Raghuveer Yadav complains of severe pain in the stomach. Dr. Rao diagnoses it as a case of acute appendicitis requiring emergency surgery. First the fracture of the leg, then suspected heart trouble in March and now an emergency surgery! The quiet shoot, which will enable him to work on his music has become a sleepless nightmare, which Raghuveer must grin and bear. The silver lining to the cloud is that the entire unit rallies around him. He has been one of the heroes of *Lagaan*, both on and off screen.

1ˢᵗ May 2000

The legendary Saroj Khan is in Bhuj for the dance direction of 'Radha kaise na jale'. This is Gracy's big moment. Part of the reason for her being cast in the role of Gauri, was her command over the Bharat Natyam style of dance. Now is the time to put her training to good use.

For the past three days, Gracy has immersed herself in mastering the dance steps. Yet, today her expression is pained, her look is tense and the footwork is awry. Something is terribly, terribly wrong. Saroj is doing her best to put Gracy at ease, Ashutosh is encouraging, yet Gracy continues on the steep path to ignominy.

Saroj Khan (centre) teaches Gracy Singh to dance like Radha

Finally, the shoot stops. No one can bear it any longer. Not Gracy, not Saroj Khan, not Ashutosh. Gracy reveals the problem. She has been wearing heavy silver earrings since January. The weight of the silver has irritated her ear lobe to the point where a small wound has formed, which is now infected.

The slightest movement causes her pain; dancing is sheer agony. So tense is Gracy about her dance that she has not dared to confide in anyone about this condition, until it is now no longer possible to conceal it.

Gracy refuses to stop the shoot. She starts on a course of antibiotics, which will provide relief within a few hours. In the meanwhile, she follows the maxim of cringing during the rehearsals and smiling during the take.

3rd May 2000

With a month long night shoot in place, Anil Mehta finally gets an opportunity to light. Most of *Lagaan* has been shot as day exterior. Now, nearly four months into the shoot, his big moment has arrived. It is difficult to summon the freshness of the early days. He has been battling wind, dust and cloudy weather. Barring Sundays, he has wielded the heavy 535 camera for nearly four months without a break. Now it seems a part of his body. Yet, that is the way things are and he must adapt to them. Anil does not complain. The ideal exists only as a figment of the imagination and that all shoots are a creative confrontation with limitations and necessities, is something he accepts as an article of faith.

The limitations for the '*Radha kaise na jale*' song are staggering. In a

Moolchand, the gaffer, checks the quality of the light

lot of shots, the camera must be able to turn 360 degrees without seeing the lighting equipment. The schedule has provided only four days to shoot the song, so there should be as few changes as possible in the lighting set-up for different camera angles. Anil meets the impossible requirements by rigging Chinese lanterns, giant balloon lights on poles that form part of the *gokulashtami* decorations – the setting for the song – and the shoot proceeds at a scorching pace.

Part of the reason for the speed of the shoot is that Anil Mehta has at his disposal a superb team of lightmen headed by the gaffer Moolchand. As the gaffer, Moolchand's job is to execute Anil's lighting instructions. With just over a dozen lightmen at his disposal, Moolchand is able to light up the massive village set and sometimes even the outskirts in astonishingly short periods of time. The reason is very simple. He has at all times had the *information* available to every other head of department.

In regular Hindi films, there is no post of 'gaffer'. The word and the post are derived from Hollywood. In Indian films, there is a head electrician who liaises with the cameraman or his assistant, but the head electrician does not have the status or access to information that a gaffer does. This again flows from our casteist hierarchy, where those who do physical labour do not enjoy equal status with those involved in purely intellectual tasks. In *Lagaan*, there has been an attempt to fight this hierarchy. The results speak for themselves.

4th May 2000

As the journey of the film continues, on the highway leading to Champaner, another journey is underway. Tens of thousands of pilgrims are walking to the *dargah* (shrine) of Haji Pir, close to the Pakistan border. The Pir, Ali Akbar, was a holy man killed centuries ago while trying to save the cow belonging to a poor woman. Generations of Hindus and Muslims have walked to his shrine flanking the Great Rann of Kutch to commemorate his martyrdom. Even after the partition of India, tens of thousands of Pakistanis are said to cross over into Kutch for this festival.

The road to the *dargah* is the Bhuj-Khavda highway leading to Champaner. Even at ten at night, the usually deserted highway is full of pilgrims. At intervals of a few kilometres, local organisations and villagers have set up tents providing free food, water and bedding for the devout travellers. I see a couple carrying a child in an improvised cloth cradle slung across two ends of a bamboo pole. I take a closer look. The child is at least five years old, which makes the bundle rather heavy. I ask the couple why the child does not walk – he appears fit and able.

"The child was born after we asked Haji Pir baba for a *mannat* (boon). So every year we make the journey on foot carrying the child to show him to the Baba."

The couple is Hindu. Their travelling companion is a middle-aged Muslim woman from their village. The couple is supremely unconcerned about the paradox of Hindus travelling on foot to a Muslim *dargah*. They have already walked eighty kilometres and have another sixty to go.

There are tens of thousands on the road, including the very old and even young girls travelling by themselves. Ultimately, half a million pilgrims will assemble at the *dargah*. For these days at least, normal social convention forbidding young girls moving on the roads at night without a male escort has been set aside. The sentiment is that all Kutchis who pay obeisance to the humble Pir are a family. The sense of unity triumphs over the sense of fear.

5th May 2000

With the *gokulashtami* sequence canned, Rachel's shoot is wrapped and the last of the British actors has now finished her work. I find myself at Bhuj airport when Rachel leaves. We hug each other warmly. After an indifferent start, Rachel had found at least some virtue in India and a great deal in *Lagaan*. In her interview with me she had spoken with passion about the light and the colours one sees all over India. I was unable to sense that some barriers and hostility still remained deep inside.

Rachel gives her last cue

15th May 2000

The entire unit trudges up Lover's Hill, for the romantic scenes between Gauri and Bhuvan. It takes ages for everyone to huff and puff their way up. I'm tempted to tell Ashutosh that there is no way that Bhuvan and Gauri could have indulged in any romance after such a climb. Wisely, I keep my mouth shut.

17th May 2000

Night shoot is in progress. Nakul hears the sound of a motorcycle on his headphones. He is furious. Teams are dispatched to the boundaries of the set but without success. Unit members scale the surrounding hilltops but they can see no vehicles moving for miles around. Teams are dispatched to the Bhuj-Khavda highway, full five kilometres away, but at 3 a.m. the Kutch countryside is fast asleep. The shoot is in grave danger of being abandoned for the night, when the source of the sound is at last discovered. Bhim Vakhani, the actor playing Kazi has fallen asleep and the sound of his snoring is resonating in Nakul's ears.

Lagaan has taught us one more lesson: sync sound and sleeping actors do not go together!

Vaibhavi Merchant and Ashutosh watch as *Ori Chhori* gets underway

21st May 2000

A shutosh has composed a song that can only be described as Indian rap. Couplets are delivered by each of the team members followed by the punch line, *"Re bhaiyya chhoote lagaan"*. The 'song' is to be rendered by the actors themselves who are thrilled at the idea of making their audio debut. Sadly, this song will ultimately be axed on grounds of length.

Today, the song is being recorded in a studio, which belongs to a local lawyer who plays the drums and has invested in this equipment more for pleasure than profit. For a sleepy little town of less than two lakh residents, Bhuj has turned out to be quite a surprise package. It has given us sixty actors, craftsmen of all kinds and now…even a sound studio! Perhaps such resources exist all over India, just waiting to be discovered.

31st May 2000

W e are back to the cricket field for what is supposed to be four days. But this time the unit is wiser. It knows that the shoot will spill over and indeed it does. Four days stretch to a week. Now the unit is subject to the full intensity of the desert heat without any respite. Temperatures rise into the forties. The rubber parts of the photocopying machine in the production office on the set simply melt and refuse to function despite installing a cooler. Actors take refuge in every available spot of shade in the afternoon, but really there is no escape.

Raghuveer Yadav has never felt quite the same after his appendix operation and really suffers the cricket ground. Nabeel Abbas, the publicity and promotion consultant for *Lagaan* commits the error of asking Raghuveer how he felt about Bhuj to which his candid reply is, "I have swallowed so much dust here, that I feel like digging deep in the soil and burying myself in this hell hole."

2ⁿᵈ June 2000

Lakha takes his famous Jonty Rhodes catch where he emerges into frame parallel to the ground to hold on to the ball. Lakha is clearly seen in the shot and so must train to be airborne. The magic is achieved with the use of a mini-trampoline, but Yashpal Sharma playing Lakha is no circus artist and has no training in this art form whatsoever. Ejaz, the fight master's assistant, does his best to train Yashpal and the mattresses buried below the earth cushion his fall. Nonetheless, Yashpal endures twenty-four takes today, without being able to can the shot. He sometimes falls on his neck, on his head, on his back and I am concerned about his well-being. Yet, Yashpal is determined to get the shot right and says he will try again tomorrow.

Lakha prepares to jump on the trampoline to take the famous Jonty Rhodes catch

3rd June 2000

Yashpal succeeds on take twenty-eight. The ball is thrown at just the right height and at just the right moment, Yashpal/Lakha takes off on the mini-trampoline, maintains his horizontal movement through the frame and miraculously, also holds on to the ball. I heave a sigh of relief. The catch is canned and Yashpal can still walk!

The rides to the set have become increasingly depressing. There is a severe drought in Kutch and the Rudrani river which we cross daily has run dry. The cracked beds of the Hamirsar and Desalsar lakes in Bhuj city have turned into grazing grounds and cricket pitches. Most depressing, every other day we spot at least one truck with cattle carcasses.

All of Kutch prays for rain, but rain will be fatal to the film. It will cause all shooting to grind to a halt. The scorching heat is often interrupted by cloudy days, yet like the clouds at the start of *Lagaan*, these clouds too are deceptive and pass without showering water and life. Moolchand anxiously trains his eyeglass upwards and the *Lagaan*ites dream the impossible dream of rain for Kutch and dry weather for the hundred acres of Champaner.

5th June 2000

Though we all suffer the heat, the morale is higher than it was in the previous round of shooting at the cricket ground. Everyone can palpably feel that the shoot is coming to an end and hope is at hand. Reena still isn't quite sure and moves around with a wooden stick in her hand, laughingly threatening to use it on anyone responsible for delays.

As in the earlier schedule on the cricket ground, this time too it is the villagers and the Bhuj actors who help to hold the shoot together with their grit and discipline. The villagers not only laugh, they also perform. From being 'crowds' they have transformed into being Vellabhai and Dangarbhai and Kanku and Ritu. They have absorbed the grammar and method of film making with astonishing speed.

The words 'cut', 'action', 'rolling' and a dozen other shooting terms in English have now entered the Kutchi lexicon. The words '*uupar juo*' ('look up'), '*badda samblo*' ('everyone please listen') and '*bau saras*' ('excellent') have entered the vocabulary of the Mumbaiwallas and even the Brits. A new language is being written in the heat and dust of shooting *Lagaan*.

The villagers focus their eyes only on the ball; no one looks at the camera

Even off screen, the villagers have come into their own. Nowhere is this more evident than among the Kutchi girls. In January, they were shy and diffident, barely able to understand or speak Hindi. Now they are confident. They know what is required of them. They know they are capable of it. Earlier Apu's assistants, including Priya, would try and bully them. Now they bully Priya and tease her about her boyfriend who has been labelled 'kanhaiya' for his philandering ways.

6th June 2000

The end of the cricket shoot completes the work of Javed Khan, playing Ramsingh. Javed Khan has been wearing shoes two sizes large, in order to change his style of walking to suit his character. Now, he may walk normally again.

With the cricket shoot *finally* over, there is a day off. Wags in the unit suggest that the day off is a ruse and the next day we'll be shooting cricket again.

Apu's assistant Priya spends a day in the village with the girls. The girls are drawn to her gentle manner. Priya has been having trouble with her boyfriend and is depressed. Kanku from Kotai village sits next to her and wraps her arm around Priya. The kindness acts as a trigger and both, Priya the psychiatrist from New York and the unlettered Kanku from village Kotai, weep soundlessly.

7th June 2000

Raju Khan (extreme right) choreographs *chale chalo*

The shooting for '*chale chalo*' has started. The heat and growing humidity are ideal for the warlike mood of the song, but the weather gods are not through with playing games with us. The fickle weather plays no small role in determining the shape the song ultimately takes. The summer winds blow huge clouds of dust into the air, obscuring visibility.

The sight triggers the creative imagination of Ashutosh and the choreographer Raju Khan who shoot the actors walking through the dust haze. Midway through the song, the wind falls stubbornly silent and the dust settles. Since the decision to shoot with a dust haze was impromptu, the storm fans required to complete the sequence are not available.

Production requests volunteers to physically pick up the sandy soil and throw it up in the air to create the dust cover behind the actors. Dozens of villagers and Bhuj actors join the setting workers and other unit members, although the dust goes into their eyes, their hair and generally cakes their bodies.

A dust storm is created with bare hands

Raju Khan tells me, "Damn this weather. One minute it's windy and dusty, the next moment it's still and clear. God is playing chess with us, but we're fighting back!"

The shot of the eleven cricketers walking with the dust billowing behind them will make its way on to posters and people's memories as one of the most dramatic moments in *Lagaan*.

8th June 2000

aju Khan wants a sunrise shot of the cricketers running up the hill with their silhouettes outlined in the light of dawn. We leave for set at 4:00 in the morning, for which we have risen at 3:00 a.m. Breakfast done, camera and rigs in place, the actors climb the hillside and wait for sunrise. Unfortunately, it is very cloudy at dawn and the diffusion created by the overcast sky creates a haze! The shot is postponed to the next day.

9th June 2000

We are now into month six of the shoot and the unit has risen yet again at 3:00 in the morning to make their way to the set. Six months back it seemed insane for hundreds of Mumbaiwallas to make their way into the desert wilderness at dawn. Now, it seems like second nature. The madness has been internalised.

Mercifully, nature is kinder today. Dawn is cloudless and the yellow-red sunrise provides the perfect background for the actors to run up the hill. Despite the vagaries of the weather we have hit back through grit and persistence. In our minds we exult, *'Koi hum se jeet na paave chale chalo!'* ('Let no one win against us. Let's walk ahead! Let's walk ahead!')

13th June 2000

Only the patchwork shots are left and even the most cynical members of the unit accept that the end is now in sight. Apu sends a message on the call sheet which indicates the goodbye mood.

The lights fade out at Champaner

"The ADs (assistant directors) would like to dedicate this call sheet to all the actors – For all the laughs, the tantrums, the complaints, for patiently tolerating the cricket ground and the home pavilion, for providing *farsan*, for losing costumes, for LPCC, for showing us the path, and most of all for the professionalism and camaraderie...*re bhaiyya lo chhoota Lagaan* (oh brother, you are finally free of *Lagaan*)!"

14th June 2000

Hangal gives his last shot today. He is perhaps the person most energised by *Lagaan*. He arrived in Bhuj looking every one of his eighty-four years, nursing a bad back and low in confidence. The determination he showed in shooting after his fall and his subsequent recovery have convinced him that there is life in the old bones yet. He has spent six months with younger people and enjoyed every bit of the attention lavished on him. He has grown at least twenty years younger. In the last days of the shoot, he has been dressing as he did in his younger days, white trousers with a white shirt tucked in. There is almost a spring in his stride. His role in the film is tiny, but even for this veteran, *Lagaan* has been an invigorating life experience.

15th June 2000

As the end approaches, the Bhuj juniors are in gloom. The past six months have been memorable. In relatively conservative Kutchi society, boys and girls even going for a picnic together is uncommon. For *Lagaan*, dozens of boys and girls have been together for six months, often through the night, without any incident. Some of the gang from Mumbai had cast admiring looks at the pretty Bhuj girls, but the unwritten law for the Mumbaiwallas was that no affairs with Kutchis would be tolerated by Production.

The six months have been a huge learning experience for the *Lagaanites* from Bhuj. They have seen just how tough and gruelling a film shoot is. They have also learned a great deal about cinema and acting. One of the young girls from Bhuj, Hency Thacker tells me, "Earlier, it never occurred to us to look at the background artists. But only if there is a background, is there a foreground. Now, I look at the background as an integral part of the frame."

The experience for the old has been no less exhilarating. For the seventy years plus group from Bhuj, *Lagaan* has been perhaps the most exciting experience of their lives. Suddenly, they have a new lease of life and a new sense of purpose.

The air of sadness of the Bhuj team finds expression in unexpected quarters. I enter the production office at night and see Reena hard at work. She looks down steadfastly at the paper on which she is writing, yet she cannot conceal the glint of tears in her eyes. I ask her what's up, but she does not respond. The next day, I see her handwriting appended to the daily call sheet. The iron lady of the shoot has melted. The trauma is over and she can be her normal self.

"The shooting of our film Lagaan is coming to an end. It has been a long and difficult shoot. But you all have managed to go through it and can now return to your normal lives and family. We will each go back with many

memories of our various experiences during the making of this film. We have laughed together, cried together, yelled at each other and comforted one another through thick and thin.

Through the last six months that we have lived together, there have been times when I have been hard on some of you. I did not get the chance to show or voice my appreciation for all the hard work and dedication of each one of you to the making of this dream.

Now that you'll are leaving, I would like you to know, that all of you have done an absolutely commendable job. Right from all the actors and technicians, to the unit members, Bhuj artists, Danabhai and his group of labourers, security, housekeeping, to all the crowds who have sat in the sun endlessly.

I would like to thank each and every one of you for your contribution in this film. For pulling along through the heat and dust; for keeping your cool through the changes in the call sheets; for your support and cooperation through the increase in the shooting schedule and for just believing in this film. My entire production team joins me in wishing all of you the very best for the future.

Kind Regards
Reena Datta"

16th June 2000

The shoot ends tomorrow. The actors cannot bear to leave the village. For six months, Champaner has been their home. Now suddenly they must abandon it and leave for Mumbai. Aamir and the other actors decide to spend the night in the village. Many others, including the financier of *Lagaan*, Jhamu Sughand join in.

Raghuveer Yadav has written a film script. After dinner, Vallabh Vyas narrates it to an appreciative audience lounging on the *khaats* outside Ishwarkaka's house. The script narration concludes well past midnight and although the next day is a shooting day, sleep does not come easily. It is a cloudy night and the moon is barely visible. Raghuveer Yadav starts singing in an inspired mood – after months of suffering, the notes are pregnant with feeling. Others join in the singing and the music resounds in the empty desert into the small hours of the morning.

17th June 2000

Ashutosh has warned Aamir that he must be awake when the unit arrives in the morning. He was asking for the impossible. As the unit streams in at dawn, they find the village square full of the sleeping residents of Champaner. There is Bhuvan snoring on a bullock cart, Lakha and Bhura sleeping on rope cots, Goli slumbering in his house. The actors are sleeping as their characters would. Reel life and real life have merged. A kind soul warns the sleepers that the director is on his way with a bucket of water. The warning produces excellent results and within moments a few dozen *Lagaan*ites rush to the toilets.

The last shot is taken at five in the evening. Ashutosh assembles the entire cast and crew and rolls the movie camera to shouts of '*Re bhaiyya chhoote lagaan*'. This has been the defining war cry of the unit. Everyone has paid their share of *lagaan* and most are now free of its burden. The shot taken, Apu announces that the entire film is now wrapped. Wild cheers break out. Bagha beats the drum. Everyone embraces everyone.

I am the only one left out, perched on a crane thirty feet in the sky with camera rolling, recording this moment for posterity. I must restrain my own emotions and separate myself from the others to play the chronicler.

Goodbye to Kutch: Aamir with Danabhai and other villagers

After half an hour of frenzied celebration, the cheers die down. Reality hits the unit. Everyone turns sombre. Suddenly, this is the end of the journey for them. Tomorrow there is no Champaner. Many break down. Some are inconsolable.

An end of shoot party has been announced which is to be held later tonight on the terrace at Sahajanand Towers. For weeks there has been talk of this party and how wrap parties are great bashes where everyone celebrates with wild abandon. Yet, when the unit members get together for one last bash, the atmosphere is almost funereal. Even the committed drinkers aren't really interested in the alcohol. It is strange and everyone can feel the strangeness of it. We had all dreamt of the day when the shoot would be over and we could go back to heart and home in Mumbai. Now, when the moment is at hand, we are unable to enjoy it.

Part of the reason for this strange feeling is that we will miss each other. Man is a creature of habit and staying together for half a year, being in certain physical spaces and circumstances, invariably creates a bond. More important, the shoot had created an enchanted world, cut off from the bureaucracy of life. There were no responsibilities, no tasks other than the mission of making *Lagaan*. The long single schedule in the midst of this great desert made the task of shooting the film larger than life. With the end of the shoot, this enchanted period in our lives was coming to an end, never to return.

20th June 2000

The entire unit has left Bhuj, barring Rao, Reena, Aamir, Ashutosh and Gracy who have stayed back to shoot stills with photographer Hardeep Sachdev. Emptied of so many occupants, Sahajanand Towers appears as a ghost building.

Then, there is terrible news. Aamir receives a phone call from Mumbai. His aunt, *chachijaan*, mother of Mansoor and Nuzhat and wife of Aamir's uncle Nasir Husain has passed away. *Chachijaan* was in good health till the last and her demise is a bolt from the blue. She had been there at the *muhurat* of *Lagaan* and her appreciation then had moved Aamir to tears. Showing her the completed film would have been an important moment for Aamir. That moment shall now never come. Reality has returned with all its cruelty. Aamir returns to Mumbai in grief.

4th July 2000

The deadline for handing the land back to the villagers ends on 11th July. The land has to be given back as it was received. Danabhai and his men have been working round the clock to tear down the village and the cricket pavilion and carry away the remains so that the farmers may till the soil in case by some miracle it rains. The *boongas* have proved to be stubbornly tenacious structures. There is only one way to speed up the process, says Danabhai and that is to burn down the village.

Danabhai's men pour kerosene on the thatched roofs. A torch is lit and Champaner is set on fire. The flames rapidly engulf the entire structure burning even the dry cow dung in the walls. Goli's house goes down, then Arjan's, then Bhuvan's... We stand at a distance watching the destruction of a fantasy. There are tears in every eye. The flames are today engulfing a little bit of everyone.

We had come to make a film, yet the film had in many ways made us.

Disaster and triumph

Six months earlier, the *Lagaanites* had lived here

GURAN: Har sant kahe, sadhu kahe — sach aur sahas hai jiske man mein, ant me jeet usiki rahey (Every saint and seer has said — he who has truth and courage in his heart, is the one who wins ultimately) — Song from LAGAAN

"If film is a larger than life experience, so is making it."
ASHUTOSH GOWARIKER
Writer - Director

14

Disaster and triumph

24th June 2000

A shutosh emerges in the offices of Aamir Khan Productions, two days after returning from Bhuj. Six punishing months away from home and in two days he's back for more. So what, that's what he lives for. "The only problem is," he says with a grin, "when I came home, Sunni had to assure the kids that the strange man with their mother is in fact their father!"

For the actors and most of the shooting unit, their work on the film is over, but with the post-production of *Lagaan* ahead of him, Ashutosh knows that at this stage he is exactly at the half way mark in completing his film. Considering the ordeal he has been through in shooting *Lagaan*, no one would have blamed him for imagining that the difficult half is done and the relatively easy half lies ahead, but as with all other judgments about *Lagaan*, this one too would have been way off the mark.

The post-production of a film consists of three major areas of work: the first is the edit, the second is the sound work and the third is the processing and printing of the film in the laboratory. No matter how well a film has been shot, unless the momentum is carried through into the edit and the rest of post-production, all the effort in the shoot may come to naught. A loose cut can bore the audience, bad background music can destroy a scene and poor laboratory work can make the most brilliantly lit film look tacky. Every task in post-production must be planned and executed with the same passion as the pre-production and shooting of the film. The director cannot let the reins loose until the release print is ready.

Ashutosh is confident of finishing swiftly. He tells Aamir, "Let's release *Lagaan* on 24th December, just before Christmas. I want *Lagaan* to be released this year."

"Famous last words!" thinks Aamir as he smiles. He estimates there is at least a year of work left on *Lagaan*.

"Great Ash! Show me the film and we'll release it this year," Aamir encourages Ashutosh.

29th June 2000

Ballu Saluja, editor

Ashutosh settles down to a life of editing at the offices of Aamir Khan Productions. With him is the pony-tailed editor of *Lagaan*, Ballu Saluja, not quite twenty-five and doing his first feature film. Ballu is just dying to tell all his party pals about his work on *Lagaan*. At this stage, he has little idea that he will not party for the next year. From this point on, his body and soul belong to *Lagaan*. His sole interface with the external world will be through his cell phone.

1st August 2000

The editing suite is overflowing with people and emotion. Aamir, Reena, Rao and Ashish are watching the first cut of only the songs. Ashutosh and Ballu look on anxiously. When the last song has been played and the lights come on, Aamir is visibly moved.

"It's working Ash. You've done a wonderful job." Aamir is not easily given to praise, so his terse reaction means a great deal to Ashutosh who is cautious.

"Aamir, we've a long way to go. Reserve your comments till the entire film is cut."

Ballu and Ashutosh get back to the editing suite as the others exit the room. The edit of *Lagaan* winds its way forward.

30th September 2000

By the end of September, Ashutosh is ready to screen a first cut of the entire film barring the climax. Many scenes are working wonderfully and the film has its moments, but at three and a half hours without the climax, it is dreadfully long. "It is there but not quite there. It is working but not quite working," comments Aamir cautiously. "Let's first cut the cricket match and see the film as a whole."

At around this time, Aamir receives a fresh round of calls from distributors interested in buying *Lagaan*. Earlier, during the shoot too, several distributors were keen on purchasing rights to *Lagaan*, but Aamir had refused to sell the film although the market was at high tide and distributors were offering to buy the film at a ratio of rupees three crore per territory. Even today, distributors are willing to pay this price, which will yield a tidy profit for Aamir. Yet, Aamir refuses. "Unless I've seen the film myself and I know the fair price of my product, how can I sell it to you?" is Aamir's response.

In distribution circles, Aamir's answer reeks of danger. Market antennae are on red alert as speculation starts.

"Why is Aamir not willing to sell the film?"

"With no dubbing required, why are they taking so long to release the film?"

"There must be serious problems, which he is not telling us."

The distributors are simply not willing to accept that anyone in the world could genuinely have the motive of not wanting to sell his product, without being personally convinced of its quality!

15th October 2000

Aamir is gearing to leave for Sydney with the *Dil Chahta Hai* unit. With his new hairstyle and trendy goatee beneath his lower lip, the contrast with the nineteenth century villager, Bhuvan, is startling. Yet, sitting in his office, his agenda today is *Lagaan*.

As with the shoot, so with the edit, cricket has been a black hole swallowing endless quantities of time. Just the digitisation of the rushes and syncing of the sound with the video has been going on for over a month. Making sense of the mammoth one thousand two hundred shots and putting them into a cogent story line will take time. The December 2000 release is impossible. In the core team there is some talk of postponing the release by two months, but Aamir has no stomach to go through the exercise of repeated postponements. They can only demoralise everyone and destroy *Lagaan*'s credibility in the market. He must be decisive. Aamir postpones the release by half a year to 1st June 2001.

Postponed by half a year for post-production and this despite no dubbing! Half the world asks Aamir and Ashutosh what on earth they are up to, but Ashutosh really has no time to reply. He must edit cricket and more cricket and still more cricket. Now, Ashutosh no longer dislikes cricket. He hates it.

6th January 2001

Through the months of October, November and December, Ashutosh has hammered away at editing the cricket match. Even in his dreams he can see Bagha dropping catches, Yardley hurling the ball ferociously and Bhuvan smashing the ball to the boundary. He is now ready to unveil his work for reactions.

The core team of *Lagaan* watches a five and a half hour cut of the film. They start at 2:30 in the afternoon, stop for an interval of half an hour and when the last shot comes on screen, it is eight-thirty at night and pitch dark outside. The audience feels like it has spent the entire day watching *Lagaan*! The length is showing; as a whole the film is not working; and as for the climax, it is a disaster! Two and a half hours of cricket is more than anyone can digest.

Editing cricket: no cakewalk

All the *Lagaan*ites know that the fortunes of the film are tied to the cricket match, perhaps the longest climax in cinematic history. If the match does not work, the film has no future.

It is difficult to even describe the emotions of the *Lagaan* team: tension, frustration, anxiety, depression. They have poured their souls into making *Lagaan* and is this what they have come up with! Fear grips their hearts. There is gloom in the *Lagaan* camp. Where have we gone wrong? What are we to do next?

7th January 2001

Aamir has not slept all night. Despite the huge problems with the cricket match, Aamir believes that *Lagaan* will ultimately be a great film. The only question is, at what cost? How much more money, effort and sacrifice will it demand before the potential of its magical script can be achieved? There is no way to tell. All that Aamir knows is that as a producer and as a creative person, this is his hour of trial. He must do whatever it takes to carry *Lagaan* to safe shores.

A day after the disastrous trial, Aamir meets with Reena and Rao.

"I want you to prepare a fresh budget for three weeks of a reshoot at the cricket ground with the entire cast including the crowds, the village actors and the British actors."

For Reena, it is as if the ground has slipped from beneath her feet. The cricket match features the entire cast of the film. It has been the biggest and most expensive portion of the *Lagaan* shoot. Reshooting the cricket match is financial suicide! This is the ultimate nightmare. The film is already wildly over budget. The market for Hindi films is now in a state of collapse. Not a single territory of *Lagaan* has been sold and there is no telling what price the distributors will ultimately pay. And now, this insane man wants to reshoot the cricket match!

They will have to go back to Kutch and back to England. They will have to begin by leasing the land all over again; preparing the pitch, building the British pavilion, renegotiating with the British actors…it will be like making a new film. Rao and Reena try very hard to explain this to Aamir.

Aamir is unmoved. "I am not saying that we *are* going to shoot, I'm only saying there is a high possibility of it. For the moment, I am only asking you to prepare the budget and this must be done with utmost secrecy. If word leaks out there will be panic and confusion."

Six months after the shoot, the cricket match is creating as much agony in its edit as it created during its filming.

8th January 2001 - 10th January 2001

A amir watches the rushes of the cricket match. Shot by shot, ball by ball, wicket by wicket he sees the original source material, the raw footage of the cricket shoot. On day 3 his writing pencil rests and so does his mind. He now knows that all the shots needed to make the cricket match work have been canned. The gruelling shoot in Kutch has not been in vain. A jewel is buried in the miles of rushes. It will take much patience and hard work to first extract and then polish it, till it glistens.

Aamir calls for another meeting with Reena and Rao. They have been working hard on the budget for the reshoot and the figures emerging are terrifying.

Aamir watches every shot of cricket

"We've got the footage!" Aamir announces to them triumphantly. "We don't need to reshoot the cricket match."

The blood flows back to the face of a very ashen Reena. Yet she cannot relax. She knows that she will face one crisis after another until *Lagaan* is released.

11th January 2001 – 25th January 2001

A hundred things are happening all at once and the production office is swamped with activity. Aamir has joined Ashutosh and Ballu Saluja in the editing suite. In the area outside the editing suite, *Lagaan's* publicity designer, Simrit Brar, watches the thousands of publicity stills on a slide projector. Ashutosh and Aamir join her to work on the posters and publicity material for *Lagaan*.

A thirty-second theatrical trailer of *Lagaan* has been cut and several thousand calendar-posters have been printed. The calendar has a bold red dot announcing the release on 1st June 2001. The posters must now be dispatched throughout the Indian subcontinent and even abroad. The production team is as overburdened as it was in the weeks before the shoot commenced.

At the far end of the office, Aamir must now wear his producer's hat and start negotiations with distributors. Sadly, times have changed and the market is in severe depression. Major films sold at a huge price have flopped, leaving distributors with heavy losses. The distributors are now offering a price at the ratio of rupees two crore per territory, one full crore less than what they were offering six months back when the film was yet to be cut.

Aamir is now confident of his product, but the market has lost faith in itself. Aamir must pay the price for his principles.

26th January 2001

A shutosh and Aamir have worked through the night of the 25th and retired only in the early hours of the morning. As they sleep, ten kilometres from what once was the shooting village of Champaner, a deep rumble emerges from the bowels of the earth and rips apart the Kutch desert. It is the worst earthquake in a hundred and fifty years in India. Over thirteen thousand people are killed under the debris of collapsing structures.

As the images of devastation appear on television screens worldwide, anxious *Lagaan*ites watch with sinking hearts their Kutch, the Kutch of Champaner and *Lagaan*, in shambles. The telephones in the production office in Mumbai never stop ringing. The *Lagaan*ites are desperate for news of friends and colleagues in Kutch. Actors and technicians trickle into the office and spontaneously, the *Lagaan* unit gets together. Everyone forgets there is a film to be completed. Everyone just wants to know how the *Lagaan*ites at Bhuj are.

Aamir and Ashutosh are devastated. Try as they might, they just cannot edit the film anymore. Ashutosh tells me later that night, "I don't know whether the people I'm seeing on screen are dead or alive. It's such a morbid situation. We just cannot work until we find out what has happened to our friends in Kutch."

Getting information is not easy. The telephone link to Bhuj has snapped. There is only one way of finding out and that is to go to Kutch. Getting to Kutch is not possible for the moment. The airport is shut, the rail link disrupted and the Surajbari Bridge, the only road link into the Kutch peninsula is shut for all but essential traffic. For the moment, we have no option but to wait.

31ˢᵗ January 2001

One year back, on 26ᵗʰ January 2000, Aamir had unfurled the national flag in Kunnaria village, which now lies in ruins

Rao and I land in Bhuj. From the skies, the city looks miraculously the same, as if for the gods, nothing has changed. Yet, for ordinary mortals, for thousands of men, women and children, their lives are fundamentally altered forever. Devastation greets us from the landing strip itself. The main building near the airstrip has collapsed. So have a large number of hangars. Either the air force was not aware that Bhuj lay in Seismic Zone V, which mandates earthquake-proof structures, or there has been deliberate neglect in construction.

The road from the airstrip to Bhuj is an even grimmer sight. Every single multi-storeyed structure has collapsed, including the air force colony where there are very large casualties. Piles of rubble seal all the entrances to the walled city of Bhuj.

Then we see Sahajanand Towers, our home for nearly a year. It has vertically split into several wings, each a separate building by itself. We can see our rooms, our homes, completely devastated. For a moment a morbid, self-centred thought flashes through our minds: what if the earthquake had occurred six months earlier when the *Lagaan* unit was still living there?

The first familiar face we see is Dr. Gyaneshwar Rao, our doctor and friend. He breaks down on seeing us. He has been through hell and beyond. Night and day he has been amputating bodies, carrying out critical surgeries and issuing death certificates. In the hours immediately following the earthquake he did this with virtually no equipment and facilities, sometimes with only scissors and knife, in a desperate struggle to save lives. In tiny Bhuj, these are all people whom he knows well.

Dr. Rao is moved to tears by our presence. We ask what we can do to help.

"No, no, we require nothing from you at least for the moment, just knowing that you care has meant everything."

For an hour, Rao and I wander through the shattered town. These are streets that we have walked a million times, these are shops where we bought toothpaste and shirts and a hundred other articles of daily use, these are the restaurants we frequented and the hotels we stayed in.

We suddenly pass Binny and Hency Thacker and their father. The sisters had acted in *Lagaan*. Now, in what used to be the main marketplace of Bhuj, they are running for their lives. I call out and they stop briefly. I catch up with them and learn that they were lucky to escape to safety although their house is completely destroyed.

They run again. I wonder why. They point out and I see that the buildings on both sides of the street hang perilously over us at an angle of 45 degrees, like a suspended death sentence. Strangely, in just an hour we are used to this sight and it no longer alarms us. Up ahead, the army has laid dynamite to bring down the tilted structures, even as onlookers run for cover.

Within two hours, we meet almost all our unit members based in Bhuj or have solid information about them. The ever-reliable Pankaj Jhala, who has been in the forefront of the relief effort, has the maximum information. One of the Bhuj actors, Deep Mehta, has died under the rubble, but all the others from Bhuj are safe.

The worst news is from Sahajanand Towers. Over forty people are dead, mainly on the upper floors occupied after we left Bhuj and also three children of our water pump operator, Bapu, who lived in a cottage annexed to the main building.

The city has been taken over by the relief mafia. A few well-intentioned people are running helter-skelter like headless chickens, but a lot of crooks, most of them outsiders to Kutch, have jumped into the fray. For the first time, I experience a traffic jam in Bhuj, caused by convoys of jeeps and trucks laden with all sorts of relief material. On several street corners we see piles of clothes donated for earthquake relief. The rich of Mumbai and Ahmedabad have emptied their wardrobes for some more *haute couture*. The clothes include mini-skirts, tight jeans and tube tops, which no Kutchi girl would wear.

At a busy junction, some young ruffians, obviously not from Kutch, stop our jeep to throw in sealed plastic sachets of mineral water. We try and explain that we do not need these, but to no avail. Obviously, they are driven by their own need to dispose off stocks rather than by the needs of the earthquake-affected people.

In the working class area where our driver Razzak lives, a group of young men dressed in suits and ties sits triumphantly on the road with a large wooden tray laden with syringes, saline and all kinds of high-end antibiotics and other esoteric drugs. "Take your pick," they offer us. There is no doctor among them.

Everywhere in the city the situation is the same. A plethora of material and an acute shortage of human organisation!

I t is late evening when we leave for Danabhai's house in Kotai village – the Kotai that built *Lagaan*'s Champaner. The bridge over the Rudrani river is cracked and for a moment I am convinced that our jeep will tumble into the chasm below. My fears are misplaced. The bridge mysteriously defies gravity and yields safe passage to Kotai.

It is nightfall when we reach the village. As the headlights of the jeep illuminate Kotai, the sight chills us to the bone. Every single house in the village is devastated. The massive stones with which the houses are built lie in giant heaps, which appear now like so many tombstones. Outside, the *choolhas* (cooking fires) flicker and families huddle around the smoking fires that are now the only sources of light and heat in the dark and chilly Kutch winter.

The jeep reaches the last house in the village. Danabhai's house, or rather what used to be Danabhai's house, is also a heap of rubble. Mammoth stones are strewn all over. I fear the worst. Rao and I get out of the jeep. I move forward, unsteady on my feet. Then we hear voices from beyond the heap of rubble. I turn a dark corner and the glow of a cooking fire warms my heart. Danabhai, his wife, his daughter Urmila and son Mahavir receive us with warmth and broad smiles. Seeing the devastation, we are terrified of asking about casualties in the village. Danabhai reads our minds and tells us what happened.

"Republic Day celebrations were about to start. Mahavir was checking the loudspeakers, when there was a rumble from the hills. For a moment, I thought it was static from the speakers, when without warning, the earth tore open. The ground shook, as wave after wave of convulsions devastated every structure. There was a mountain of dust in the air blinding everything from sight. It was horrible. Fortunately, because of the Republic Day celebrations, most of us were in the village square and not inside any structure. The moment the tremors subsided, we ran around the village checking for anyone missing. A three-month-old baby was trapped under the rubble. We frantically removed the stones, but by some miracle, the boulders had interlocked in such a manner, that the baby escaped without a scratch."

We listen riveted, unable to respond.

Danabhai's wife and daughter prepare a wonderful meal of *rotlas* and *sabzee*. We are embarrassed by the hospitality and the stench of death has robbed us of our appetite. To Danabhai's way of thinking, death and life must co-exist and food is the very essence of life. We end up actually enjoying the meal. After dinner we head for the limitless open-air bedroom where everyone sleeps. The *Lagaanites* in Kotai gather and the earthquake stories pour in.

The organisation of the Kotai villagers is in sharp contrast to what we witnessed in the city of Bhuj. The relative paucity of material resources is more than compensated by the manner in which the villagers are organised.

Danabhai has unloaded the foodgrain officially made available by the government in the village square, set up a diesel driven *chakki* (flour mill) and placed tankers carrying fresh water in the village square for anyone who needs these.

"Why should one compromise one's self respect by standing on the road, foraging from passing relief trucks?" he asks.

We have lost one member of the *Lagaan* unit in Kotai – Merabhai. The story of his death is chilling. On the morning of 26th January, Merabhai along with two other family members had left for Bhuj city to visit his nephew who had been admitted to Bhuj Civil Hospital after an unsuccessful suicide attempt. When the tremors started, Merabhai and his two relatives tried to escape and perished as the hospital building collapsed. Meanwhile, the nephew who had been tied to the hospital bed on account of his repeated attempts at suicide was unable to run. Miraculously, the rubble fell all around him. When help arrived, they had only to cut the ropes that bound Merabhai's nephew to his bed and he walked unscathed, even as his kith and kin perished. The ropes in some way tethered him to life and survival.

The men who struggled to survive, perished and the man who wanted to die, survived. The irony is inescapable.

The stories continue.

Rao and I gaze at the starlit night grappling with the apparent senselessness of it all. The morbid thought refuses to go. If the earthquake had occurred six months back, few, if any, of us would have survived! Yet, today we were listening to the stories of the survivors who are still smiling, grateful to be alive and confident of their ability to stand on their feet again. How many of us, we wonder, would have been so cheerful.

February 2001 - May 2001

R ao and I return from Bhuj, with the news that almost our entire team has survived. We also take the first steps towards organising relief by sending Ashok Shinde from the production team with a truck loaded with material to make tents for the Kotai villagers.

Five thousand miles away, the British actors from *Lagaan* plan an event to raise money for Kutch. They are relieved to hear that everyone they know is well and now want to raise money for earthquake relief. From Mumbai, Bangalore, Chennai, wherever the *Lagaan*ites are, money pours in for the relief efforts. While the money will enable the tenacious villagers of Kotai to rebuild their shattered village, it more importantly reaffirms at a concrete level, the unique bond within the *Lagaan* team.

Aamir and Ashutosh heave a sigh of relief. A huge load on their hearts has lifted. The editing of *Lagaan* may now resume.

N ow a hundred things are happening all at once. The primary process is the edit or rather the creative war that ensues in the editing suite. The edit of the pre-cricket match portion of *Lagaan* is being finalised. The producer-father and the director-mother of *Lagaan* are pulling in opposite directions. Aamir wants to slash the length of *Lagaan* as much as possible, while Ashutosh wants to stay true to the original script. The mother as always is more emotional about the baby and the father stricter and more demanding.

Fortunately, these contradictory pulls work well for *Lagaan*. Left to himself, Ashutosh might perhaps have not trimmed *Lagaan* as much as he now does. Left to himself, Aamir might have cut the film to the point where the beauty of the story might have been affected. Together, their attrition helps mitigate each other's excesses.

On the twenty-seventh of February, it is back to the cricket field, but this time, the match is for real. Sound recordist Nakul Kamte and his assistant, Steven, are at Mumbai's Wankhede stadium for the first cricket test between India and Australia. Their mission: recording the the cheers and applause of the crowds. Although Nakul has miles of digital audio tape with the sound of roaring crowds, every inch of it, for obvious reasons, has Kutchi words on it. Also, the roar of a full house of fifty thousand at the Wankhede stadium would be far greater than that of the villagers dispersed over the Kutch hills during the shoot.

Getting permission to record the sound has not been an easy task and Aamir has had to use his friendship with Sachin Tendulkar to pull it off. Yet, it is Sachin himself who is now Nakul's nemesis. If Nakul is to record crowd sounds that are of any use to *Lagaan*, the audience must stop yelling, "Sachin! Sachin!" But this is Mumbai and Sachin is the ultimate icon. It is only after Sachin gets out that Nakul gets the cheers and applause that will ultimately be used in *Lagaan*.

Ashutosh, Aamir and Ballu edit the cricket match. They cut and cut and cut. Search and search and search. Pull out shots that were meant for some other place – put in the reaction shots and gradually, gradually, gradually almost like a stone taking a shape as the sculptor works on it, the climax starts emerging.

With so much grief caused by a match of one inning, the trauma a two-

Maharaja Puransingh (Kulbhushan Kharbanda) with Col. Boyer (John Rowe): their reactions during the match help the climax come alive

innings match would have caused is unimaginable.

Although the edit demands total focus and attention, it is no longer possible to postpone the other processes that must commence if the film is to release in June. Rahman is planning to leave for England in March to work on a play for Andrew Lloyd Webber. Work on the background score must commence immediately. Ashutosh, Aamir and Ballu Saluja move with the editing suite to Chennai. Ashutosh works with Rahman at night and with Aamir and Ballu in the day. It is a superhuman effort and Ashutosh is punishing his body, but with the end so close he just cannot let up.

Lagaan is proving so difficult to edit, because its script is highly ambitious. Consciously and otherwise the potential of the script is playing on the minds of Ashutosh and Aamir. Does the film achieve its script? Does it have the same power and beauty? Repeatedly, they find the film falling short and they must work and rework the edit until they get there.

The film seems to fall short of the script partly because of its length. At over four hours it is too long. Determining which scenes should be axed is no easy task.

Numerous screenings are held for different kinds of audiences. The same audience sees screenings with different scenes having been cut. It is not easy to watch one's film dozens of times with a critical eye, but the feedback of the audience proves critical in guiding Ashutosh and Aamir in the right direction. It is through this agonising and demanding process that clarity is achieved.

Aamir wants to cut the film to under three and a half hours, but Ashutosh is holding out. There are some scenes he simply will not let Aamir touch. Aamir presses his point as well as he can and then gracefully retreats, as the director has the last word. Finally, the editing scissors fall still. The film is fully edited - all three hours and forty-two minutes of it.

The delay in the edit has taken its toll. Nakul Kamte must complete the sound design of the film in less than a week. Anil Mehta has far less time than he needs to work on the colour correction and the laboratory in Hyderabad, which is experiencing teething troubles must print in far less time than they would have liked. This is just the way film making is. The ideal is a mirage and whether it is Ashutosh Gowariker, Anil Mehta or Nakul Kamte, each must work under the limitations that the situation presents.

J ust when Aamir and Ashutosh think that the discussion on the length of the film has been concluded, there is an unexpected call – from Aditya Chopra.

"Aamir, I heard that Lagaan is nearly four hours long. As a friend and as a colleague in the industry I want to tell you about the problems we faced with Mohabbatein, because of its length. You can only have three instead of four shows and you can never make up the loss in revenue. Also, the audience finds it difficult to sit for so long. I suggest you cut your film to under three hours."

Aamir thanks Aditya profusely for his concern and informs Ashutosh who is in Chennai, about Aditya's call.

Ashutosh refuses to respond. They are too far down the line for any spot response.

"Aamir, let's sleep it over and talk in the morning."

That night, Ashutosh introspects, thinking not of Aditya Chopra's call, but about what had prompted him to make Lagaan. His mind's journey leads him back to his moorings and the vision that had inspired him. He had begun with wanting to make a film that he, Ashutosh Gowariker, believed in. Now, if he cut the film any further, it would no longer be the film he wrote and believed in. Rather than slash the film in a hit and miss search for a box office smash, he decides to stick by the Lagaan he has always believed in. The die is now cast for one of the longest films ever released in India!

O n 1st April 2001, a programme on the music of Lagaan is aired on national television as a prelude to the worldwide release of the film's music album on 6th April 2001. This is the first time that any footage from Lagaan is being screened publicly. I co-direct the programme with Sankalp Meshram. Exactly a year back, I was appointed director of the making of Lagaan and on the same day a year later, I make my directorial debut. I hope there is no organic connection between my professional graph and All Fool's Day!

I n Mumbai, the local press has reproduced an article written by Rachel Shelley in The Guardian of London. It is a portion of Rachel's diary during the shoot. In large part, it is a litany of Rachel's complaints, many absurdly petty, but seeing it in press a few weeks before the worldwide release of the film, it outrages *Lagaanites* in England and in India. Then, the unkindest cut: Rachel's diary reveals the cricket secret. For three long years, thousands of people keep a secret and one single person, one of the heroines of the film at that, spills the beans!

8ᵗʰ June 2001

F inally, the actors get to see *Lagaan*. A.K. Hangal, Kulbhushan Kharbanda, Raghuveer Yadav, Rajendra Gupta, Sri Vallabh Vyas and the rest of the Champaner eleven pack into the preview theatre at Famous Studios in Mumbai along with Paul Blackthorne, Jamie, Katkin and Charlotte from England. Each has acted in several films and some like Hangal are veterans of hundreds, but perhaps no other film has made the kind of demands on them as has *Lagaan*. An important part of the life of every actor is embedded in the reels of film that will now unwind. Their moment of truth has arrived.

This is perhaps the most curious screening of *Lagaan*. Practically everyone watching the screen is also on it. As happens with most actors, each one is concentrating on himself or herself. How well have I done? Could I have played this scene better? Why has this scene of mine been cut? These are the questions that typically agitate actors when they first view their films. The *Lagaan* actors begin watching the film in this mode, but soon the power of the narrative takes over and the actors are able to distance themselves from their individual performances. They laugh and cry and sigh as if this is a story they are hearing and viewing for the first time.

When the lights come on for the interval, Paul Blackthorne is deeply agitated. "It's bloody magnificent!" he proclaims repeatedly. Paul cannot believe the artistic beauty of what he is seeing. He runs up and down the stairs of the building in which the theatre is located, until he can calm himself down sufficiently to be able to watch the second half of the film.

When the lights come on after the end credits, the actors are incredulous. What is on screen has proved to be every bit as large as what had happened during the shoot. All the suffering and privations are validated. The film has justified its endless demands.

Raghuveer Yadav had suffered ill health throughout the shoot of *Lagaan*. His six months in the Kutch desert turned out to be so traumatic, that by the conclusion of the shoot, he had few kind words to say about *Lagaan* or Kutch. Now, nearly a year later, he sees *Lagaan*, is moved to tears and hugs Ashutosh. A.K. Hangal's scenes, which he heroically shot despite the injury to his back, have been cut to reduce length and yet Hangal loves *Lagaan*. The Brits watching a Hindi print without subtitles are ovewhelmed.

For all this, the actors cannot help but feel anxious. Will the film work commercially, they wonder. Will the audience respond as the actors have? Will 'the weird story about villagers in the British Raj' carry the mainstream viewer? As yet, there is no way to know.

10th June 2001

The *Lagaan* team is in Bhuj for the first public screening of the film. In an atmosphere suffused with emotion, eight hundred Kutchis put aside their personal tragedies to see themselves or their work on screen. They love the film. Now they know that all the apparently senseless cheering and clapping and sighing and laughing had a purpose after all! It has all come together to tell a wonderful story and they are an integral part of it.

They are proud of their work and of *Lagaan*. After the screening, the *Lagaan* team dines together after a year of separation. The tearful reunion continues way past midnight.

The next morning, the *Lagaan* unit rises early and makes its way to the village of Kotai. Aamir Khan Productions has been involved with the post- earthquake relief effort in Kotai and the production team has been to Kutch several times, but this is the first time that Aamir, Ashutosh, Nitin Desai and the actors are here.

A world of warmth: Danabhai wraps a shawl around the author

The Mumbai team moves around the village meeting old friends, seeing their shattered houses and finally catching up with the devastating earthquake. A large amount of money has been collected for earthquake relief. The villagers feel that their share would be best used in rebuilding their houses. A week later, Reena and Rao will visit Bhuj to set these plans into motion.

Everyone then assembles in Danabhai's house. A traditional Kutchi breakfast is served with *chaas*, buttermilk. Danabhai felicitates every single member of the *Lagaan* team from Mumbai by draping a shawl around the person. A different villager honours each *Lagaanite* from Mumbai in this manner. The shawls have been woven by one of the villagers present, a national award-winning weaver who lives in Kotai. It is an emotional moment. Residents of a devastated village, simple rural folk with big hearts, are felicitating us.

We move to the site where the village of Champaner once stood. Ever since the *ghanan* song came on screen last evening, it has poured heavily and the imporous soil is waterlogged. There is nothing to indicate that a film was shot here. We miss our beautiful Champaner and our hearts are filled with sadness and longing. Barring the walls of a solitary village well, there is no sign that our village once proudly stood here. We peer into the dark interior of the well. It is full of water. The fantasy of water has turned into reality, at least for the moment.

The *Lagaan* team assembles on the hilltop, where the Champaner temple once stood. For miles around, we can see the barren countryside of Kutch. So much has changed, both within and without. The *Lagaan*ites unconsciously make a journey back in time.

We had arrived, perhaps no differently from another film unit, driven by the need to work and succeed. Driven above all by ambition. Hundreds of restless souls, seeking to be more than they were, to achieve more than they had. Perhaps this is true of any profession in the world, but in the very public roller coaster career of films, there is never a moment of stability. Never the feeling that yes, I have achieved what I sought to do. I am now secure. Even an Aamir Khan seeks to be *the* Khan of the industry. Ashutosh seeks to emulate the great masters Guru Dutt and Bimal Roy. Veteran actors like Rajendra Gupta seek from *Lagaan* a recognition they feel they deserve, but do not fully enjoy.

There are but four days left for *Lagaan* to release and soon each will know whether *Lagaan* has given them the success they sought. This is the last time they will be together in this *karmabhoomi*, the land where *Lagaan* was made, without knowing whether *Lagaan* has made their careers. The thirty-odd actors and technicians are remarkably calm. Something in this soil tells them that they have received from *Lagaan* far more than success or failure. The journey of making the film has been larger than any possible outcome. Four days later, this will sound false. It will be affected modesty if the film is a hit and sour grapes if the film flops. Today, no one can deny them this truth. As they sit on the hilltop they must savour the moment so that they may remember it forever.

15th June 2001

The heads of department and the principal cast are together in Sun City, South Africa for the worldwide premiere of *Lagaan*. Despite the holiday atmosphere, Reena and Rao cannot stop worrying. The printing of the film has been a desperate race against time. Although prints have by now reached the far corners of the world, the prints for the city of Mumbai were still in process when they boarded the flight for South Africa. This last lot of twenty prints was to have been printed overnight and dispatched by the early morning flight from Hyderabad, which reaches Mumbai at nine in the morning. Any glitch in the printing or cancellation of the flight will mean cancellation of shows in Mumbai!

As the *Lagaan* team boards the bus from the airport, Rao calls Mumbai and learns that the Mumbai prints have reached the theatres with minutes to spare! Finally, the production team may relax. *Lagaan* is ready for screening worldwide. Although there are a few hours still for the Sun City show, in India, the first show at twelve o'clock is now due to start.

Suddenly the *Lagaan*ites are desperately homesick. They had arrived excited about the worldwide premier in Sun City. Now they just want to go home and watch the film with a paying audience. They have appeared for an examination, their examiners are in the process of declaring their results and here they are missing out on all of it.

After two and a half years of writing, a year of pre-production, six months of shooting and a year in post-production, in two hundred and sixty theatres all over India, the lights grow dim and there is a hush in the audience as the coin imprinted with the bust of Queen Victoria spins rapidly and the opening credit comes on. *Lagaan* finally releases.

In Sun City, the *Lagaan* team is eating breakfast or pretending to do so when the first show in India approaches its end. A cell phone rings. Thirty pairs of ears perk up. It is Ashutosh's sister Ashlesha. She, along with her parents, is watching the first show at Gaiety theatre in Mumbai and is choking with tears.

"Ashu, you guys don't know what you're missing."

Ashlesha describes what's been happening. For the last two hours, the audience has laughed at Guran, admired Bhuvan, hated Captain Russell and smiled at Gauri. Now, the climax has started and for the audience it is the finals of the World Cup and India's honour is at stake.

Their pent-up emotions explode, cheering each British wicket that falls, sighing at every boundary hit by Russell. Some dance in the aisles. Some stand on their chairs. Some stare at the screen transfixed. Everyone is transported to 1893 Champaner and the distance between the viewer and the viewed has been obliterated.

Ashlesha is in the theatre and her mobile phone is on. At the other end, in Sun City, South Africa, thirty heads butt each other trying to listen to the phone. They can hear the audience clapping and cheering. They can hear the audience shout, "Come on Kachra. Hit a six!" "Bhuvan! Bhuvan!"

Thirty pairs of ears can hear only the speakerphone until the end credits come on. Thirty pairs of eyes are brimming with emotion. Ashutosh's wife Sunita bursts into tears and hugs him. It has been a long and difficult journey for the couple.

While the rest of the *Lagaan* team goes wild with jubilation, Aamir and Reena quietly embrace each other.

Aamir and Ashutosh hold on to each other forever. *Lagaan* has severely tested their powers of endurance, a test that has forged a deep bond.

Later that day, big guns of the industry see *Lagaan* at Sun City. Rakesh Roshan catches hold of Aamir and Ashutosh after the show and tells them,

"You'll don't know what you'll have made."

Aamir and Ashutosh thank him profusely, but Rakesh Roshan goes on.

"No, you're not understanding what I'm saying, you'll really don't know what you'll have made. You've made a classic!"

Randhir Kapoor, Karishma Kapoor, Hrithik Roshan, Sunil Shetty, Preity Zinta and several other stars present at Sun City are ecstatic about the film.

The screening at Sun City has been a huge success and the reports from India are ecstatic, but the *Lagaan* team cannot fully believe it, until they see the film in an Indian theatre with a paying audience.

19th June 2001 onwards

Ashutosh, Aamir and the *Lagaan*ites who were in Sun City finally watch the film in Mumbai. They move from theatre to theatre studying the audience reaction and in each place it is the same: audience reaction has transformed into audience interaction. Even as the screen speaks to the audience, the audience speaks to the screen and urges on the characters.

When Captain Russell challenges Bhuvan to accept the wager, the audience responds, "*Haan kah Bhuvan!*" ("Say yes Bhuvan!") When Bhuvan hits a six, the theatre is on its feet. When it rains at the end of the film, the audience weeps.

This is the big moment Ashutosh and Aamir have been waiting for. They have connected with the man on the street for whom the film was made. The 'weird story about villagers in the British Raj' has captured the soul of India.

Javed Akhtar sees *Lagaan* in several theatres and tells Aamir, "In my career spanning three decades, I have been a part of some of the biggest hits on Indian screen and seen audiences react. Yet, never in my life have I seen an audience reacting to a film as they do to *Lagaan!*"

Children playing cricket on the street name themselves Goli and Tipu and Guran. All over India, hundreds of newborns are named Bhuvan.

In Mumbai, tickets are simply not available for the first ten weeks. The distributor and the staff in the production office are hounded for tickets until they are compelled to virtually go underground. Even Aamir is unable to obtain tickets for friends.

Perhaps as important as the reaction of the audience is the reaction of the film industry. The entire industry in a rare show of unanimity applauds *Lagaan*, as if the film belongs to each one of them. They are proud that one of them has shown the courage and ability to make such a film.

Amitabh Bachchan reviews *Lagaan* and calls it "A perfect film."

Shekhar Kapoor says, "I thought I had made a good film when I made Bandit Queen, but *Lagaan*…"

Lagaan sweeps a slew of trophies at all the Indian film industry awards.

Recognition and honour come from unusual quarters. *Lagaan* is included as a case study in team building by the Indian Institute of Management, Indore. Many companies conduct workshops on team building using *Lagaan* as their primary resource material. Top corporates and industry associations invite Aamir and Ashutosh to speak about team building. Ironically, more than the on screen team building in *Lagaan*, it is the off screen team building for *Lagaan* they would like to speak about.

Lagaan is a huge hit in the non-resident Indian circuit in the United Kingdom and America. But Ashutosh is convinced that his film deserves more and wants to enter it in the festival circuit.

Lagaan's international success creates history. At the Locarno Film Festival in Switzerland, an audience of eight thousand five hundred Europeans views *Lagaan*. Being strangers to cricket does not stand in the way of their being swept off their feet by *Lagaan*. The Swiss Alps resonate with cheers that have been heard earlier in the cities and towns of India, in Ratlam and Akola, in Burdwan and Madurai. When Captain Russell asks Bhuvan whether he accepts the wager, the Germans shout, "Ja! Ja!" the French urge, "Oui" and the Italians exhort, "Si! Si!"

The day after the screening, several European newspapers headline the *Lagaan* screening. One proclaims: "Miracle at the Piazza!" *Lagaan* is voted as the best film from out of the three hundred and fifty films from all over the world screened there, upstaging films starring such greats as Robert de Niro and Marlon Brando. Ashutosh receives the *Prix du Public* award before a mammoth audience that gives him a standing ovation.

The director of *Mission*, Roland Joffe, the celebrated British composer, Sir Andrew Lloyd Webber and other creative giants pay rich tributes to *Lagaan*.

Then, the icing on the cake. *Lagaan* is selected as India's official entry for the Academy Awards in the category of best foreign language film. Given India's dismal track record at the Oscars, getting *Lagaan* noticed is an uphill task. Aamir and Ashutosh camp for a month in Los Angeles...and as with so many other things about *Lagaan*, the impossible becomes the possible. On 12th February 2002, dozens of *Lagaan*ites spontaneously gather at Aamir's house and a hush envelopes those packed in front of the television set as the five films nominated in each category are announced. Even before the announcement: "*Lagaan* from India," is completed, a war cry bursts out, "*Re bhaiyya chhoote lagaan!*"

The party goes on till the small hours of the morning, by which time the *Lagaan*ites are in work mode, with plans being drawn up for the next round of work in Hollywood. The wild horse of *Lagaan* gallops on.

The initial reaction of Aamir and Ashutosh to *Lagaan*'s success is unexpected. They receive the success with equanimity...and then with growing irritation. Irritation at their own inability to fully enjoy the moment. The overwhelming emotion is of having no emotion, of being numb, unable to enjoy or rejoice in its success. Somehow, making the film has taken too much out of them, and now with the end of the journey, they are left for quite a while with a feeling of emptiness. Curiously, this sentiment echoes in the hearts of the *Lagaan*ites all over the world.

Perhaps the big thing about *Lagaan* was that what had happened off screen was much larger than what happens on screen. The sense of achievement was in the journey itself, in climbing the mountain, not reaching the top. This journey has now run its course and the *Lagaan*ites know this.

Even years later, as the film *Lagaan* dims from public memory, for all those who endured the trials of 1893 Champaner, the memories of that eventful journey are what will always endure.

———————————